GLOBAL COMPETITION AND TECHNOLOGY

Also by Robert Pearce

GLOBALISING RESEARCH AND DEVELOPMENT
(*with Satwinder Singh*)

INTERNATIONAL ASPECTS OF UK ECONOMIC ACTIVITIES
(*with Peter J. Buckley*)

PROFITABILITY AND PERFORMANCE OF THE WORLD'S
LARGEST INDUSTRIAL COMPANIES (*with John H. Dunning*)

THE GROWTH AND EVOLUTION OF THE MULTINATIONAL
ENTERPRISE

THE INTERNATIONALISATION OF RESEARCH AND
DEVELOPMENT BY MULTINATIONAL ENTERPRISES

THE TECHNOLOGICAL COMPETITIVENESS OF JAPANESE
MULTINATIONALS (*with Marina Papanastassiou*)

THE WORLD'S LARGEST INDUSTRIAL ENTERPRISES
(*with John H. Dunning*)

US INDUSTRY IN THE UK (*with John H. Dunning*)

Global Competition and Technology

Essays in the Creation and Application of Knowledge by Multinationals

Robert Pearce
Reader in International Business
University of Reading

First published in Great Britain 1997 by
MACMILLAN PRESS LTD
Houndmills, Basingstoke, Hampshire RG21 6XS and London
Companies and representatives throughout the world

A catalogue record for this book is available from the British Library.

ISBN 0–333–67183–X

First published in the United States of America 1997 by
ST. MARTIN'S PRESS, INC.,
Scholarly and Reference Division,
175 Fifth Avenue, New York, N.Y. 10010

ISBN 0–312–17634–1

Library of Congress Cataloging-in-Publication Data
Pearce, Robert D., 1943–
Global competition and technology : essays in the creation and
application of technology by multinationals / Robert Pearce.
p. cm.
Includes bibliographical references and index.
ISBN 0–312–17634–1 (cloth)
1. International business enterprises. 2. Technological
innovations. 3. Competition, International. I. Title.
HD2755.5.P398 1997
658'.049—dc21   97–18621
                                                 CIP

This book is printed on paper suitable for recycling and made from fully managed and
sustained forest sources.

10   9   8   7   6   5   4   3   2   1
06   05   04   03   02   01   00   99   98   97

Printed in Great Britain by
The Ipswich Book Company Ltd
Ipswich, Suffolk

Contents

List of Tables

Acknowledgements

The papers in this book deal with a number of issues relating to the positioning of R & D, and creative operations generally, in MNEs. The development of the ideas embodied in the analysis has benefitted enormously from enjoyable and creative association with research students and co-researchers. Therefore my greatest debt of gratitude goes to the co-authors of seven of the chapters.

My first survey-based analysis of decentralised R & D in MNEs was carried out with Satwinder Singh and provides two chapters here. The extension of analysis of R & D into its role in the repositioning of MNE subsidiaries, and ultimately as a factor in the changing strategic nature of MNEs themselves, benefitted enormously from work with Marina Papanastassiou (initially as a PhD student and subsequently as a research fellow). Three chapters here cover aspects of our joint work. The extension of these ideas into new geographical/political environments and different industries is now being tackled by my current PhD students Julia Manea and Kam Pooni, and I am pleased to be able to include encouraging examples of their endeavours.

I am also extremely grateful to Jill Turner for undertaking the daunting task of turning the originally separate papers into a stylistically coherent overall manuscript, with great efficiency and patience. Finally, I would like to thank the editors and publishers of the *Journal of Economics of Business* for permission to reprint the material in Chapter 3 (originally published in vol. 1, no. 2, 1994).

ROBERT PEARCE

Notes on the Authors

Julia Manea is studying for a PhD at the University of Reading.

Marina Papanastassiou teaches at the Economic University of Athens and is a visiting fellow in the Economics Department, University of Reading.

Gurkanwal Singh Pooni is studying for a PhD at the University of Reading.

Satwinder Singh teaches at Gyosei International College, Reading.

Part I
Strategic Evolution and Technology in MNEs

1 Global Interdependence, MNE Strategy and Technology

Technology has always taken a central position in analysis and evaluation of multinational enterprises (MNEs). It is the key theme of the papers in this book that now the strategic *re*positioning of technology is a vital element in the evolving behaviour of these companies as they take a central position in the global competitive interdependencies of the late twentieth century. Increasingly MNEs know they must use their *global* environment creatively as the basis for the acquisition of knowledge and the innovation of new products, and not merely as an extension of the market in which they can apply *nationally*-derived technology and centrally-innovated products. Individual MNE subsidiaries increasingly take responsibility for discerning and accessing creative attributes of their local environment (e.g. market characteristics and trends, technological heritage and research capabilities). Where subsidiaries can develop such individualised local technical competences within their own scope they move from a state of dependence within the MNE to one where they assert their position in interdependent group-level programmes of knowledge-creation and product-development. The ability to articulate these decentralised programmes, seeking to access the extended range of creative perspectives available in their globalised operations, enables MNEs to widen and deepen the progress of their technology trajectory and its commercial application.[1] These new perspectives on MNEs' approaches to the intensification of globalised competition also have resonances in the restructuring of valuable established theories.

3

The main theoretical dimensions of an understanding of the ability of firms from national origins to extend their operations effectively into a multinational environment are encompassed in the eclectic framework of Dunning.[2] Firstly this suggests that such firms need an *ownership advantage*, in the form of some source of unique firm-specific competitive asset that provides the basis of a sustainable demand for a product (embodying the attribute) in overseas markets. Next the framework discerns the need for *location advantages*, in order to explain why the good or service embodying the ownership advantage is best produced overseas (rather than exported from the home country of the MNE, where traditionally it would have been presumed to have been created and to have achieved its original commercial innovation). Finally it is necessary to explain why the use of a firm's ownership advantage in an overseas country needs the extension of the value-adding activity of that firm into that location, rather than the transfer (e.g. by sale or licensing) of the asset itself to an indigenous firm that might then make better use of it in its home environment. That is, why do firms often continue to retain the internalised use of their key competitive attributes, even when this involves their emergence as MNEs through the initiation of overseas value-adding activities? The *internalisation advantages* that have been invoked to explain this usually involve elements of failure in the markets for such intermediate products.

The early expositions of the eclectic paradigm (e.g. Dunning 1977, 1980) clearly discerned a key position for technology in two of its three elements. Thus the long-standing acceptance of knowledge as a key competitive attribute of successful firms led to the almost automatic endorsement of technology as a likely source of the ownership advantages possessed by those enterprises capable of competing globally.[3] Similarly the pioneering interjection of the concept of internalisation into MNE theory by Buckley and Casson (1976) chose knowledge as a prime illustration of the relevant types of market failure for intermediate goods.[4] By contrast the initial views of location advantages provided little role for host-country technological capacity, instead focusing on factors such as local market size and the availability of standardised inputs (e.g. labour, raw materials). This enshrines a view of MNEs in which they expect to transfer established group technology to overseas operations, and select the location for subsidiaries according to host-country ability to supply the relevant complementary inputs in a cost-effective manner. Nowadays, we argue throughout this book, MNEs do acknowledge the existence of distinctive technology and research competences in many countries and often build these into their subsidiaries' operations and into their global knowledge-generation programmes. Thus technology becomes a potential location advantage of host countries, implying also that MNEs increasingly take the view that location factors should be viewed in a dynamic context (i.e. as contributing to technology evolution rather than simply to applying it effectively). Host countries may then move from a position of technological dependence to one where they contribute positively to technological interdependencies in MNEs.

The emergence of technology as a location advantage also has implications for its nature as an ownership advantage. Previously it was possible to see technology as a stock which (reflecting its possession of some public good characteristics)[5] could be transferred relatively cheaply throughout an MNE's operations. In the more dynamic competitive context the flow of new technology (and its improved commercial application through innovation) now becomes vital, with the increased need to widen (globalise) the sources of knowledge inputs then emerging in the manner envisaged above. Against that background the technology-related ownership advantage in contemporary MNEs becomes the current stock of knowledge *plus* the ability to build on it and increase its effective application through the articulation of world-wide creative programmes. With all MNEs potentially having similar access to the global technology environment those that develop the best skills in monitoring those potentials and assembling an optimal portfolio of decentralised operations into an effective international network will benefit most. Alongside the firm's established knowledge stock itself these organisational skills may also now be seen as another key component of an MNE's technology-based ownership advantages.

The new perspectives on technology also extend the scope of internalisation decisions in MNEs. This now involves not only how best to secure returns from existing technology but also how to most effectively access the increasingly decentralised sources of new technology inputs. In terms of the first facet of this we may speculate that the emergence of interdependent globalised approaches to the creation and application of knowledge in MNEs make it even less likely that such leading firms will find it viable to adopt externalised routes for securing rewards from their most important technologies. To internalise the technology competences of foreign countries MNEs are most likely to set up R&D units there, employing local scientists who embody elements of the distinctive local knowledge heritage. Thus the substantial growth in overseas R&D units in MNEs is viewed here as not a random and *ad hoc* occurrence, but very much as a core element in the emergence of carefully articulated globalised approaches to technology. Nevertheless the operations of such subsidiary labs may also be augmented (or in some cases substituted for) by the adoption of externalised contractual collaborations with host-country facilities (e.g. University, industry or independent labs). Therefore the global technology programmes of MNEs may balance externalised and internalised operations.[6]

Another piece of pioneering theorising which contributed in a significant way to the understanding of the location of creative activity in globally-competing enterprises was the original product cycle of Vernon (1966). The first stage of this cycle sees the new product innovated in the home country of the enterprise, and targeted initially at that market. In the second stage, when the product reaches a degree of maturity, overseas demand will begin to emerge. This will eventually reach sufficient levels in the larger and more developed foreign markets to encourage the setting up of production facilities in them in order to achieve a more competitive supply (including perhaps some degree of product adaptation). In the final stage the product has become very standardised and the market for it very intensively price competitive. This may then involve the relocation of production to mainly export-oriented plants in low-cost (especially low-wage) economies.

A key element in the centralised (home-country) location of the innovation process in the original product cycle is that, in its pure form, it assumes that the firms involved start with no overseas operations (so that one of its major contributions was to explain the emergence of foreign production operations in technologically-dynamic enterprises). An implication of the absence of overseas activities is that the firms have no reliable source for detecting market trends and technological developments outside the home country. Since effectively communicated access to such knowledge is central to an efficient innovation process this suggests that technological creation and product development will occur where the relevant information can be most clearly discerned and communicated, i.e. in the home country. However, the second phase of the product cycle predicts the emergence of overseas marketing and production facilities, and once these have settled into their host-country environments they can alter the nature of the product cycle and, indeed, of the enterprise itself. Certainly these overseas subsidiaries can monitor key trends in their local environment and communicate this knowledge to the parent (home-country) operations. This means that, at least, the innovation process can be informed by a much wider range of knowledge inputs. Beyond this, however, scope exists for overseas subsidiaries to play a much more proactive role in the innovation process in firms facing the challenges of global competition.

The overseas subsidiaries set up in the second stage of the original product cycle will seek to extend the local market beyond that already achieved by exports from the

home country, and to do this will acquire detailed knowledge of the local market needs (through a marketing unit)
and adapt the product in response to this (through creative
engineering personnel or a full-scale R&D unit). Taken
with ambitious and entrepreneurial local managers many
of these subsidiaries (especially those in distinctive high-
income markets and with access to original and high-quality local technology and research capacity) will seek to
acquire roles which transcend being mere implementers of
technology that is already embodied in fully-defined products (only susceptible to peripheral adaptation). At the
same time the intensification of global competition means
that firms innovating a significant new product cannot
afford to wait for it to 'trickle down' to overseas markets
in the relaxed manner of the original product cycle. The
approach to innovation itself now needs globalised perspectives, with returns actively maximised in each key
market. This means the new product must be introduced
in each market very quickly and in forms that respond to
distinctive characteristics of these markets. This, in turn,
provides a more proactive and creative role for the ambitious subsidiaries discerned earlier. In a particular region a
subsidiary with the necessary level of managerial dynamism and functional scope can acquire the core knowledge
of the new product and derive from it a product variant
that is appropriate to its own market segment.

This view of a contemporary approach to innovation in
MNEs in effect brings together the first two stages of the
original product cycle. Certain centralised responsibilities
are likely to remain, co-ordinating basic and applied
research and from them deriving the core technology of
the new product. The second stage is then speeded up to
near simultaneity, with a range of variants of the new
product being created in separate regional subsidiaries in
the manner described above. Adding these new perspectives to the original product cycle allows us to discern two
distinctive roles for overseas subsidiaries in the contemporary MNE. The intensity of global competition in many
industries is such that even innovation-oriented companies

cannot rely solely on product originality to secure adequate returns, optimal production efficiency also needs to be pursued. Thus there remains a role for subsidiaries that concentrate on the cost-effective production of established products, in the manner of the third stage of the product cycle. Secondly we have those subsidiaries that accede to the more creative product-development role. These subsidiaries build individualised competences that reflect, and help respond to, distinctive local assets and attributes. But they may do this most positively, from the point of view of their parent MNE, when their creativity retains strong interdependencies with the broader technical and commercial progress of the overall group. Through such differentiation, and widening of scope, in their overseas subsidiaries we can envisage modern MNEs that can respond to, and benefit competitively from, increasing heterogeneity in the global economy.[7]

We can see the MNE as a 'well-established phenomenon in evolution' (Papanastassiou 1995, p.iv). The original theorising of Dunning and Vernon initially provided us with crucial understanding of the factors that enabled national companies to become established international players. The continuing strength of these works is that they help us to subsequently articulate the ways in which these companies then interact in a dynamic fashion with the evolving global economy. The evolutionary processes in MNEs can be seen as an initial response to exogenous changes in the international environment that then themselves become key forces in the further evolution of the global competitive situation. The chapters in this book concern themselves with various aspects of the ways in which the new strategic approaches of MNEs (especially those related to their activities involving the creation and application of technology) both respond to, and help to intensify, the forces of international competition and the globalised pursuit of efficiency.

Central to much of the analysis here is the view that in their new globalised technology strategies MNEs access a number of what are essentially still *national* science bases in order to enhance their own *inter*national competitiveness. The issues that may emerge from that apparent asymmetry are discussed and evaluated in Chapter 2. In Chapter 8 we look at a particularly distinctive case of this interdependence between MNEs' strategies and the development of a national science base, i.e. that of Romania, a transition economy. Here it is suggested that under communist central planning Romania developed a strong research and technology capacity which did not feed through into an innovative commercial potential (an incomplete and biased national system of innovation). The ability of MNE subsidiaries to speed up the effective commercial application of local technology is discussed as a relevant potential in this case.

The new decentralised approach to technology can be seen as just one aspect of MNEs' broader strategic response to increased international heterogeneity, with interdependent global networks of subsidiaries encompassing distinctively different roles and motivations. Using US data, Chapter 3 tests the determinants of the different roles played by MNEs' overseas subsidiaries. In Chapter 7 the US data is again used to relate subsidiary roles (and also some host-country characteristics) to the research- intensity of US MNEs' operations in particular foreign locations. This reflects further on the various ways in which overseas subsidiaries are built into the global strategies of MNEs and particularly on the way that decentralised R&D can support these new competitive approaches. Using survey evidence on MNE subsidiaries' operations in Europe, Chapter 6 also investigates both their strategic roles and their technological scope. A key facet of the latter is whether or not the subsidiaries acquire the support of R&D units, and if so their roles and motivations. Chapter 9 focuses on the European R&D operations of Japanese MNEs, with some evidence on how these activities fit into broader technological perspectives of Japanese companies seeking to extend their global competitiveness.

The internationalisation of R&D in MNEs is at the centre of three other chapters. In Chapter 4 we look at aspects of R&D decentralisation through a survey of parent (home-country) labs in MNEs, with the expectation that they can elucidate on the overall aims of a globalised programme and on the various ways that overseas labs can fit into this. A complementary survey is discussed in Chapter 5, this time seeking the views of individual overseas labs in MNEs. Factors helping to determine the specific roles played by such units are discussed, as well as their perceived interdependencies with other operations in the MNE group. Chapter 10 uses a survey of parent labs in the chemicals and allied sector to analyse aspects of the process of globalisation of technology. Here a valuable element is the ability to discern interesting differences between subsectors (i.e. industrial chemicals, pharmaceuticals, biotechnology). Finally, Chapter 11 seeks to draw some policy-related conclusions from the range of evidence discussed.

Notes

1. Ernst and O'Connor (1989, p. 23) note that the presence of new generic technologies make autarchy impossible, so that all players in global competition 'have to rely, at least to some degree, on external sourcing of scientific and technical inputs through a combination of joint ventures, contract R&D, consultancies, licensing and know-how agreements, collaboration with University laboratories, technology "scanning" and so forth'.
2. For a detailed exposition see Dunning (1988, Chapters 1 and 2).
3. See Pearce (1993, pp. 32–4) for a survey of empirical studies that investigated the position of technology (usually proxied by research intensity) as an ownership advantage.
4. 'There are certain markets in which the incentive to internalise is particularly strong. The strongest case of all concerns the market for various types of knowledge' (Buckley and Casson 1976, p. 39). Buckley and Casson's further discussion (1976, pp. 39–40) amplifies this view.
5. As Teece's (1976, 1977) evidence on the cost of intra- group technology transfer shows it was always dangerous to overstate its public good nature.

6. Ernst and O'Connor (1989, p. 23) suggest that the effectiveness, cost and speed of external technology sourcing 'depends on the company's in-house technical capability as much as on the scientific and technical infrastructure accessible to the firm'. In similar terms Cohen and Levinthal (1989, p. 593) argue 'that firms invest in R&D not only to pursue directly new process and product innovation, but also to develop and maintain their broader capabilities to assimilate and exploit externally available information'.

7. Thus important recent theorising indicates a change in the MNE from a hierarchical to a heterachical organisation. See Hedlund (1986, 1993), Hedlund and Rolander (1990), Birkinshaw (1994).

2 The Implications for Host-Country and Home-Country Competitiveness of the Internationalisation of R&D and Innovation in Multinationals

2.1 INTRODUCTION AND BACKGROUND

The sources from which MNEs can create, develop and sustain competitiveness have widened, both geographically and institutionally, and new organisational practices are being evolved by these enterprises in order to use in an optimal manner the technological opportunities that are opening up to them on a global scale. These new technological opportunities can be seen as paralleling and complementing new priorities in marketing strategy, which in many industries requires extensive responsiveness to decentralised (national or regional) consumer demands, both for new products and for established products that more fully acknowledge differentiated tastes and other idiosyncratic and distinctive market characteristics and needs. This chapter reviews recent research which analyses and documents the emerging decentralised technology strategies in MNEs, in which their pursuit of global competitiveness seeks to harness to group needs the wide range of knowledge and research inputs available from the scientific communities of the various countries in which they have established subsidiaries, but at the same time also seeks to apply such new group-level knowledge in these countries in the most commercially-effective manner.

Clearly this perspective on MNEs' strategic approaches to the creation and application of technology means that these enterprises may both absorb crucial knowledge inputs from what are still predominantly seen as nationally-generated science bases and, somewhat later and perhaps after considerable refinement and evolution of the knowledge, pass it back as new products that have been, at least to some extent, developed in a manner that responds to the distinctive local-market needs. This, in turn, suggests that what may, in its most developed form, be seen as the emergence of a globalised approach to innovation by MNEs has crucial, and potentially varied and widespread, implications for both the host and home countries of these corporations. This chapter seeks to interpret the recent analyses of the new approach to the generation and use of commercial technology in MNEs in terms of its effects on host-and home-country competitiveness.

Central to the implementation of the broader perspectives of the new global technological scope of MNEs has been the generally enhanced position of overseas R&D facilities in their operations. A key part of the background to the chapter then starts from two developments in the internationalisation of R&D by MNEs over the past quarter century.

Firstly, *quantitatively*, it appears that an increasing number of MNEs have established an increasing number of R&D facilities outside of their home country (see Pearce and Singh 1992a, pp. 58–64; Pearce and Singh 1992b, pp. 182–187).

Secondly, *qualitatively*, there is clear evidence that the roles played by such overseas R&D facilities have extended in scope and have taken more central positions in the technological operations of the MNEs.

The first important extension of the roles of overseas laboratories in MNEs is essentially a contemporary upgrading of their more traditional *demand*-side role, which was previously perceived as being limited to the *adaptation* of existing products and production processes so that they might conform to the needs and conditions of particular host countries' markets. Now this traditional role is seen to be increasingly superseded by the more substantial and ambitious demand-side function of *developing* distinctive new products that respond more completely to the particular characteristics of leading countries and regions (groups of countries).

Alongside the upgrading of the established demand-side role of overseas R&D in MNEs there is some clear suggestion of a newer *supply*-side influence. In this case MNEs locate R&D facilities overseas in order to secure access to particularly strong and distinctive pools of scientific expertise in areas of science that are likely to be relevant to the longer-term evolution of the technological competence of their operations. Here it is not what a host country needs in terms of product-development work that influences the decision to set up a laboratory, but what it can supply in terms of the quality of its science base.

Though these two types of evolution in the roles of decentralised R&D in MNEs can be seen as reactions to different changes (the nature and intensity of market competition and the widening distribution and increasing specialisation of technological and research capacity), it can also be suggested that an optimal use of the potentials opened up in responding to them can be seen as a move towards a more systematic approach to organising innovation itself on a global scale (i.e. a global-innovation strategy).

The logic for the emergence of a global-innovation strategy in MNEs follows from two generalised trends in the competition of the key players in many industries over perhaps the last 30 years or so.

The first of these trends has been an ever increasing emphasis on innovation of radical new products as a key element in sustaining the competitiveness and profitability of the leading enterprises. This may be notably exemplified by the change over this time of Japanese firms from a position as cost-competitive producers of well-established mass-market products, to leading-edge innovators of many of the most important and radical new product concepts; this in turn intensifying the competitive environment of companies from the traditional industrial economies. Along these lines the results (Table 2.1) of a questionnaire survey by Granstrand and Sjolander (1992) of the perceptions of technology executives in leading enterprises with

Table 2.1   Importance of managerial issues as perceived by technology executives in multitechnology corporations in USA, Japan and Sweden[1]

	Japan	Sweden	USA
Keeping pace with new product technologies	2.82	2.33	2.75
Escalating R&D spending	2.27	1.17	2.12
Pressure for shorter innovation lead times	2.54	1.83	2.88
Shorter market lifetime of products	2.64	1.67	2.62
Pressure for more frequent introduction of new generation of products	2.45	2.00	2.50
Pressure to acquire technology from outside the company	2.09	1.17	2.12
Pressure for technological protectionism	1.82	0.83	1.88
Pressure for scientific protectionism	1.64	0.67	1.50
Pressure to acquire technology from abroad	1.73	0.67	2.00
Increased complexity (fusion) of technology	2.70	1.67	2.50
Increased fusion between science and technologies	2.45	1.00	2.00
Demand for higher quality	2.82	3.00	2.88
Average for 12 technology issues[2]	2.33	1.50	2.31
Average for 16 non-technology issues[3]	1.76	1.59	1.74

Notes:
[1] Scale: 0 = unimportant, 1 = of minor importance, 2 = important, 3 = of major importance.
[2] Unweighted average of above individual responses for the 12 issues.
[3] Unweighted average of individual responses for the 16 issues.
Source: Granstrand and Sjolander (1992, Table 9.1, p. 185).

regard to the most important current managerial issues demonstrated the increasing significance of the more radical product-creation activities in defining contemporary competitiveness. Thus whilst 'demand for higher quality' and 'keeping pace with new product technologies' may be considered to reflect a continued need to sense and respond to trends in market needs and technological developments in established product areas, other well endorsed concerns such as 'pressure for shorter innovation lead times', 'pressure for more frequent introduction of new generations of products' and 'shorter market lifetimes of products' all point towards a more fundamental and dynamic creativity as now being an essential element in competitive strategy.

The second of the trends has been the increasing internationalisation of the markets and the production networks of the leading corporations, and the change in their modes of international competition from the import-substituting supply of relatively isolated markets to the use of integrated networks of specialised facilities to supply what is now perceived as a global market in the most effective way possible (UNCTAD 1993). This global-supply strategy, however, not only pursues cost-effective production but also market responsiveness. Firms have found it necessary to respond to the distinctive needs of particular segments of the global market.

The juxtaposition of the implementation of a global-competition strategy and the need for sustained innovation in a MNE's approach to competitiveness, ultimately implies that its global-marketing and global-production strategies need to be allied with a global-innovation strategy. Thus the process of innovation needs to be directly and immediately responsive to the broader dimensions of the MNE's pursuit of global competitiveness.

It may be suggested that a fully-developed global-innovation strategy will seek to encompass three objectives. The first of these will be to secure the most effective performance of the programmes of precompetitive research that will allow the company to extend and reinforce its underlying technological competence in a manner that will eventually provide for its long-term commercial evolution through the introduction of major new product generations. Though the results in Table 2.1 ('escalating R&D spending') suggest that research costs may be of some concern in this objective, the main aim will be to secure high-quality inputs in all the areas of science that can make a contribution to these precompetitive research programmes.

The second objective of a global-innovation strategy is to get new products into *all* the world's key market areas with the greatest viable speed, in order to maximise the available competitive edge and retain it as long as possible. This aggressive approach to all the main global markets, within the process of innovation itself, is then further elaborated in the third objective of the strategy. This is to not only get new products into separate key markets quickly, but also in forms that respond to the distinctive needs of their consumers and to the problems and potentials of their production environments.

The modelling of a fully implemented global-innovation strategy sees these three objectives being achieved through a two-phase approach, both of which are likely to involve the use of overseas R&D laboratories by MNEs. The aim of the first phase is to derive the outlines of a new product concept, the nature of which extends the scope of the industry in quite radical ways. At this stage the characteristics of the new concept fully define what the product does, and the way in which it does it, without providing complete details of the precise form in which it will be offered to consumers, or the way in which it is to be produced. In this first phase the MNE will use all the basic-and applied-research resources available to it in order to create the new technology that underpins the innovative new product concept. The work of this stage is likely to be carried out by a global network of pure-research labs, which seek to access all the areas of technology where specialist inputs are needed. Thus, as Cantwell's (1991) research has shown, the range of technologies

needed by firms in many technologically-dynamic industries has widened, whilst the forces of agglomeration have
tended to narrow the areas of outstanding scientific capacity of many countries. In this situation it is logical for
science-based MNEs to pursue an optimal selection of
research inputs to their precompetitive research by tapping
into the specialist capabilities of several countries.[1] Such a
decentralised network is, however, likely to be decisively
coordinated by a central laboratory, probably located in
the MNE's home country, which will take the ultimate
responsibility for the formulation of the new product concept. This first phase clearly aims to achieve the first
objective of a global-innovation strategy, with its successful implementation being predominantly influenced by
supply-side (quality and scope of national science base)
factors.

The second and third objectives of a full scale global-
innovation strategy are secured through its second phase.
Here a second set of decentralised product-development
laboratories take up the outlines of the new product concept and seek to define its detailed characteristics, and the
precise form of the production process, in order to meet
the specific needs of their own markets and production
conditions. This second phase then allows the new product
to reach global markets through a series of more or less
simultaneous differentiated innovations. This results in a
set of product variants, each of which meets the detailed
needs and conditions of a separate national or regional
market. In this phase demand-side factors clearly move
into a more influential position.

The background so far discussed clearly establishes the
potential for overseas R&D facilities in MNEs to play
distinctive and differentiated roles, which involve specialisation in different types of scientific work. To provide a
context for this, relating to the different needs and phases
of a global-innovation strategy, we can derive a distinction
between types of research and development. This is essentially a modification to our area of analysis of a quite
familiar sequential taxonomy.

The taxonomy starts with *basic research*, representing fundamental investigation in the broad area of science that is of interest to the firm. Such basic research is not implemented to solve a specifically defined problem, or to meet a currently perceived commercial objective of the company. We may therefore say that the basic research phase ends when a particular piece of scientific output *is* perceived to be providing an idea that *might* underlie an important commercial possibility.

The next, *applied research*, stage of the taxonomy then picks up the basic research output and moves it forward in the light of what should become an increasingly clear commercial possibility. In our typology the applied-research phase then ends with the definition of the broad outlines of the new product concept.

In its conventional application this taxonomy then concludes with a *development* stage, in which the product concept derived from applied research is refined into a commercially-innovated product (along with its associated production process). However, in the context of an approach to innovation in a MNE two alternative paths could occur at the development stage. In the first possibility the innovation process is essentially centralised, with the definitive product derived and implemented in, probably, the home country through the efforts of centralised R&D, marketing, engineering and management personnel. This sequence, in the context of the contemporary MNE, would then often add on an additional phase to the process, namely *adaptation*. Thus overseas subsidiaries in the group may find it necessary to adapt the product and/or the production process, in fairly minor or peripheral ways, to meet host-country needs or aspects of the production environment. In this approach, therefore, overseas subsidiaries carry out *adaptation development* when necessary. In the second alternative the development/innovation stage itself is decentralised, making the process responsive to the needs of a global-innovation strategy. The needs of contemporary global competition indicate that the eventual adaptation of a centrally-innovated product to overseas markets may be too slow and inadequately responsive. So adaptation development in overseas subsidiaries is replaced by a more complete attempt to be locally responsive, through an individualised local development process. Thus the overseas subsidiaries now perform their own more comprehensive *innovation development* stage, in order to, in effect, implement the second phase of a global-innovation strategy.

2.2   MNEs' INNOVATION AND HOST COUNTRIES

The previous section has elaborated some specific background perspectives on the increasing decentralisation of creative work in MNEs, indicating that this may be seen as a means of articulating the role of technology in the pursuit of a genuinely globalised competitiveness. This section applies the focus of the analysis more directly on the host country, dealing with two main issues. The first of these is the manner in which a MNE's R&D in a particular host economy can play specific roles which reflect the country's position in, and contribution to, the firm's world-wide generation and application of technology. Secondly, the implications of this for the competitiveness of the host economy are discussed.

A number of useful taxonomies of overseas R&D laboratories have been derived (Ronstadt 1977, 1978; Hood and Young 1982; Haug, Hood and Young 1983; Hakanson 1981; Cordell 1971, 1973; Pearce 1989). Here we discuss three types of overseas laboratory, each of which, in its pure form, would perform a distinctive role in supporting its MNE's operations.

The first role we can define for a R&D laboratory of a MNE operating in a foreign country is to help a producing subsidiary there to use the MNE's current technology, as embodied in existing products and their associated production processes, as effectively as possible. Its main function is, therefore, *adaptation development*, either of the product so that it may meet the distinctive characteristics of the subsidiary's market, or of the production process in order that it may use most effectively the production environment of the host country. Laboratories that focus on this role we may term Support Laboratories (SL). These SLs are then limited to supporting the ability of production subsidiaries to use existing technology to succeed in already determined target markets. It is no part of the objective of a pure SL to in any way extend the technologies, or market scope, of the part of the MNE's operations it supports.

The most obvious position for a SL is to support the ability of a traditional import-substituting subsidiary to supply its host country with the relevant parts of the MNE group's established product range. However the pressures of contemporary globalised competition have now rendered such import-substituting operations decreasingly viable (Pearce 1992), and this has led to the emergence of export-oriented subsidiaries that play a closely defined role in their MNE's wider strategy. One such role is that of a rationalised product subsidiary (RPS),[2] which operates within a network of similar subsidiaries to facilitate the optimally-efficient supply of a wider regional (or global) market. Thus an RPS could produce a very limited part of the MNE's relevant product range (with other parts supplied by other RPSs in other countries) for supply to the wider market, or it could produce component parts for assembly elsewhere, or it could perform one stage of a vertically-integrated production process. Where an RPS-type role replaces an import-substituting operation, the need for even the limited technological inputs of a SL are likely to diminish, most notably because the host-country market is now only a small part of the one to be supplied. The specifications of the product will have been defined in the light of the needs of the wider market, and it is the aim of the RPS to supply it efficiently. Though some adaptation of the production process to make best use of local conditions might be possible even this is likely to be limited, as the MNE will allocate products to an RPS that are already the most in line with its particular production capabilities. Though R&D is thus unlikely to be needed at the level of an individual subsidiary in a RPS network, some support for the whole system may be relevant. If, for example, a US MNE sets up a network of RPSs to supply its established US product range throughout the European market, a quite extensive SL might be needed to adapt the products and processes to European circumstances. This SL could then be established alongside a leading RPS in the network or, for reasons of group-level politics, independently of any producing operation. Overall, though, the evolution away from import-substituting operations seems likely to have diminished the position of SLs amongst MNEs' overseas R&D units (Pearce and Singh 1992a, p. 115).

As the limited adaptation role of SLs declines in relevance more ambitious positions can be found for overseas R&D laboratories in the pursuit of global competitiveness by MNEs. One of these is for an R&D unit in a particular country to work as a closely-integrated part of a subsidiary there (i.e. alongside the subsidiary's management, marketing, engineering, etc. personnel) to *develop* a distinctive product which can be supplied to a regional (e.g. European), or even global, market. Thus, unlike the SL, it is the objective of this type of lab, which we may term a Locally Integrated Laboratory (LIL), to actually extend the scope of the subsidiary, and therefore of the MNE, by using all the resources available in a creative collaboration which expands the competitive product range of the group, rather than merely ensuring the effective use of an established one. Thus we envisage a LIL being encompassed within a world (or regional) product mandate subsidiary (WPM or RPM), which receives from the MNE parent a mandate to take full responsibility for the creation, production and marketing of a distinctive product. It is in this way that the laboratory integrates with other local functional inputs in order to contribute to the full range of skills needed to derive the product, achieve its effective production and marketing, and to ensure its further competitive development. Such a WPM/RPM operation would share with an RPS the advantage (compared with an import-substituting subsidiary) of achieving production efficiency through access to export markets which allow them to obtain optimal scales of production. The extra dynamic advantage of the WPM type operation is that it greatly extends the creative scope of a MNE by making full use of a range of talented resources either in, or accessible to, the subsidiary.

We may, in fact, define more formally a role for RPM/ LIL type operations within a systematic global-innovation strategy of the MNE. Thus we have envisaged the first phase of a global-innovation strategy as deriving the broad outlines of a new product concept, which generally extends the scope of the industry. To benefit as much as possible from this we noted that the initiating firm needs to get the product into all key markets as quickly as possible, and in ways that respond fully to the distinctive consumer needs and production conditions of each of these markets. In each important market a particular subsidiary may then be given RPM responsibility for the effective implementation of the product concept, in a way that maximises its competitiveness in the unique circumstances of that region. To achieve this the RPM subsidiary's LIL will have full access to the centrally-derived technology defining the broad outline characteristics of the new product, so that it can work with its allied marketing, engineering and management personnel to ensure that its own distinctive variant is developed (i.e. *innovation development*) in a way that is fully responsive to the region's needs and potentials. Amongst the market-responsive types of labs LILs now prevail over SLs (Pearce and Singh 1992a, p. 115).

The third possible role that can be distinguished for overseas R&D laboratories, or the second that plays a part in a global-innovation strategy, is to provide basic or applied research inputs into a programme of precompetitive work organised by a MNE. Thus a laboratory that focuses on such work would not be allied (in the manner of a LIL) with other operations (i.e. production and/or marketing) of the MNE in the same country. Instead its alliances are with similar laboratories of the MNE in other countries, and especially with a parent laboratory which is expected to coordinate the overall research programme. Therefore we may refer to this type of facility as an Internationally Interdependent Laboratory (IIL). A pure IIL, therefore, would have no responsibility for dealing with the current competitiveness of subsidiaries in the same country. Its interest is rather with contributing to the expansion of the basic scientific knowledge available to the MNE, from which future generations of products can be derived. Thus the broad range of technology relevant to many of the more dynamic industries, and the distinctive scientific and research capacities of particular countries, means that a MNE wishing to access all the facets of scientific expertise required to ensure a balanced programme of speculative precompetitive research can benefit from having a network of IILs. Each of these IILs can then carry out basic or applied research, building on the special strengths of the science base of its host country and supplying results that complement those of other contributing IILs, that have themselves accessed other specialised sources of expertise. Such a network of IILs can then contribute to the first phase of a global-innovation strategy, by providing inputs into an overall programme of basic and applied research from which a central coordinating laboratory can ultimately derive the new product concept that the second phase implements internationally (through LILs) as described earlier. This now seems to be the most prevalent of the three types of lab (Pearce and Singh 1992a, p. 115).

Implicit in the lines of argument so far developed is the view that increasingly the ability of individual MNE subsidiaries to develop their own technological and creative competences may determine the role that they take in the group's pursuit of competitiveness. This may be seen as a reversal of a traditional direction of causation where a role determined in response to other factors then dictated the technology to be acquired and used. Thus the earlier perspective accepted that factors predominantly related to market orientation and the availability and cost of physical inputs to the production process would define the roles to be played by individual subsidiaries in MNEs. This role then dictated a subsidiary's technological needs, with the traditional expectation that these would then be supplied from within the group's existing knowledge capacity. Then the upper limit to the individual technological capacities required within such a subsidiary would be the ability to assimilate the relevant knowledge effectively, and to discern the need for, and to secure the effective implementation of, such product or process adaptation as might be needed to make the established technology fully applicable to the subsidiary's market and production conditions.

In the more contemporary perspective:

> the emergence in subsidiaries of creative competences (managerial, technological, marketing) that provide a scope that extends beyond that needed in the more traditional roles underwrites their pursuit of, and accession to, the higher-value-added product development activities that increase both their own autonomy and the wider competitiveness of their group. Ultimately the skills and technology available to the subsidiary will determine its role, rather than an externally-allocated role determining its needs with regards to such assets. Thus subsidiaries go through a creative transition [Papanastassiou 1995; Papanastassiou and Pearce 1996] in which distinctive attributes increasingly differentiate their position in the group, whose overall competitive scope is thereby extended. The ability of a subsidiary to achieve an effective creative transition both depends upon, and enhances the return to, a host country's knowledge (scientific and educational) background.
>
> (Papanastassiou and Pearce 1994b)

These views indicate that to varying degrees the technological competence of subsidiaries in MNEs reflects a distinctive intermeshing of group-level knowledge capacity and their own individualised abilities and perceptions, which in turn reflect the wider scientific and knowledge (educational) background of their host country.

The implications for host-country competitiveness of the expanded technological scope of MNEs' overseas subsidiaries can be seen to have two distinctive dimensions. The first of these relates directly to the competitiveness of current industrial activity based in the host country, covering primarily the production operations of the MNEs that are located there but also encompassing the efficiency of local firms that may supply or compete with them. The second dimension of host-country competitiveness that may be influenced by the presence of MNE scientific activity relates to the longer-term evolution of the local science base itself, and its ability to support the development of indigenous industry.

In terms of the first of these dimensions it is a long-standing argument (e.g. Kojima 1978) that host-country competitiveness (and efficiency and welfare in general) can be enhanced if MNEs' technology complements currently available local production factors in a manner that boosts their productivity to levels that extant indigenous technology did not permit within local firms. In the traditional argument therefore a positive interpretation of technology transfer by MNEs was that it enabled some host countries to realise a potential comparative advantage that was embodied in certain local productive factors, but that could not be utilised competitively due to inadequate scope of existing local technology. The negative critique of this traditional process emphasised the possibility that the technology the MNEs used in certain countries would *not* be appropriate to their circumstances (demand characteristics or productive conditions) and might then seriously distort the industrial and technological development of these economies.

The forms of MNE behaviour postulated in the earlier parts of this chapter suggest that in the contemporary situation the indigenous technological competence of many countries has now achieved levels that permit it to play a much more active role in the innovation processes of MNEs, and to do so in ways that explicitly seek to min-imise the dangers of a damaging mismatch between the corporation's technology and host-country conditions and needs. Thus local scientific capacity, applied through the MNE subsidiaries' laboratories, may mediate in the application of new group-level technology to production operations located in the host country in ways that enhance their efficiency and competitiveness. Where this process is implemented effectively it would be the case that the operations of the MNE labs build on complementari-ties between their group technology and host-country scientific competences in ways that achieve distinctive (otherwise unavailable) improvements in welfare. However if the laboratories' operations are productively *efficient* (Dunning and Pearce 1994) in these terms, by achieving a synergistic use of inputs from two sources, it needs to be asked how the benefits of this are *distributed* between the partners, or more explicitly (since the MNE has specific target benefits articulated in global strategies as already observed) 'what are the rewards to the host country?'.

The second host-country issue relating to the commit-ment of parts of its scientific competence to MNE R&D activities is how this will affect the extent and direction of the development of the local technological capacity itself. In many countries support for an extensive, high-quality and distinctive local science base is seen as an integral part of, and source of, their *sovereignty* that would then be expected to contribute to the *self-reliance* of an effective locally-owned industrial sector. Does the involvement of parts of the host-country science base in MNE operations limit its growth and narrow its scope or does it assist its expansion and widen its experience, perspectives and hori-zons? Faced with the heterogeneity of MNE overseas lab roles, unique answers to these two sets of questions cannot be provided. However, by looking at the activities of the three basic types of laboratory, some clear ideas about sources of benefits or costs to host countries can be derived (Pearce 1989, 1994).

A pure SL will limit its operations to the adaptation of existing products, and their associated production processes, to local needs and conditions, so that MNEs would only need to hire competant and knowledgeable, rather than especially creatively talented, local scientific personnel for such operations so that (even in a tight labour market) the opportunity cost to local firms (gaps left in their laboratories) will be small, with it being relatively easy for them to train replacements from a new intake. The problems that will be posed to SLs are most likely to relate to technology that has obtained strong firm-specific dimensions, so that

> it may share a technological background that is common throughout much of the industry, but this has been endowed with explicit properties that represent the comparative advantage which the firm depends on to market it successfully. It is likely to be inappropriateness of these firm-specific elements, the commercial embodiment of the technology, for a particular environment that set the challenge to the SLs. Because of this it is likely that where a SL cannot fully resolve a particular adaptation problem it will seek help elsewhere in the group, where the essential characteristics of the problematic technology are understood, rather than through other host-country scientific institutions, whose technical background may be wider but less attuned to dealing with difficulties in commercial implementation.
>
> (Pearce 1994, p. 306)

This background to SLs' operations indicates that they are not likely to make a substantial contribution to the growth of the longer term, more dynamic and independent technological competence of either the MNE subsidiary or the host country. Thus

> a SL only encounters a particular piece of technology after all the creative decisions concerning its basic

manifestation, in terms of product and process, have been made, [so that] the SL's own creativity is a very truncated and essentially dependent one. Thus its personnel are unlikely to be in a position to learn the wider types of expertise needed to develop a more broadly-based innovation capability.

(Pearce 1989, p. 113)

However, more short-term benefits may accrue to a host country from SL operations as a direct result of the MNE's local production operations acquiring increased competitiveness. Thus consumers may get products that better suit their needs, at reduced prices (if production operations became more efficient users of local inputs), whilst the subsidiary's higher output may generate more local employment, increased purchases from local input suppliers and enhanced payment of local taxes.

The product-development aims of a LIL (working with associated local management, marketing and engineering personnel) in effect seek to establish a distinctive source of subsidiary-level competitiveness that reflects both the needs and competences of the host country. This locally-generated competitiveness should allow the RPM/WPM subsidiary that incorporates a LIL to provide a host country with all the direct benefits of a SL, plus a distinctive and independent export capacity that would not usually be expected from a SL.

As a result of their more ambitious aims LILs are likely to need to hire rather more distinctively talented local scientific personnel than SLs. These are then likely to have a higher opportunity cost to local enterprises that may be seeking to build up their own teams of creative personnel. However longer-term benefits may be available to the indigenous science base if these personnel later return to local firms or institutions with levels of competence that have been augmented during their work in the MNE.

Central to this is the interactive nature of LIL work. An important facet of this is the need of the LIL to liaise closely with central R&D in the group in order to become fully acquainted with the background technology (the broad characteristics of new product concepts) which it is to implement for its unique market. The temporary secondment of LIL personnel to central laboratories as part of this process may not only deepen their knowledge of the relevant technology itself, but also broaden their range of expertise by demonstration of techniques in the management of research programmes.

(Pearce 1994, p. 307)

While the MNE thus provides the background to the technology that is to be used by the LIL, the problems that may emerge with respect to its application to particular conditions may need collaboration with another set of knowledge sources. Therefore to enhance its capacity in this respect the LIL may also collaborate with local research institutions that may be familiar with the peculiarities of the specific environment, e.g. industry-funded laboratories or perhaps other firms.

In its pure form an IIL is set up in a particular country entirely in response to the quality and areas of specialisation of the local scientific community, with no mandate to help local production operations to enhance their competitiveness through product or process adaptation or development. Therefore none of the direct short-term sources of benefit that may flow to the host country through SL or LIL work are available. Thus the more important benefits or costs of IILs are likely to relate to the manner in which their activity enhances or retards the longer-term development of the capabilities of the host country's science base.

In this context it is immediately relevant to note that IILs are likely to employ especially talented local scientists, whose abilities extend well beyond the types of routine competence that could be adequately replicated through the training of new recruits. The propensity of IILs to compete such high-opportunity-cost local scientists away from indigenous firms is obviously likely to compromise the longer-term competitiveness of the locally-controlled component of the host-country industrial sector. On the other hand the employment of top local scientists in the perhaps more challenging and stimulating environment of a MNE's IIL may ultimately provide compensating benefits. Firstly

> it may be that local firms could not have provided adequate challenging opportunities to such outstanding scientists and, if they were not given such an opportunity in the IIL, they might otherwise have migrated. Since such outstanding researchers are likely to play a stimulating and constructive role in the wider host-country scientific community, as well as in the firm which employs them directly, their retention in the country may still have useful benefits.
>
> (Pearce 1994, p. 308)

Secondly when scientists work in a MNE's IIL they enter a much broader technological environment, which provides them with substantial opportunities for communication and collaboration with other talented personnel throughout the MNE group. In these interactions they may expand both their scientific knowledge and also their insights into important aspects of the initiation, organisation and coordination of major research projects, which they may later have the opportunity to apply within indigenous firms or scientific institutions. Finally it is IILs, among the lab types, that would be most likely to establish links with independent host-country scientific institutions. Once again such links may not only enable the MNE to access a further dimension of useful scientific expertise but also enhance the experience and scope of the collaborating institutions.

2.3   MNEs' INNOVATION AND HOME COUNTRIES

The discussion of the two preceeding sections has fully delineated the view that contemporary MNEs, responding to the forces of increased competition on a global scale, are increasingly decentralising their approach to the generation, application and regeneration of their technological competences. For many MNEs this crucial element in their strategy incorporated a systematic approach to R&D which embodies a strong role for overseas laboratories. A key issue underlying the analysis of this section therefore becomes the implications of this mode of behaviour for the home countries of leading technology-based MNEs. If a country's leading technologically-dynamic competitive enterprises increasingly adopt a decentralised approach to the acquisition and use of their scientific strength will this slow down the growth of its science base and lower the quality (or narrow the scope) of work that it undertakes? Does the manner in which a MNE extends its pursuit of the scientific basis for its *global* competitiveness lessen its contribution to the sustained *national* competitiveness of its home country?

A valuable perspective on the nature of the balance between home country and overseas creative activity in MNEs can be obtained through reference to data on patenting in the USA.[3] The data on each patent granted records the location of the research facility originally responsible for the innovation, and the firm to which the patent has been granted. Work carried out by researchers at the University of Reading and the Science Policy Research Unit of the University of Sussex made it possible to establish the ultimate ownership of patents in cases where they had been granted to affiliates of MNEs. This meant that for a large number of the world's leading industrial enterprises[4] data was available on the total number of patents granted to the group in the USA in a particular year, and the number of these that were attributable to research performed outside of the MNE's home country. In Table 2.2 the growth rates of the overseas patenting and total patenting of these enterprises from 1969/72 to 1987/90 are presented, broken down by the home country of the firm. Table 2.3 presents the share of overseas patents in total patents by home country of firm

over the period. Though the patent data clearly suggest
that the role of overseas creative activity in the evolution of
MNEs' technological operations varies significantly
according to the enterprises' home countries, some hypotheses regarding the implications for the home countries'
science bases may be discerned.

The most remarkable case indicated by the patent data is
that of Japanese companies' scientific expansion. For
Japanese firms the data on growth of total patents presented in Table 2.2 strongly verifies the perception that,
over the past two decades, these enterprises had a commitment to the creation of new knowledge that greatly
exceeded that of their leading rivals. Thus whilst Japanese
firms' patenting in the USA increased almost six times over
the period 1969/72 to 1987/90, the patenting growth rate
only exceeded 50 per cent for Germany, France and the
Netherlands among enterprises from major competing
countries. Reflecting this the Japanese firms accounted for
6.1 per cent of all patents taken out by the leading enterprises in the USA in 1969/72 and for 30.3 per cent in 1987/
90. US patents attributed to the overseas operations of
Japanese MNEs doubled over the period 1969/72 to 1987/
90, which is a growth rate well above the average for all the
leading firms, though below that for France and Germany.
Since the growth rate of *overseas* patenting by Japanese
MNEs is still relatively low compared to that for their *total*
patenting, Table 2.3 reveals a fall in the overseas share. It
can also be seen in Table 2.3 that the share of patents in
Japanese companies that are attributed to their overseas
activity is still much lower than that of their leading rivals.

Overall these figures for patenting in Japanese MNEs
seem to imply that the emerging overseas R&D in these
companies is playing a major *supporting* role within the
strong firm-level momentum towards the creation and
implementation of competitive new technologies. Thus the
Japanese case appears to be a classic example of overseas
R&D playing a role which is complementary to a parallel
expansion of R&D operations in the MNE's home country. As Japanese enterprises emerged from an era of com-

Table 2.2   Growth rates in US patents granted to the world's largest firms, by home country of firm

1969/72 = 100

	Overseas patenting					Total patenting				
	1969/72	1973/77	1978/82	1983/86	1987/90	1969/72	1973/77	1978/82	1983/86	1987/90
USA	100.0	133.9	117.2	114.2	121.7	100.0	112.0	89.8	74.4	75.9
Japan	100.0	163.3	135.2	186.7	210.5	100.0	228.5	290.7	389.7	597.6
Europe	100.0	132.9	111.7	104.8	132.3	100.0	147.9	131.1	111.5	129.3
EU	100.0	123.9	103.2	104.4	136.7	100.0	144.3	129.6	112.2	132.4
UK	100.0	107.6	77.7	73.0	88.7	100.0	111.2	85.8	69.2	81.9
Germany	100.0	144.7	154.8	160.7	221.3	100.0	167.3	163.7	141.7	165.7
France	100.0	149.3	123.6	145.3	292.0	100.0	158.0	140.7	129.3	150.7
Netherlands	100.0	137.1	115.8	129.1	177.1	100.0	145.9	122.5	120.5	165.6
Other Europe	100.0	167.1	143.9	106.1	115.5	100.0	166.1	138.7	108.1	113.8
Sweden	100.0	161.6	168.8	181.4	174.7	100.0	149.2	120.7	113.4	111.0
Switzerland	100.0	164.8	133.7	88.8	98.0	100.0	167.9	135.8	94.9	101.4
Total	100.0	134.2	114.3	109.5	130.1	100.0	127.2	111.4	102.1	120.0

Source: US patent database held at the University of Reading with the support of the Patent and Trademark Office, US Department of Commerce.

petitiveness based on the cost-effective production of relatively well-established products in Japan and sought to move into phases of industrialisation that involved, firstly, a growing emphasis on more sophisticated higher value-added products and, subsequently, more substantially innovative new products, it may be suggested that they became increasingly aware of severe limitations in the ability of the Japanese science base to support such an evolution. These developments coincided with expanded overseas production in these Japanese enterprises, and thus their growing familiarity with the technological and marketing capacities and environments in other developed countries. It is therefore plausible to expect that at the same time as their scientific needs motivated a vast commitment to new R&D activity in Japan it was also feasible to build into these programmes overseas R&D inputs in areas of science where established competence in other countries was clearly of outstanding quality. It may then be that the global-scanning capacity of Japanese MNEs meant that the strongest expansionary emphasis on R&D in Japan was in areas that these companies could perceive

Table 2.3   Share of total US patents granted to the world's largest firms accounted for by their overseas R&D, by home country of firm

| | Per cent | | | | |
	1969/72	*1973/77*	*1978/82*	*1983/86*	*1987/90*
USA	5.0	5.8	6.5	7.6	8.0
Japan	2.6	1.9	1.2	1.3	0.9
Europe	28.8	25.9	24.6	27.1	29.5
EU	27.4	23.5	21.8	25.5	28.3
UK	45.4	43.9	41.1	47.9	49.2
Germany	12.8	11.0	12.1	14.5	17.1
France	8.2	7.7	7.2	9.2	15.9
Netherlands	50.4	47.4	47.7	54.0	53.9
Other Europe	36.2	36.4	37.6	35.5	36.8
Sweden	18.0	19.5	25.2	28.8	28.3
Switzerland	44.5	43.6	43.8	41.6	43.0
Total	10.3	10.9	10.6	11.1	11.2

Source: As Table 2.2.

as being initially the least disadvantaged there, with their R&D overseas then tapping into the science bases of other countries in disciplines where the host comparative advantage was most formidable. Thus the needs and vision of Japanese MNEs may have not only provoked the massive rise in Japanese R&D, but also have helped to define its specific areas of competence in ways that allow it to develop distinctive comparative advantages. This emerging home-country competence will, in turn, allow Japanese MNEs to use the rest of the global technological environment in a more creative complementary manner.

By contrast with Japan the other two countries (Germany and France) that recorded very notable growth rates of overseas patenting (Table 2.2) also revealed a significant rise in overseas patenting as a proportion of total patenting (Table 2.3). This reflects the fact that the rise in their overall patenting (Table 2.2) was relatively modest.[5] In such cases it seems likely that some, at least, of the overseas R&D *substitutes* for work that might have been carried out through an expansion of R&D at home. Here then it seems plausible to suggest that for these MNEs the implementation of overseas R&D may often represent *restructuring* within a programme whose overall magnitude is relatively unchanged (rather than being a distinctive *complementary* increment in a *growth* programme for R&D, as in the Japanese case). The first implication of the rise in overseas R&D in these countries' MNEs (which are obviously likely to be amongst their most technologically-dynamic and innovative enterprises) seems likely to be that there is some slowing in the growth of their use of their home-country science base (less employment of local scientists and collaboration with local universities, etc.), though this remains substantial and central to the development of the groups' technological operations. Against this the *quality* of the MNEs' commitment to, and activity in, the home-country science base should rise. Thus as these companies increase their use of specialised high-quality decentralised R&D laboratories the home-country operations will increasingly focus on, and help to further build up, those scientific disciplines where the country already has an established comparative advantage. Further, by combining these outstanding local competences with improved access to complementary expertise (in areas where local capability may be weaker) through their overseas R&D units, the MNEs may broaden the further evolution of the most notable areas of home-country scientific capacity (by allowing them to interact synergistically with expanded research perspectives) and deepen their ability to contribute to commercial competitiveness.

The third type of case that can be discerned in the patenting data is that represented most decisively by the US and UK (also to some extent Switzerland) where the dominant factor is a notable decline in overall patenting (Table 2.2). In both cases this resulted in a modest rise in the share of overseas patenting in total patenting (Table 2.3), though overseas patenting was also essentially stagnant in these countries' MNEs (rising only slightly in the US case and falling in the UK). It may be considered that it is US and UK MNEs that pioneered the implementation of overseas R&D units, and therefore that many of them have for sometime been in the position of having fully-developed and balanced globally-integrated networks of labs, built around the specialised use of the distinctive competences of various countries' science bases, including that of their home country. When group-level factors cause the need for retrenchment in R&D operations in MNEs where such balanced global R&D networks are in place it is logical that the withdrawal should affect both home-country and overseas facilities in roughly comparable proportions. The problem that this represents for the US and UK as home countries to MNEs is, therefore, that when these leading companies make global cutbacks in their R&D the reductions they make at home tend to be in scientific disciplines that represent particular areas of national strength. This then illustrates the point that whereas the incorporation of overseas R&D in the research portfolios of companies that are expanding their scientific horizons quantitatively and qualitatively (e.g. Japan) may benefit their home countries, by encouraging an increased specialisation in their areas of greatest scientific comparative advantage, this also becomes a source of vulnerability as it is then these leading technological sectors that are most likely to be subject to substantial cutbacks if a country's main MNEs enter a period of research retrenchment.

The evidence so far discussed in this section generally supports the view that there is an underlying momentum in MNEs (albeit one that is differentiated in terms of its strength and nature between enterprises from different home countries) towards the decentralisation of their research and innovation operations. It also appears (Pearce and Singh 1992a, 1992b) that in a notable majority of cases the parent laboratories of the MNEs that embody such technology decentralisation see their overseas R&D operations as part of globally-integrated networks rather than as autonomous operations. Thus the implementation of such overseas R&D facilities seems likely to represent the most effective contemporary means of continuing the evolution of a MNE's established technological trajectory. This can then be achieved through both the widening and the deepening of the MNE's technological operations, with the extended network of R&D units capable of both adding new complementary areas of scientific competence (new disciplines) to the group's scope and also enhancing its capacities in its more well-established traditional areas of work.

Viewing these expansions of scope as an integrated evolutionary process suggests that, whatever adjustments may occur in the home-country's day-to-day research contributions, the centralised scientific decision makers of MNE groups are likely to retain the vital role of custodians of the overall perspectives on their enterprise's technological development and its contribution to future competitiveness. Clearly the performance of this role, and the decisions resulting from it, should represent and balance the needs and potentials of group-wide operations. Nevertheless it is likely to constitute the efficient extension and expansion of a scientific and commercial tradition that has historically been formulated in the predominant light of home-country conditions. Therefore it can plausibly be suggested that, even with no conscious home-country bias, the decisions taken regarding overall group-level programmes of scientific work and commerical innovation are very unlikely to take radical directions that would then diminish the potential contribution to their implementation of home-country facilities or personnel. The global imperatives of their contemporary decision making obviously will influence the long-term development of MNEs' overall technological and commercial competences, and certainly are likely to alter the parent companies' contribution to the generation and application of these competences, but, it can be hypothesised, the new intragroup balance is not likely to lessen such MNEs' contribution to their home-countries' competitiveness.

Overall it seems likely that home countries of MNEs have little reason to fear for the competitiveness of their own industrial sector when these particular companies increase their commitment to overseas R&D and adopt a more globalised perspective on technology and innovation. The investigations have clearly shown that a significant component of overseas R&D in MNEs does aim to enhance the competitiveness of the companies' operations in particular countries/regions by allowing them to apply group technology more effectively there. However there is no suggestion that the ability to use host-country scientific resources in this way has any significant influence on front-line decisions with regard to the balance between home-country and overseas production, which will be determined by a range of quite conventional supply and demand factors articulated through the strategic needs of contemporary global competition. It does seem that when a MNE has become familiar with a particular region through its initial activity there the perception of high-quality and entrepreneurial technological, marketing and managerial competences in a particular subsidiary may then provide the basis for an enhanced level of ambition in that subsidiary, perhaps as a core element in extending the depth of the

MNE's competitive commitment to the region. This form of evolution, however, is unlikely to imply any diminution in support to the competitiveness of home-country operations. Indeed the home-country production facilities are still likely to themselves comprise a central part of operations in a key market or region and may therefore benefit from *their* position in the global strategy, by being able to use local technological resources to focus on enhancing their own distinctive competitiveness.

The analysis has indicated other perspectives with regard to MNEs' commitment to the more precompetitive (basic or applied research) areas of scientific investigation. Here it has been suggested that implementation of global approaches to the performance of such work, in pursuit of the most effective underwriting of the technological basis for the MNEs' longer-term commercial development, may result in a narrowing of the home-country research effort in these companies around the country's areas of greatest scientific ability. How much diversity and how much specialisation is desirable in a country's science base and research capacity may clearly vary between countries according to, for example, their technological heritage and competitive ambition. Here we can only note that the likely effect of MNEs' evolving strategy in this area is to contribute to forces moving towards increased agglomeration in the home-country's technological capacity, which may mean taking it closer to the desired optimum or further past it into an excessive degree of specialisation.

A further point to recall in this regard is, however, that the home-country science facilities in a MNE are likely to embody responsibility for retaining the essential overview of the group's technological competences and their broad evolution, i.e. they have the unique understanding of its technological trajectory. This means that whatever may happen to the scope of their own current in-house research activity, the parent scientific units in MNEs are likely to have access to an extremely valuable global vision of technological progress which ultimately may benefit the richness of the home-country science base.

2.4   CONCLUSIONS

This chapter has reviewed selected evidence on the nature and aims of decentralised R&D operations in MNEs, placing the interpretation of this against a perception of the manner in which these enterprises are moving towards a strategic approach to *globalised* dimensions of innovation and the sustained pursuit of competitiveness. MNEs have traditionally accepted the need to adapt established products to meet the distinctive tastes and characteristics of particular host countries or regions. The greater depth of understanding of and commitment to these host economies that is thus achieved, taken with the intensified competitive pressures on leading global firms, has then led to the frequent desire in ambitious subsidiaries to be able to react more profoundly to local conditions and potentials through a more complete commitment to the *development* of distinctive products. One aspect of this is the belief in such subsidiaries that the quality of the local science base can support such ambitious activity, by permitting the recruitment of adequately-skilled personnel for in-house work (the subsidiary's own R&D unit) and by allowing for a complementary supportive collaboration with other local scientific institutions (e.g. university laboratories). Where such interaction then reveals especially strong basic research capacities in a host country's science base, relating to particular strengths in areas of investigation that are relevant to the needs of the longer-term precompetitive research programmes of the MNE, a further dimension of involvement may emerge. Here then a country may host specialised basic or applied (but mainly precompetitive) laboratories, that operate in a manner that is more or less autonomous from other MNE operations in the same location, in order to provide high-quality specialised inputs to a globally-coordinated group-level programme. However, it is out of the increasing intermeshing of the *global* technology objectives and programmes of MNEs, and what are still usually essentially *national* science bases that potentially significant policy dimensions may emerge.

As a background to elucidating these issues let us assume (Pearce and Papanastassiou 1996) that there remain significant areas of potentially important scientific investigation that are unlikely to be funded adequately by private enterprises, even very large and globally-competitive MNEs. Thus crucial areas of speculative precompetitive (basic and applied) research may be very expensive, involve high levels of risk and uncertainty, and provide results that may be difficult to appropriate adequately. If private enterprise will not risk funding these areas of research it may be considered vital that some authority does support them, in the interest of the long-term capacity of science to enhance welfare and solve problems. Assume further that, for the present, the most likely sources of funding for such precompetitive science (that ultimately may make a major contribution to defining a country's technological comparative advantage) emerges at the national level (or at most at the level of a regional group of countries) rather than at the global level. Then if, in the ways analysed in this chapter, key users of these national science bases are MNEs (i.e. *nationally*-created elements of science support the development of *internationally*-oriented firms) then important issues may emerge with regard to the attitude and policy response to these developments of both home and host countries.

However the first of these issues may be whether it is in fact necessary or appropriate to concern ourselves too much with the country-level consequences of MNEs' new approaches to globalised perspectives on technology creation and application. Thus

given the increasingly globalised operating perspectives of leading firms, and the probable global-viewpoint of most researchers (in the sense that they see themselves as primarily motivated to achieve progress in their areas of science, rather than as motivated to help science to benefit explicitly their own country) isn't it very narrow to ask how the MNEs' R&D can benefit individual countries?

(Pearce and Papanastassiou 1996, p. 98)

It is certainly important that national attitudes should not move towards a kind of research mercantilism, which could occur if a country was host to laboratories of foreign MNEs but at the same time also the home country of other MNEs which themselves possessed labs overseas. The government of a country in this situation could try to maximise the benefits it gets from foreign laboratories' operations in the country and also those secured by its own MNEs' labs abroad in order to, in some sense, create a balance-of-research surplus. Such manipulation would be likely to severely compromise the genuine welfare-creating potentials of an internationalised firm-level approach to R&D.

Nevertheless as long as precompetitive research is not going to be wholly, or adequately, funded by private companies, and as long as the wider research and technological-education infrastructure is predominantly created and supported at the national level, there may be reasons for fearing the results of countries becoming concerned at the use of their science base by MNEs.

Two quite obvious and complementary reasons may be suggested for this fear (Pearce and Papanastassiou 1996, pp. 98–9):

Firstly, if a government begins to suspect that a large share of the benefits of the scientific infrastructure it supports are attained in the global operations of foreign MNEs, rather than in the effectiveness of its own national industrial base (and, of course, especially that part of it taken by indigenous enterprises), it may cut back severely on such funding. If many leading industrial countries gain the same viewpoint, and implement the same response, the result could be a significant global decline [in official support for science and especially basic research] and a slowing of overall technological progress. Secondly, if a government notes that its own MNEs are performing large amounts of their R&D overseas and that the global efficiency of their operations gains from this, with ultimate benefits to the home country, it may decide to take a free ride on this situation and cut back support for domestic science. Again if a number of countries perceive the situation in this way the overall effect on R&D inputs and scientific progress may be negative.

Overall then it seems that national perspectives within the process of technological globalisation by MNEs remain a matter of concern. Earlier analysis has clearly suggested that the process possesses the potential to enhance the ability of science to contribute to an improved generation of economic welfare, but that also uncertainties and suspicions about the way such benefits

> are distributed may ultimately compromise the effectiveness of the process, through technological protectionism or even opportunistic behaviour by governments. To analyse the nature of the implications of the globalisation process for individual countries, therefore, does not imply an ideological constriction of the conceptual scope, but rather that securing all its possibilities does require acknowledgement and understanding of different dimensions of interest amongst contributing parties.
>
> (Pearce and Papanastassiou 1996, p. 99)

How then may host and home countries of MNEs articulate policy positions that support the wider creative perspectives of these companies' global technology strategies whilst still ensuring that these strategies also operate in ways that provide benefits to the competitiveness and technological scope of their own local economy?

A broad policy prescription for host countries, based on the line of argument just put forward, is that the interjection of foreign MNEs' laboratories into their economies should not compromise governments' commitment to a sustained backing for technological evolution through support for education at all levels, the development of scientific skills in the labour force, and for certain areas of R&D. The quality of this science base can then attract valuable elements in MNEs' operations, which in turn may help improve the effective application of science in order to enhance the competitiveness of industry based in the host country (indigenous as well as foreign controlled). This then points to the more specific point that if a government wishes to take a detailed policy stance on the role of R&D in inward investment it should approve operations that add to the competitiveness of MNE production activity in its economy. This is most likely to be achieved when the work of local scientists enables a MNE's technology to be applied most effectively, i.e. in a manner which allows local production operations to supply products that meet the precise needs in the firm's target markets in the most cost-effective manner. We have suggested that this is most likely to occur when a LIL plays a role in WPM/RPM subsidiary product development operations.

A second benefit that host countries can seek through the operations of MNE laboratories is the expansion of the knowledge and scope of the local personnel that secure employment in them. This too is likely to be a potential that is extensively available through LILs, where local scientists may increase both their scientific knowledge through familiarity with the newer elements in the MNE's technology (which they then develop and apply to their subsidiary's specific needs), and also their functional scope by closer familiarity with the wider organisational aspects of programmes from applied research through to commercial development. Some of these benefits may also emerge from IILs where local personnel are certainly likely to be involved with key elements in the MNE's most scientifically ambitious work and may again expand their own scientific horizons notably, along with valuable experience of the organisational aspects of such complex basic research programmes. However IILs provide no direct feedback to current host country competitiveness and may also be employing some of the country's most talented scientists, with therefore a considerable opportunity cost to local industry's creative scope. Support for the prestigious quality of work in IILs may therefore be a somewhat misguided policy, with wider and more immediate benefits likely to emerge from the LIL/RPM package which targets competitiveness directly.

The growing tendency in contemporary MNEs for their overseas subsidiaries to take increased responsibility for their own distinctive competitiveness need not be a source of any substantial policy concern to the home countries. Thus it is unlikely to be responsible for any reduction in the status of home-country production operations. The increased competitiveness that the overseas subsidiaries develop within their own operations is mainly an attempt to expand their market (more suitable products produced more efficiently) through a degree of responsiveness that could only be achieved using local in-house creative resources. In any case this is likely to occur within a wider decision process that will already have determined the desirability of decentralised production in key market areas as part of a logical contemporary global strategy. Creative operations in overseas subsidiaries thus develop their allocated market rather than, in any way, win it away from home country exports, i.e. reduce home-country competitiveness in a quantitative sense. More positively home-country production facilities are likely, within the same global strategy, to gain an enhanced mandate to focus on the supply of a key market area of their own (the local market and perhaps adjacent regional markets) and concentrate on developing distinctive technological competences to do so.

In terms of the use of more precompetitive (basic and applied research) areas of scientific investigation, the earlier discussion did illustrate the manner in which increasingly globalised perspectives on the acquisition of such inputs in its MNEs might help to narrow the range of truly world class disciplines within a country's science base.

Here, however, the behaviour of the MNEs would appear to be a reinforcing reaction within a more widely driven process of agglomeration, and thus not one that would merit a policy response aimed at restricting the MNEs' globalised programmes. Nevertheless home countries might view the overall process of the narrowing of their quality science base as quite a vulnerable one, and could perhaps provide support for certain complementary and supportive areas of research that are not currently benefitting from the natural agglomerative momentum. Finally we can observe that even if MNEs are narrowing the range of research they perform in the home country when they take a global-network approach to precompetitive investigation, the fact that such decentralised programmes usually remain subject to parent (home-country) laboratory coordination and supervision helps considerably to maintain a clear monitoring of evolving world science in the main areas relevant to the MNEs' longer-term competitive evolution.

Notes

1. The relevance of 'increased complexity (fusion) of technology' in Table 2.1 confirms this perspective.
2. See Pearce (1992), Pearce and Papanastassiou (1996, pp. 32–6).
3. The data on the geographical origins of patents granted in the USA have been compiled at the University of Reading in collaboration with the Science Policy Research Unit at the University of Sussex. The data on US patent counts were prepared by the Office of Technological Assessment and Forecast, US Patent and Trademark Office, with the support of the Science Indicators Unit, US National Science Foundation. The opinions expressed in this paper are those of the author and do not necessarily reflect the view of the Patent and Trademark Office or the National Science Foundation.
4. The data covers all the firms from the sample of the 792 largest industrial enterprises in the world in 1982 analysed by Dunning and Pearce (1985, pp. 8–11) for which patenting records were available, plus 41 additional companies excluded from that sample but where patenting was extensive.
5. At more modest growth-rate levels Sweden and the Netherlands reveal some of the same patterns.

3 Motivation and Market Strategies of US Foreign Direct Investments: An Analysis of Host-Country Determinants

with Marina Papanastassiou

3.1 INTRODUCTION

During the past quarter-century there has been a major change in the predominant mode of strategic behaviour adopted by leading multinational enterprises (MNEs) in many industries. Up until the 1960s the prevalent approach was what Porter (1986) termed a multidomestic strategy, in which MNEs' overseas subsidiaries focused on supplying the local markets of the countries in which they operated with products whose characteristics had already been essentially defined in the home country (or another major market) of the MNEs.[1] Each subsidiary thus had, to a great degree, its own competitive environment, with its rivals limited to other incumbents of that local market, be they indigenous firms or subsidiaries of other leading MNEs in the industry. In this context competition between MNEs could be seen as predominantly a series of separate contests between quite autonomous subsidiaries in specific national markets.

However, a range of developments (see Pearce 1992, pp. 39–42) led to an increasing internationalisation of the background to competition. MNEs could no longer rely on a set of autonomous import-substituting subsidiaries, focused uniquely on the supply of their host-country markets, to provide the basis of a sustainable posture. Such a *multidomestic* strategy needed to evolve into a much more clearly perceived *global* strategy. Though it is often dangerous to abandon the attempt (which had often been quite a natural part of a multidomestic strategy) to respond to the distinctive needs of important individual markets, a global strategy requires an MNE to make the most effective use of all its worldwide assets in order to optimise its ability to compete on a global scale. Leading MNEs now compete with each other through their integrated globalised operations, rather than through a fragmented set of isolated confrontations of individual subsidiaries. As an element in this approach to global competitiveness the MNE needs to integrate the resources of each of its overseas subsidiaries as effectively as possible into its international network of operations. Very often this has meant a fundamental refocusing of an individual subsidiary's role, away from supply of the host market towards an export-oriented position in the MNE group's global network of facilities. These export-oriented subsidiary roles, and their implications for host countries, are a central theme of the conceptual argument and empirical investigation of this chapter and they will be elaborated upon in the next section.

Though MNEs now see their behaviour and targets in an essentially globalised perspective, host countries (even when to some degree integrated into wider economic communities) still have to determine their own policies for resource development and welfare creation at the national level. Nevertheless the presence of MNE operations is one of a number of factors that indicate that the most effective strategy for the use and development of a nation's resources needs to be articulated in the light of its position in the international economy. A key aspect of such issues is that a country should be concerned to derive policies that not only permit an internationally competitive use of its current resource base, but that also fully respond to the need to regenerate sources of competitiveness and enhance the level of local value-added in production and exports. Countries thus need to perceive their industrial progress as a process of *creative transition*, in which the current sources of competitiveness are not seen merely as a static comparative advantage, but rather as providing the resources for the development of new sources of technological capacity which endow the sector with a more self-supporting dynamic capability. Exemplifying this concept of creative transition has been the evolution of countries (e.g., Japan and the Asian newly industrialising countries) which were able to initiate an industrial base by producing established products in a more price-competitive manner (due, notably, to low labour costs) and were then able to greatly increase the value- added in their output by moving to a situation in which indigenous technological capability allows them to innovate and market important new products.

It is a central element of our thesis here that there exists a natural tendency for the roles of export-oriented subsidiaries of MNEs to evolve in a manner which parallels and supports the type of creative transition that would be valuable to host countries. The next section develops this thesis further. Section 3.3 then introduces the empirical tests, with the two remaining sections reviewing the results and drawing some conclusions.

3.2 SUBSIDIARY ROLES AND CREATIVE TRANSITION

As we have observed, developments in the international economic environment induced MNEs to adopt new approaches to competing worldwide, with these changes having major implications for the role played by subsidiaries in individual host countries. Our analysis of the roles played by MNE subsidiaries can be seen as based around two choices. The first choice is that involving a refocusing of the subsidiary's basic orientation away from supply of the host-country market towards export markets. The second choice is then that between two very different types of export- oriented subsidiary. To elaborate on these choices, and the natural evolution that may to some extent be involved in them, we can use a taxonomy of three types of overseas subsidiary operation.[2]

The first type of subsidiary is that which played the import substituting role within a multidomestic strategy. This has been termed a truncated miniature replica (TMR). The subsidiary is a *replica* in the sense that it produces, and sells in its host-country market, most of the product range of the parent company and other leading subsidiaries in the group, thus reproducing their behaviour in those respects. However, many such subsidiaries are *miniature* replicas since their local markets do not permit them to achieve the scale of production of the group's leading operations. This is one of the reasons why these subsidiaries were often very inefficient producers. Further these facilities are *truncated* in the sense that they lack certain functions that would be present in a healthy independent operation. In particular they have no scope to create products for their market, being dependent on externally-derived product and process technology. Similarly management is constrained to implementing the local operation essentially in the image of established MNE group practices, with little room for innovative behaviour. This suggests that TMRs are not only likely to suffer *static* inefficiency in their current production, but lack any *dynamic* scope to enhance the capability of host-country industrialisation.

Inevitably, developments eventually exposed the limitations of such TMR subsidiaries. Declines in protection and improvements in international transportation increasingly opened these operations to very damaging import competition. Furthermore the rise of new MNEs (especially from Japan), which from the start emphasised efficiency throughout their global network, also underlined the vulnerability of TMRs. However, simple closure of a subsidiary was often not an acceptable option to MNEs, since the country's market remained important and might be extensively damaged by unfavourable publicity following the withdrawal from local production. Thus a restructuring of the subsidiary to take on an export-oriented role was frequently considered the more viable form of evolution. A further choice was then available in terms of the nature of the exporting subsidiary.

Perhaps the natural exporting successor role for TMRs is that of a rationalised product subsidiary (RPS). Here the subsidiary focuses on the specialised production of a very limited part of the established product range (perhaps even selected component parts or a separate stage in a vertically integrated production process) which, given access to the MNE's existing worldwide market for these goods, it is able to carry out at a scale which allows the achievement of full efficiency. Local demand for those parts of the MNE's product range not produced in the RPS can be met by imports which have themselves been manufactured in other, similarly specialised, RPS plants located elsewhere. Thus the feasibility of extensive intra-group trade allows MNEs to establish an international network of producing facilities that contribute to strong cost-based competitiveness. The key step forward taken by the RPS is that its specialised production role allows it to avoid the damaging efficiency connotations of the miniature aspect of TMRs. Also, of course, its specialisation means it is no longer a replica of other units. This, however, is less obviously progressive since its role *is* still defined within the existing product and process technology of the MNE group. It will generally be *allocated* its position in the network (in the light of host-country factor availabilities and costs), rather than *earn* it through its own creativity and advocation of its distinctive attributes. Thus the RPS will be at least as truncated in its functional scope as was the TMR. The role of management is to execute the production of current products for supply in externally determined quantities, with no scope for marketing or other creative initiatives.

We, therefore, perceive this RPS approach to investment as based on a static view of host-country comparative advantage, basically in line with the trade theory approach of the Heckscher–Ohlin model. It can thus be argued that such operations would be unlikely to provide the basis for a distinctive long-term development of the host country.

Indeed many host countries that have successfully started development around this type of approach (notably several of those countries now described as the Newly Industrialised Countries) have needed to evolve through a process of *creative transition*, in which resources have been committed to upgrading their location characteristics and deriving an indigenous creativity. This then involves a deliberate move towards the establishment of an independent local technical capability, away from the dependent implementation of the existing results of foreign innovative capacity. Forces pressing for such an evolution may also emerge, within the MNE, at the subsidiary level. The competitive and outward-looking environment occupied by the RPS (compared with the protected and inward-looking situation of the TMR) may cause its managers to take a more ambitious view of their own potential and of creative resources (technological, engineering, marketing) available in the host country (if not already in the subsidiary). They may then advocate a fundamental widening of the subsidiary's role, from the production of current products, to the creation, production and marketing worldwide of new products.

Such a widening of the functional basis of these export-oriented operations to incorporate more creative local inputs (technology and marketing), coordinated and motivated by much more entrepreneurial subsidiary-level management, led to world (or regional) product mandate subsidiaries (WPM or RPM). These operations are generally perceived[3] as subsidiaries which are mandated by their parent MNE to create a distinctive new product, and take responsibility for its further competitive evolution, its production and its marketing (either worldwide [WPM] or in a substantial regional market [RPM]).[4] MNEs using WPM operations may therefore be able to tap into a much wider range of creative resources as an integrated part of their global activity. Thus a network of WPM facilities can both contribute strongly to the evolution of the MNE group's competitive ownership advantages (in a manner absent from RPS operations), whilst still responding efficiently to the distinctive location advantages of different production sites.

The role of central management in a MNE moving towards the use of WPM subsidiaries then becomes much more one of evaluating and balancing programmes of geographically-decentralised independent creative initiatives, rather than imposing the implementation of an essentially centralised programme on a network of dependent RPSs.[5] However, the MNE group may still supply some centralised services to its network of WPM facilities. Thus a given WPM subsidiary may decide, at its own discretion, to secure some scientific inputs from a central group laboratory or to use a group-level global marketing network to supply at least part of its international market. WPMs can therefore retain autonomous *responsibility* for obtaining some functions, without needing to implement a complete range of their own facilities.[6] Indeed it is this intermeshing of host-country creative inputs into the wider programmes, and alongside the existing assets, of the MNE that may provide the longer-term benefits of WPM subsidiaries to the countries in which they are based. Thus talented host-country personnel may not only be able to more completely utilise their current abilities in such subsidiaries, but may also greatly enhance them through the wider perspectives offered in the context of WPM work. Further the MNE-motivated context of seeking innovative global competitiveness should cause the local personnel committed to it to gain a clearer perception of the potential value of their own, and their country's, capability. If these abilities and perspectives can spillover into the wider host-country economy then they can strongly support its wider creative transition.

The global perspectives of the MNE, as implemented through the roles played by their subsidiaries in individual host countries, and the way their transformation responds to the challenges and opportunities of an interdependent world, can therefore boost their host countries' understanding of their potential in the *global* economy. With such an image clearly perceived by host-country policy makers, they can comprehend the need for the operations of MNEs to go beyond the short-term benefits of RPSs (e.g. employment, balance of payments effects) towards the creative transition that will provide the country with a sustained ability to create dynamic comparative advantages of the type brought by WPM facilities.

This perspective suggests that host countries need not be passive recipients of investment that merely *allocates* them a role in centrally-determined MNE programmes, but may be able to *claim* a distinctive position in mutually-beneficial creative operations. There can then be an evolutionary interaction between host countries and MNEs, which provides mutual benefits in which host-country characteristics may help shape the development of the competitive ownership advantages of an MNE, which when implemented can, in turn, enhance competitiveness of its host-country subsidiaries.

3.3   TESTS AND HYPOTHESES

In order to obtain some empirical elaboration of the strategic choices discussed in the previous section we test the determinants of the degree of export-orientation of US MNE subsidiaries' operations in various countries. Broadly these tests help to discern the factors underlying the basic choice between inward- and outward-oriented operations. However, the hypotheses developed for certain of the independent variables can also relate to the second choice, i.e. that between RPS and WPM type of exporting. The basic data used is derived from US Department of Commerce Benchmark Survey of Operations of US MNEs. More detail of this, and of the sources for the independent variables, is included in Appendix 3.1.

The tests are carried out for an all industries sample (i.e. including petroleum and services), and for all manufacturing. Three different export-orientation ratios are incorporated in the tests.

The first of these ratios measures, for each host country, 'total exports as a percentage of total sales' of US MNE subsidiaries (EXPTOT). It was possible to test this ratio for the all industries and manufacturing samples, including separate tests for developed and developing country sub-samples (see Table 3.1).

The second ratio tested was 'exports to the US as a percentage of total sales' (EXPUS). This was tested for the same samples as EXPTOT (see Table 3.2), except that a high number of zero values for manufacturing in LDCs precluded meaningful separate tests for this subsample. Finally the remaining ratio covered 'exports to other countries as a percentage of total sales' (EXPOC), and was tested for the same samples as EXPTOT (see Table 3.3). Because these dependent variables are constrained (to values between zero and one hundred), and all samples included some limit values, our multiple regression tests are carried out using the tobit technique rather than OLS.

One expectation that we hold with regard to potential differences between the two component ratios (i.e. EXPUS and EXPOC) is that exports to the US will be much less likely than exports to other countries to include supplies from WPM type operations. This is because it remains likely that the creation and innovation of products primarily targeted at the US market would be carried out there[7] rather than within overseas subsidiaries. Use of overseas subsidiaries to supply US markets is likely to remain motivated by cost and efficiency factors (i.e. RPS operations).

The independent variables used to test the various export-orientation ratios will be introduced in detail below. Initially we recall that many of these variables are developed in an attempt to distinguish the relative presence of RPS and WPM types of operations. It will be seen that an underlying assumption in the articulation of the role of several of these independent variables is that export-oriented facilities are more *footloose*, and therefore more likely to be either encouraged or discouraged by certain aspects of the local environment that would be less likely to influence the extent of host-country-market-supplying operations. However, this traditional view is somewhat modified within the context of our analysis of the different export roles. Thus while we would expect RPS facilities to still be quite footloose in this way, we believe this is likely to be much less the case for WPMs. This is the implication of the fact that WPMs are based on much more distinctive attributes of local inputs, which are therefore less likely to be available in alternative locations than the more homogeneous inputs sought by RPSs. In a sense then the possibility of supplying these quality inputs provides host countries with an element of bargaining power *vis-à-vis* WPMs that they do not possess *vis-à-vis* RPSs. We now proceed to introduce the independent variables and the hypothese relating them to the export orientation.

(i) GDP

We include GDP as an indicator of the potential size of the host-country market. Our clear hypothesis here is that, where host- country markets are relevant to the operations of US MNE subsidiaries, a negative relationship will emerge between GDP and the measures of export orientation. Thus it may be argued that the higher is GDP the more likely it would be that US subsidiaries would take on a predominantly import-substituting role, with a primary focus on the local market and no systematic interest in the development of export capability. A detailed aspect of this would be that the larger is the host-country market the more rewarding it may be to create distinctive product variants to meet the specific characteristics of that market, which may then lessen the range of foreign markets to which the subsidiary's output might have been applicable. Against this is the possibility that large host-country markets may induce high levels of cost efficiency in subsidiaries' local production (through realisation of economies of scale) which may generate some spillover exports, which could weaken the negative sign expected in this case.

Turning to the export-based strategies, we would still expect a negative sign on GDP to persist to some extent for the case of WPM operations. Thus, though export markets are a central part of WPMs' product-development activities, the host country is also very likely to be a natural part of the market area targeted. With this being so, it would again be a logical prediction that the higher the host-country GDP the more important its share of a WPM's overall market. So, by comparison with the import-substitution case previously outlined, the share of exports in WPM operations is likely to be generally very much higher, but is still likely to be negatively related to GDP. By contrast our view of RPS operations is that they are likely to have negligible interest in host-country markets, so that GDP would have little influence. Therefore in cases where RPS operations predominate, the relationship between GDP and our measures of export orientation would be relatively weak.

(ii) Wage and wage bill productivity (WBP)

As indicated in the development of the conceptual background in the first two sections, host-country labour costs may be a crucial factor determining the role of US MNE subsidiaries' operations. The annual average wage per worker (WAGE) is introduced to test this.

We would expect that if decision makers look predominantly at the wage rate, and if cost factors are a key influence on the establishment of export-oriented facilities, then the variable WAGE would be negatively related to the share of exports in sales. This, as already suggested, does involve the view that productivity of labour is not also taken into account. However, it remains our interpretation that where the negative sign does emerge this would indicate the prevalence of predominantly cost-based RPS operations. By contrast, in the case of WPM operations a key attraction of relevant host countries would be the availability of personnel with the particular types of original creative abilities needed to generate such a subsidiary's distinctive competitive potential. If WAGE is, in such a case, considered as an indicator of quality (with cost now taking a much lower priority) then a positive relationship between this variable and the measures of export orientation can be hypothesised.

As previously observed, it may be a deficiency of WAGE that whilst focusing on the *cost* of labour as a decision variable, it does not allow for the way in which firms might also need to take productivity into account in determining the role of subsidiaries in particular countries. We therefore also include a wage bill productivity variable (WBP), which measure sales ($) per $ of wage paid. Our most decisive prediction for this variable is of a positive relationship with the measures of export orientation in the case of RPS operations. Thus highly cost-efficient labour is generally assumed to be a key factor attracting these very strongly export-focused subsidiaries. However, a positive sign for WBP could also reflect the presence of WPM operations. This would follow from the possibility that the high productivity that contributes to a high value of WBP may reflect the local inputs of the types of skilled creativity and innovativeness that lead to the successful export of high-value-added differentiated products by WPM subsidiaries. Nevertheless pursuit of the type of cost effectiveness reflected in WBP is much less of a priority for WPMs, whose dynamic focus on longer- term product development (compared with the RPS's need to emphasise effective short-term supply of existing products) may lead to extensive employment of high-wage scientists, marketing personnel and managers whose contribution lowers WBP without compromising the basis of a WPM subsidiary's export capability. In such a case the positive relationship between WBP and measures of export orientation can be broken, with insignificant, or even negative results.

(iii) Collective bargaining (CB)

In order to investigate further dimensions of the employment environment, we include a variable that reflects the prevalence of collective bargaining in production operations in host countries. Thus the collective bargaining variable (CB) is measured as the percentage of US MNE subsidiaries' production workers in a particular country that are covered by collective bargaining agreements. This may complement the cost and efficiency variables (WAGE and WBP) by providing an indicator of more qualitative aspects of the employment environment. Indeed CB may serve as a proxy for wider aspects of the social context within which US MNE subsidiaries operate.

Underlying our broad hypothesising with respect to CB is the general view that such environmental influences are more likely to affect the willingness of MNEs to implement relatively footloose export operations than those tied to the supply of the host-country market. If high values of CB are interpreted as symptomatic of potentially difficult or confrontational environments (perhaps with the potential for damaging upward pressure on costs), then our line of argument clearly leads to the prediction of a negative relation between CB and the export-orientation ratios. A secondary aspect of this (alluded to earlier in general terms) is that *within* export activities those crucially dependent on the production environment (i.e. RPSs) will be more affected by influences such as CB than those embodying a wider range of inputs and functions in pursuit of more creative aims (i.e. WPMs). Though we need not abandon the predicted negative sign for CB, we may anticipate that the relationship with export orientation would be somewhat weaker in those cases where we believe WPMs to be relatively prevalent. In such situations the distinctive capabilities of skilled and creative local workers may prepare MNEs to work around any potential difficulties implied by high values of CB, in ways that they would not do for unskilled production labour. Furthermore the opportunity to apply their expertise to interesting projects set up by WPM subsidiaries of MNEs may lead such talented host-country workers to themselves take steps to mitigate any unfavourable implications of high levels of formal collective bargaining requirements.

(iv) Education

We include in our tests two measures of host-country education levels, namely 'number enrolled in secondary education as a percentage of the relevant age group' (SEC ED), and 'number enrolled in higher education as a percentage of population aged 20–24' (HIGH ED). The purpose of this is an attempt to distinguish between circumstances conducive to the implementation of RPS and WPM operations.

Though clearly not in a strict sense a rigorous distinction we argue that a positive relationship between SEC ED and the measures of export orientation would be most likely to reflect the presence of RPS, since secondary education would imply the presence of adequate skills to implement the relatively routine production of the established products exported by these facilities. By contrast we would argue that a positive relationship between HIGH ED and the export ratios would be more likely to reflect the availability of the types of highly-trained and individually-creative managerial, marketing and technological personnel that could provide the basis of innovative WPM operations.[8]

(v) Incentives and performance requirements

Governments may influence the environment for FDI by either offering encouragements or by setting behavioural targets. These may affect the willingness of MNEs to set up subsidiaries, or help determine the type of operation. Thus the last two country-characteristic variables that we incorporate are incentives (INC) and performance requirements (PERF REQ). The measure of incentives used is the percentage of respondents to a US Department of Commerce survey that received incentives offered by the host country, whilst the measure of performance requirements (PERF REQ) is the percentage of respondents to the same survey that had undertaken to operate within some particular form of regulation or limit. From the host-country point of view incentives may be seen in a rather quantitative sense, as a general attempt to stimulate the flow of foreign direct investment into the country. Performance requirements, however, may have a more qualitative aspect, by attempting to induce particular types of behaviour by investors that would fit in with previously determined host-country objectives.

From the point of view of MNEs incentives may be perceived positively, either because of the actual assistance they provide, or because willingness to offer them is interpreted as indicative of an overall favourable host-country environment for foreign firms. From this broad perspective our hypotheses for INC are developed as for other environment characteristics (e.g. collective bargaining). Thus we suggest that export operations will generally respond more strongly than host-country market operations (positive relationship with export ratios), and that the RPS operations that are more conscious of the need for immediate efficiency will be more responsive than WPMs.

Our hypothesis for PERF REQ is that of a negative relationship with the export ratios that, once again, would be strongest in the case of the more strongly efficiency-motivated RPSs. This interpretation partly incorporates a general perception of performance requirements as symptomatic as a somewhat unsympathetic host-country attitude to foreign-controlled operations. More directly, however, it reflects the unwillingness of MNEs to have their desired behaviour patterns altered by such regulations, especially in the case of export operations. This would clearly be the case when the MNE views such performance requirements as embodying arbitrary and unrealistic demands which reflect bad planning and perhaps generate short-term and uncertain perspectives. However, it is plausible that when performance requirements reflect sensible plans related to the long-term potential of the host country MNEs may not be so deterred by them, and may in fact view them as helping to define a clear and reliable environment.

(vi) Country and region dummy variables

Finally we include a number of country or region dummy variables. These seek to take account of the influence of geographical proximity or special trading arrangements that might have an effect on exports even after taking account of the market, cost and other environmental influences covered by the previous variables. Thus Canada and Mexico are given individual dummies because of their extensive borders with the USA, whilst Japan, as a rather distinctive host country also has its own dummy.

Another dummy covers members of the EEC. Since, in our tests, it is the non-EEC European countries that serve as the omitted dummy we believe that a positive sign for the EEC dummy would indicate a particularly strong tendency to allocate specialised export-oriented roles to subsidiaries in these countries, as a direct response to the free-trade arrangements available in the community.

Dummy variables are also included for Latin America, Asia (including Australia and New Zealand), and Africa and the Middle East. We have no strong *a priori* expectation that membership of these areas would induce different exporting performance by comparison with the non-EEC European countries that serve as the omitted dummy.

3.4 RESULTS

(i) GDP

Throughout the tests it is the negative sign for GDP that prevails among the significant results. The strongest source of this relationship seems to be for EXPOC for developed countries, which reflects a relatively strong role for import substituting and/or WPM operations, whilst the insigni-

Table 3.1 Regressions with total exports as a percentage of sales (EXPTOT) as dependent variable

	All countries		Developed countries		Less-developed countries	
	All industries	*Manufacturing*	*All industries*	*Manfufacturing*	*All industries*	*Manufacturing*
GDP	-0.3054 *D-1*	-0.6084 *D-1*	-0.5716 *D-1**	-0.6944 *D-1***	-0.1158	-0.5166 *D-1*
	(-1.0905)	(-1.6447)	(-2.1572)	(-2.4529)	(-1.2435)	(-0.3592)
WAGE	0.1366	-0.6722	4.7635 ***	1.5504	-0.1835	-0.8248
	(0.2429)	(-0.6230)	(3.3576)	(1.1025)	(-0.2511)	(-0.3589)
WBP	2.1724 ***	-2.5394	-1.1993	-6.4135	2.7022 ***	-1.7250
	(3.8506)	(-1.1967)	(-1.2587)	(-1.3554)	(3.8581)	(-0.5612)
CB	-0.1847	-0.8297 ***	-0.4058	-0.8768 **	-0.4155 *D-1*	-0.5668 *
	(-1.2047)	(-3.5017)	(-1.6088)	(-3.0337)	(-0.2402)	(-1.9245)
SEC ED	0.6014 *D-1*	0.8405 *D-1*	-0.1586	-0.1571	0.9433 *D-1*	0.6157
	(0.2455)	(0.2414)	(-0.5084)	(-0.5269)	(0.3420)	(1.2374)
HIGH ED	0.4245 *D-1*	0.1242	0.2265 *D-1*	1.8719 *	-0.4771	-1.3134
	(0.0977)	(0.2104)	(0.0286)	(1.9235)	(-0.9782)	(-1.5906)
INC.	-0.4995	0.1301	-0.1479	1.3210	0.4352	0.9697
	(-0.9559)	(0.2143)	(-0.2508)	(1.3237)	(0.5657)	(0.8703)
PERF REQ	-0.3766	-3.3177 *	7.8075 **	-0.2396	-0.6234	-4.0397
	(-0.2849)	(-1.6459)	(2.8622)	(-0.0675)	(-0.4428)	(-1.5235)
Canada	7.0347	17.596	14.907	-0.3363 *D-1*		
	(0.3177)	(0.6469)	(0.7869)	(-0.0014)		
Mexico	5.2091	3.1586			5.7520	13.327
	(0.2386)	(0.1211)			(0.2573)	(0.4296)
Japan	-11.416	-0.6453	32.601	8.8272		
	(-0.3176)	(-0.0144)	(0.8788)	(0.2289)		
EC	21.066 **	37.539 **	36.935 ***	38.667 ***		
	(1.9817)	(2.6123)	(3.7125)	(3.6146)		
Latin America	7.4101	-15.842				
	(0.7162)	(-1.1174)				
Asia	-3.2130	-9.8388	-4.7875	-43.147 ***	-12.486	13.690
	(-0.2698)	(-0.6166)	(-0.4302)	(-3.3059)	(-0.9659)	(0.6470)
Africa and Middle East	0.8283	-52.695 **			-1.5450	-31.347
	(0.0629)	(-2.6208)			(-0.1407)	(-1.2950)
R^2	0.5570	0.6135	0.7815	0.8661	0.6916	0.7125
n	50	45	22	21	28	24

Notes:

n is the number of observations. In the notation *D-X*, *X* is the number of 0 to be inserted after the decimal point. Figures in ( ) are *t* values.
* Significant at 10% ** Significant at 5% *** Significant at 1%

Table 3.2 Regressions with exports to US as a percentage of sales (EXPUS) as dependent variable.

	All countries		Developed countries		Less developed countries
	All industries	Manufact uring	All industries	Manufact uring	All industries
GDP	0.5457 D-2 (0.2264)	0.2914 D-1 (0.9406)	0.7229 D-2 (0.5176)	0.5025 D-2 (0.5233)	-0.1331 (-1.3277)
WAGE	-0.1776 (-0.3767)	-1.4436 (-1.5195)	1.4080 * (2.0687)	-0.8171 D-1 (-0.1459)	-0.2889 D-1 (-0.0368)
WBP	0.5088 (1.1524)	-4.9084 ** (-2.0120)	0.8468 D-1 (0.1553)	-1.0548 (-0.5612)	0.6685 (1.0406)
CB	-0.3568 D-1 (-0.2751)	-0.7231 *** (-3.2476)	0.2452 (1.6509)	-0.1338 (-1.0168)	-0.3520 D-1 (-0.1869)
SEC ED	0.1824 (0.8697)	0.4335 (1.4314)	0.1956 (1.1680)	0.1545 (1.2657)	0.8396 D-1 (0.2769)
HIGH ED	-0.5882 (-1.5755)	-1.5575 *** (-2.7415)	-0.4503 (-1.0022)	0.3394 D-2 (0.0102)	-0.8780 (-1.6420)
INC	-0.7833 * (-1.7160)	0.6080 (1.1382)	-0.4122 (-1.2005)	0.3982 (1.0203)	-0.1239 (-0.1501)
PERF REQ	1.3156 (1.1605)	-4.9315 *** (-2.6969)	3.8836 ** (2.6447)	-2.1280 (-1.3976)	1.6299 (1.0615)
Canada	20.234 (1.0936)	56.567 ** (2.4734)	19.106 (1.8005)	27.058 ** (2.8393)	
Mexico	-1.9430 (-0.1067)	23.643 (1.1291)			6.4810 (0.2745)
Japan	-11.688 (-0.3842)	-38.889 (-1.0632)	7.3588 (0.3703)	-4.9297 (-0.3604)	
EC	0.3003 (0.0327)	8.6919 (0.7018)	1.3210 (0.3029)	1.2555 (0.3687)	
Latin America	8.4687 (0.9411)	20.461 (1.5906)			
Asia	3.8860 (0.3727)	13.432 (0.9689)	4.4384 (0.6838)	-3.7861 (-0.8890)	-4.9544 (-0.3579)
Africa and Middle East	8.7376 (0.7330)	-130.85 (-0.0201)			-0.2837 (-0.0227)
R^2	0.4511	0.6899	0.7211	0.8120	0.3797
n	50	45	22	21	28

Notes:

n is the number of observations. In the notation D-X, X is the number of 0 to be inserted after the decimal point. Figures in ( ) are t values.

* Significant at 10%   ** Significant at 5%   *** Significant at 1%

Table 3.3   Regressions with exports to other countries as a percentage of sales (EXPOC) as dependent variable

	All countries		Developed countries		Less-developed dountries	
	All indu-stries	Man-ufacturing	All indu-stries	Man-ufacturing	All indu-stries	Man-ufacturing
GDP	-0.2084 D-1	-0.5915 D-1 †	-0.5985 D-1 *	-0.7234 D-1 †	0.6375 D-2	0.4662 D-1
	(0.9312)	(-2.0637)	(-2.2335)	(-2.6212)	(0.1080)	(0.3821)
WAGE	0.2913	0.5861	3.6279 †	1.8824	-0.5011	-1.0479
	(0.6148)	(0.7208)	(2.7103)	(1.3714)	(-0.9168)	(-0.5544)
WBP	1.9007 ‡	0.5283	-1.6453	-6.9161	2.3017 ‡	1.2237
	(4.1003)	(0.3350)	(-1.6047)	(-1.5327)	(4.6868)	(0.4760)
CB	-0.2032	-0.4590 ‡	-0.7498 †	-0.8049 †	-0.6944 D-2	-0.2293
	(-1.5366)	(-2.6259)	(-2.7108)	(-3.0233)	(-0.0575)	(-0.9501)
SEC ED	-0.6011 D-1	-0.3088	-0.2824	-0.2532	0.5321 D-1	-0.2505
	(-0.2934)	(-1.1358)	(-0.9002)	(-0.8803)	(0.2831)	(-0.5633)
HIGH ED	0.5663	1.3594 ‡	0.3499	1.7123	0.1816	0.8733
	(1.5916)	(2.7495)	(0.4331)	(1.8266)	(0.6026)	(1.2005)
INC	0.2398	0.1371	0.4336	1.4262	0.5595	0.4434
	(0.5694)	(0.3038)	(0.7144)	(1.5095)	(1.1768)	(0.4834)
PERF REQ	-1.8436 *	-0.4290	3.1882	0.8147 D-1	-2.1497 †	-2.2001
	(-1.6654)	(-0.2827)	(1.1249)	(0.0254)	(-2.1319)	(-1.0015)
Canada	-10.072	-26.549	-2.7886	-22.237		
	(-0.5658)	(-1.2693)	(-0.1467)	(-0.9781)		
Mexico	14.331	-4.3071			0.8553	14.311
	(0.8130)	(-0.2191)			(0.0622)	(0.5401)
Japan	-13.644	6.8291	19.676	13.815		
	(-0.4709)	(0.2004)	(0.5325)	(0.3719)		
EC	21.992 †	32.615 ‡	36.435 ‡	39.245 ‡		
	(2.5428)	(2.9303)	(3.6657)	(3.7336)		
Latin America	4.7092	-33.018 ‡				
	(0.5602)	(-2.9012)				
Asia	-7.7604	-24.129 *	-12.295	-42.805 ‡	-14.146	7.5403
	(-0.7869)	(-1.9574)	(-1.0796)	(-3.2838)	(-1.6945)	(0.4214)
Africa and Middle East	-9.1251	-35.771 †			-7.7426	3.8544
	(-0.8555)	(-2.4375)			(-1.1106)	(0.2026)
R^2	0.6180	0.7228	0.7738	0.8786	0.7995	0.2919
n	50	45	22	21	28	24

Notes:

n is the number of observations.

In the notation D-X, X is the number of 0 to be inserted after the decimal point.

Figures in ( ) are t values.

* Significant at 10%   † Significant at 5%   ‡ Significant at 1%

ficant result for developing countries for EXPOC may indicate (by our hypotheses) a much more important role for RPS in that case. The insignificance of GDP in the tests of EXPUS is compatible with our view that RPS style exports are likely to prevail in US MNEs' exports to their home country, with host-country markets rarely likely to affect the scale of production.

(ii) Wage and wage bill productivity

In the results for EXPOC (and as these are also reflected in the results for EXPTOT) we find some tentative support for the expectation that US MNEs' WPM operations would be most prevalent in developed countries, with a much stronger focus on RPS in LDCs. Thus Table 3.3 shows that for both all industries and manufacturing WAGE is positively signed and WBP negatively signed for developed countries, which our hypothesising suggested to be a pattern most compatible with the needs of innovative and skilled WPM activity. By contrast for LDCs in these tests of EXPOC, WAGE is negatively signed and WBP positive (though surprisingly significantly so for all industries but not manufacturing), the combination which we feel is more likely to reflect the cost-based orientation of RPS. Overall the results in Table 3.2 are somewhat disappointing in view of our expectation that EXPUS would be much more decisively related to cost-based influences.

(iii) Collective bargaining

The negative sign predicted for the variable CB clearly prevails throughout our results, with all the clearly significant cases taking this sign. This confirms that this indicator of qualitative aspects of the employment environment is one that affects MNEs' decisions with regard to the type of operations implemented in particular countries. In particular it supports our view that such aspects of host-country environments are more likely to affect decisions with respect to the viability of export-oriented production than those relating to supply of the local market.

However, the indications that can be discerned within these results do not substantiate our expectation of a stronger negative effect of CB on RPS, compared with that on WPMs. Thus in Table 3.3, CB is more strongly negatively related to EXPOC for developed countries (where WPMs are believed to be relatively prevalent) than for developing countries (where RPS are likely to predominate). Similarly CB has less obviously negative effects on EXPUS (Table 3.2) for developed countries, despite the fact that we believe these exports to the US to be distinctively cost based, than for EXPOC for developed countries (Table 3.3) where we anticipate a greater role for WPMs.

(iv) Education

In the results for EXPOC reported in Table 3.3, we find a positive sign on HIGH ED combined with a negative sign for SEC ED in the case of manufacturing operations in developed countries. Despite lack of significance this can be seen, in the light of our articulation of the hypotheses for these variables, as representing some degree of indicative support for our expectation of a strong role for WPM operations in this case. However, the fact that a similar pattern is repeated (only a little less strongly) for manufactured exports from LDCs, a case where RPS operations would have been clearly expected, works against over-confident interpretation of the result. For EXPUS (Table 3.2) the prevalent pattern of positive signs in SEC ED and negative signs on HIGH ED is clearly compatible with our expectation of a predominant role for cost-based RPS in overseas supply of the US market, and of little need for the creativity of WPM.

(v) Incentives and performance requirements

In the tests of EXPOC (Table 3.3), INC is persistently positively signed (i.e. incentives tend to stimulate export operations somewhat more than local-market sales), though never significant. The strongest of the results in this table is that for manufacturing subsidiaries in developed countries. In line with our hypotheses we may tentatively suggest that in this case it is WPM operations that are finding incentives particularly valuable in supporting the longer-term perspectives of a transition to more creative activities. For EXPUS incentives are less clearly stimulating to export operations (though INC is still positively signed for manufacturing). If we are correct in believing that exports to US are more likely to be the output of RPS than WPMs, this result again counters our expectation that it would be the former that were most responsive to incentives.

The negative effect of performance requirements on exports emerges most clearly for the variable EXPOC in LDCs (Table 3.3). This is in line with our view that such requirements are perceived as most seriously compromising by subsidiaries seeking to make the optimum use of host-country location advantages in pursuit of competitive production of existing products. For EXPOC PERF REQ loses its negative sign for developed countries. This may be the result of an ability of many developed countries to set up performance requirements that do not deter export-oriented operations, but rather may encourage them by establishing a more collaborative environment in which foreign subsidiaries feel understood and secure. This in turn may reflect developed country governments' knowledge of the experience and needs of their own MNEs. For EXPUS the expectation that performance requirements would particularly deter the cost competitive operations that are believed to prevail in this case is only supported for the manufacturing sample.

(vi) Country and region dummy variables

The strongest result amongst the dummy variables is that for EC countries in the tests of EXPOC. This may be mainly attributed to intra-community trade, responding to the opportunities created by the institutional arrangements established by the community. Thus, apart from these community conditions, many of the same trading opportunities would have been available to the other European countries which comprise the 'omitted dummy' region.[9] In line with this the EC dummy is not significant (i.e. EC subsidiaries' behaviour is not different from that in other European countries) for exports to the US (EXPUS).

The dummy for Canada is consistently negative in the tests of EXPOC, reflecting geographical and institutional isolation. As would be expected, this changes for EXPUS, where the Canadian dummy is clearly the most strongly positive, especially for manufacturing. For Mexico the strongest dummy result is the positive one for manufactured exports to the US, whilst for Japan the negative sign in the same test is the most distinctive result.

As might be expected, the dummy variable results for Latin America in Tables 3.2 and 3.3 suggest that, at least in manufacturing, US subsidiaries in that region have a greater than average tendency to focus their export capability on supply of the US market. US subsidiaries in both Asia and Africa and Middle East seem to have generally rather low export orientations, especially as reflected in EXPOC (Table 3.3).[10]

3.5 CONCLUSIONS

In broad terms (though not always in precise detail) the results confirm our view that the export orientation of US MNEs' overseas subsidiaries responds to host-country characteristics in ways that reflect an increasing scope for widely different motivations within such operations. The results of this study are compatible with our belief that the implementation of global-competition strategies by MNEs involves not only the pursuit of optimally-efficient networks of dispersed *production* facilities (i.e. RPS), but also an increasing desire to use the *creative* resources of a wide range of locations in order to broaden the base of their innovative capability (through WPM subsidiaries). Thus it appears that as host countries get richer the export orientation of US MNE subsidiaries may become rather less dependent on the pure cost effectiveness of the local labour force, and more responsive to elements of skill and creativity, which may instead generate competitiveness through the innovative development of differentiated products. As emphasised in the introduction, this intermeshing between the more dynamic and innovative functions of the MNE and the creative potential of host countries will substantially widen the contribution that MNEs may make to sustained development. Whereas RPS may provide a valuable first step, by increasing the scope for the use of a country's current productive resources (a quantitative benefit), WPMs can take their contribution beyond this by (in a more qualitative manner) providing the country's more distinctively talented personnel with the opportunity to help to develop a unique source of competitive advantage within the MNE's global portfolio of assets. The global competitiveness of MNEs may now derive from the ability to utilise a geographically-dispersed range of ownership advantages, many of which, whilst compatible with the group's broad competitive programme, may have distinct location-specific (or subsidiary-specific) characteristics with regard both to their creation and implementation. The momentum to regenerate these sources of competitiveness means, in effect, that MNEs take a more dynamic view of the location advantages of host countries, seeing their own corporate evolution as inextricably intertwined with the development of national capability.

Notes

1. Thus the process of internationalisation of production had frequently followed the precepts of Vernon's (1966) original product cycle. The restructuring of operations discussed here may then be,

to some extent, discerned in Vernon's subsequent (1979) reformulation of the product cycle argument.

2. Analyses which have contributed to the derivation of a taxonomy of subsidiary types include Crookell and Caliendo (1980, pp. 61–2); Wex (1984, pp. 4–6); White and Poynter (1984, pp. 59–61); Young *et al.* (1987, pp. 155–8); Cordell (1971, pp. 29–30); D'Cruz (1986, pp. 80–7); Crookell (1986, pp. 104–7).

3. For a definition of World Product Mandates, see Bonin and Perron (1986, p. 161); Poynter and Rugman (1982, p. 60); Rugman (1983, p. 79); Wex (1984, pp. 18–19); Wolf (1983, p. 91).

4. For illustrative examples of the origins and roles of selected WPM facilities see Bartlett and Ghoshal (1986, p. 90); McGuinness and Conway (1986, pp. 147–56); Rugman and Bennett (1982, pp. 60–1); Witten (1981).

5. See Pearce (1992, pp. 54–5). Also Bartlett (1986, p. 382) has suggested that a challenge facing global companies is to 'upgrade the role of national units from that of implementer or adapter of centrally directed policies and strategies, to that of contributor and partner in the development and execution of the company's worldwide strategies'. Bartlett adds (1986, p. 384) that this 'requires important changes in individual attitudes and interpersonal relationships. To ensure that local capabilities are enhanced, instead of depleted, and that the entrepreneurial spark is fanned not doused, the challenge is to coopt rather than subjugate the national units into a global role'.

6. For an elaboration of this point in the context of R&D and marketing see Pearce (1992, pp. 52–4).

7. In a manner that still reflects the traditional arguments relating to the first stage of the original product cycle (Vernon 1966).

8. An obvious problem with tests of these distinctions using these education variables is the high correlation between them shown in Appendix 3.2. However, when, in the various tests, subsidiary regressions were run omitting either SEC ED or HIGH ED the result for the remaining variable changed little from its value when both variables were included. Certainly in no case did changes occur which changed the patterns depicted in Tables 3.1 to 3.3. Thus multicollinearity seems to be less of a problem in interpreting these variables than might have been anticipated.

9. Except in tests of developing country subsamples, when Latin America plays this role.

10. The particularly strong negative dummy results for Asia in the developed country analysis of Tables 3.1 and 3.3 covers Australia and New Zealand, and at least partially reflects their geographical isolation.

Appendix 3.1: Source of data

Dependent variables

The ratios EXPTOT, EXPUS and EXPOC were calculated from US
   Department of Commerce, Bureau of Economic Analysis, *US Direct
   Investment Abroad: 1982 Benchmark Survey Data*, Tables III.E.3;
   III.E.4; III.E.5.

Independent variables

GDP – is measured in billions of US \$. The source was The World
   Bank, *World Development Report 1984*, Table 3, pp. 222–3.
WAGE – is measured as thousands of US \$. It is derived from US
   Department of Commerce (*op. cit.*), Tables III.F.3. and III.F.6.
WBP – is calculated from US Department of Commerce (*op. cit.*),
   Tables III.F.6; III.E.3; III.E.4: III.E.5.
CB – is calculated from US Department of Commerce (*op. cit.*), Table
   III.F.13.
SEC ED *and* HIGH ED – the source of both of these variables was The
   World Bank, *World Development Report 1985*, Table 25.
INC – is the percentage of respondents in a country who received
   incentives there. It is calculated as the average for three types of
   incentive; i.e. tax concessions; tariff concessions; subsidies. The
   source is US Department of Commerce (*op. cit.*), Table II.I.1.
PERF REQ – is the percentage of respondents in a country who
   operated under performance requirements there. It is calculated as
   the average for five types of performance requirement; export a
   minimum amount; import no more than a certain amount; acquire
   a minimum amount of inputs locally; employ a minimum amount of
   local personnel or add a minimum amount of local labour content to
   products; transfer technology to the host country; maintain a specified ratio of exports to imports, or of earnings of foreign exchange to
   expenditures of foreign exchange. The source is US Department of
   Commerce (*op. cit.*), Table II.I.3.

Appendix 3.2: Correlation matrix[1]

		(1)	(2)	(3)	(4)	(5)	(6)	(7)	(8)	(9)	(10)	(11)
(1)	EXPTOT	1.000										
(2)	EXPUS	0.614	1.000									
(3)	EXPOC	0.783	-0.011	1.000								
(4)	GDP	-0.246	-0.244	-0.119	1.000							
(5)	WAGE	0.049	-0.166	0.196	0.312	1.000						
(6)	WBP	0.646	0.429	0.481	-0.193	-0.094	1.000					
(7)	CB	-0.180	-0.284	-0.001	0.065	0.254	-0.274	1.000				
(8)	SEC ED	0.027	-0.350	0.309	0.194	0.501	-0.139	0.269	1.000			
(9)	HIGH ED	-0.170	-0.470	0.152	0.270	0.390	-0.354	0.382	0.684	1.000		
(10)	INC	-0.422	-0.345	-0.267	-0.157	-0.349	-0.449	0.184	-0.001	0.051	1.000	
(11)	PERF REQ	-0.205	0.195	-0.414	-0.221	-0.474	-0.064	-0.070	-0.623	-0.493	0.446	1.000

Note:
1. Covers all countries and all industries.

Part II
Overseas R&D and
Technological Diversity
in MNEs

4 Motivation and Organisation of Decentralised R&D

with Satwinder Singh

4.1 INTRODUCTION

It is a familiar argument that the emergence of global strategies in leading enterprises has involved the balancing of factors encouraging an increased emphasis on the distinctive needs of overseas markets with the more traditional factors believed to favour a continued concentration on the centralisation of key functions. Thus the need to maximise global competitiveness is seen as requiring a full response to the characteristic needs of each major market and also the need to optimise the use of each country's productive potential, either to supply its local market in the most competitive way or to incorporate efficient capacity in a wider strategy (i.e. as export-platform facilities). Operating against the moves towards the decentralisation of activity provoked by these perspectives may be such familiar centralising influences as the need to fully recognise economies of scale (in production, R&D, management, etc.) and the importance of sustained close communications between the key decision makers from various functional areas (e.g. marketing, R&D, engineering, planning).

For a long time it was believed that innovation was a factor which played a major role in the sustained influence of centralised activities and held back the emergence of truly distinctive elements in overseas operations. This perspective was very influentially enshrined in the original product cycle (Vernon 1966), where it was indicated that various factors (notably the need to facilitate close interfunctional communications during the implementation of

81

important innovations) would lead to the introduction of new products being focused on home-country markets, with a certain amount of subsequent adaptation (to products or processes) occurring to support their competitiveness in overseas markets. One of the most important recent developments in thinking on global strategies has been to recognise the need for, and viability of, a much more geographically dispersed and differentiated approach to innovation (Bartlett and Ghoshal 1989, 1990). Thus true global competitiveness needs new products to reach all major geographic market segments quickly and in forms that respond to the unique needs and characteristics of these markets. This geographical widening of the key technological and creative processes of firms is clearly likely to benefit from a dispersion of their R&D activities through the increased establishment of overseas laboratories. It is the purpose of this chapter to present some survey evidence on the manner in which overseas R&D facilities in MNEs support a more differentiated approach to the creation and application of knowledge in support of widening global strategies.

Against this background in the increasing need of MNEs to use overseas R&D to support the effective implementation of global strategies, our survey analysis recognised three broad sets of factors which are perceived as influencing the extent and nature of such work. The first of these are *demand-side* factors. Thus overseas R&D is likely to be frequently motivated by the need to make the most effective response possible to the needs or potentials of different markets and/or production environments, where the required creative work (adaptation or development) is likely to be most efficiently implemented in facilities located in close association with the other functions (production and/or marketing) which define the problems to be addressed.

We also seek to investigate the relevance of *supply-side* influences on overseas R&D. One facet of these influences includes several characteristics of technology creation which have traditionally been alleged to constrain the ability of MNEs to effectively decentralise their R&D. These include the need to fully realise economies of scale in R&D, the need to keep R&D centralised in order to max-imise the security of important knowledge, and the diffi-culty of handling the communications involved in an effectively decentralised approach to R&D. Against this can be placed the more positive facet of supply-side influences, such as that MNEs have become much more sensitive to the existence of strong and specialised scientific capabilities in particular foreign locations and aware of the possibility of usefully co-opting such inputs to support their global strategies.

Since we have observed that the interest in overseas R&D has developed alongside the need for MNEs to strengthen their ability to respond to the demands of global competition through the effective implementation of a global strategy, the third set of influences recognised are *competitive* factors. At one level these competitive factors involve the ways in which decentralised R&D is required to support the overall competitiveness of the group, e.g. by developing distinctive new products or by contributing to the derivation of important new techno-logy. At another level overseas R&D units may implement some aspects of their operations as a response to oligopo-listic competition within the technological environment, i.e. in response to moves initiated by R&D facilities of rival companies.

The role of overseas R&D in leading enterprises[1] was investigated through a questionnaire sent to 623 parent laboratories, i.e. either corporate level R&D units (physi-cally located at corporate headquarters, or otherwise dis-tinguished as the corporate unit) or the main R&D facilities of major divisions in diversified firms. Satisfac-tory replies were obtained from 245 of these.[2] The next section of the chapter investigates the influences on over-seas R&D in terms of the demand-side, supply-side and competition factors discussed earlier, and then analyses the nature of specialisation between parent and overseas sub-sidiary units with regard to the performance of five types of R&D. The third section derives some perspectives on the nature of coordination and interdependence in overseas R&D as perceived by the parent units. The last section derives conclusions on the nature and roles of overseas R&D in MNEs.

4.2 MOTIVATION AND SPECIALISATION OF OVERSEAS R&D

We now seek to interpret results from various parts of the questionnaire that was sent to parent labs in order to assess the relevance of the three types of influences on overseas R&D discerned in the introduction.

(i) Demand-side factors

Those parent labs that had overseas R&D facilities were asked to assess six factors which might have influenced the type of work done in those affiliated units abroad. They were requested to grade each factor as 'never relevant', 'sometimes relevant' or 'nearly always relevant'. Three of these factors represent demand-side influences on R&D.

As might have been expected the 'need to adapt the product for the local market' was a widely pervasive influence on overseas R&D, being rated as 'nearly always relevant' by 81 (67 per cent) of 121 respondents and 'never relevant' by only nine (7 per cent), thus providing an average response[3] (AR) of 2.60 (see Table 4.1). Though somewhat less prevalent than product adaptation, parent labs also saw the 'need to adapt production techniques to local conditions' as also very influential on overseas R&D. Thus 60 (51 per cent) of 118 respondents considered this factor as 'nearly always relevant' and only 19 (16 per cent) as 'never relevant' (i.e. an AR of 2.35). UK firms (an AR of 2.75) seemed to be particularly influenced by this factor, as were firms in food, drink and tobacco (2.82) and metal manufacture and products (2.80).

Table 4.1   Parent laboratory evaluation[1] of factors influencing the type
of work done in overseas R&D units

| | *Influencing factor (average response)[2]* | | | | | |
	A	B	C	D	E	F
By industry						
Food, drink and tobacco	1.60	2.27	2.10	2.73	2.82	2.78
Aerospace	2.00	2.00	1.50	1.50	2.00	2.00
Industrial and agricultural chemicals	1.89	2.13	2.00	2.81	2.48	2.39
Petroleum	1.67	1.50	2.17	2.67	2.27	2.50
Electronics and electrical appliances	2.00	1.94	1.63	2.67	2.29	2.33
Industrial and farm equipment	1.67	1.78	1.63	2.44	2.00	2.00
Metal manufacture and products	1.80	2.20	1.40	2.60	2.80	2.40
Motor vehicles (including components)	1.75	2.13	1.67	2.75	2.38	2.63
Office equipment (incl. computers)	3.00	2.50	2.00	2.50	2.50	2.00
Photographic and scientific equipment	2.40	1.60	1.60	2.00	2.20	2.00
Pharmaceuticals and consumer chemicals	2.21	1.79	1.43	2.36	2.00	2.14
Other manufacturing	2.00	1.56	1.63	2.56	2.33	2.75
Total	1.89	1.92	1.76	2.60	2.35	2.37
By home country						
USA	1.85	1.87	1.68	2.54	2.31	2.29
UK	1.63	2.00	2.04	2.48	2.75	2.40
Other Europe	2.13	1.96	1.59	2.76	2.30	2.46
Japan	2.07	1.93	1.67	2.64	2.43	2.43
Other countries	2.00	2.00	3.00	3.00	2.00	3.00
Total	1.89	1.92	1.76	2.60	2.35	2.37

Notes:
1. Respondents were asked to rate a factor as 'never relevant', 'sometimes relevant', 'nearly always relevant'.
2. Average obtained by giving a value of 1 to 'never relevant', 2 to 'sometimes relevant', 3 to 'nearly always relevant'

Influencing factors:
A – a distinctive local scientific, educational or technological tradition conducive to certain types of research project.
B – cost factors.
C – only room for a small number of basic R&D laboratories.

(*Contd. overleaf*)

D – need to adapt product to local market.
E – need to adapt production techniques to local conditions.
F – need to develop distinctive new products for the local market.
Source: Pearce and Singh survey.

Though seen by the parent R&D units as somewhat less influential than the adaptation of current products, the more ambitious demand-side role of developing new products in response to distinctive needs of local markets was also rated as very important. Thus 56 (49 per cent) of 115 respondents considered the 'need to develop distinctive new products for the local market' to be 'nearly always relevant' and only 13 (11 per cent) believed it was 'never relevant' (an AR of 2.37). Industries in which overseas R&D was particularly motivated by product development were food, drink and tobacco (an AR of 2.78), motor vehicles (2.63) and other manufacturing (2.75).

Elsewhere in the questionnaire parent labs that had considered implementing overseas R&D but had eventually decided not to do so were asked to evaluate a number of factors relating to their rejection of such units. Demand-side factors did not seem to play such a strong role in these decisions. Thus when asked to evaluate the possibility that 'none of our overseas markets are large enough to require separate R&D support', only nine of 30 respondents rated this as a 'major cause of rejection', whilst 11 believed it to be 'of some influence' and 10 'irrelevant to the decision' (an AR of 1.97). Similarly only eight of 31 respondents felt that 'none of our overseas markets are sufficiently distinctive to require separate R&D support' was a major cause of decisions not to implement such research which, with 11 considering this influence as irrelevant, gave an AR of 1.90.

When respondents that had not actively considered the implementation of overseas R&D were asked to evaluate factors that might lie behind this lack of interest, 'no, or very limited, foreign market' was rated as of little relevance. Thus 36 (57 per cent) of 63 parent labs believed this factor to have had 'no influence on consideration of foreign R&D', 11 (18 per cent) felt it may have been 'of some influence on excluding possible foreign R&D', and only 16 (25 per cent) rated it as 'a major factor ruling out consideration of foreign R&D' (an AR of 1.68).

(ii)   Supply-side factors

It is increasingly suggested that part of the motivation for the emergence of geographically-dispersed R&D in MNEs lies in the perception that certain overseas sites have distinctive strengths which can be harnessed to play specialised roles in a group's R&D programme. To test this parent labs with overseas R&D were asked to evaluate the influence of 'a distinctive local scientific, educational or technological tradition conducive to certain types of research project'. Only 22 (19 per cent) of 118 respondents considered that this influence was 'nearly always relevant', though 61 (52 per cent) felt it was 'sometimes relevant' (an AR of 1.89). MNEs from Other Europe (an AR of 2.13) and Japan (2.07) were most likely to respond to this influence in their overseas R&D, and those from the UK (1.63) least so.

When the parent labs that had considered but not implemented overseas R&D were asked to evaluate possible reasons for rejection, one offered factor was that 'no overseas R&D locations have the expertise to rival home country units'. The replies suggested that the relative availability of scientific expertise was perceived as of surprisingly limited importance by the parent labs. Thus of 30 replies 14 considered the factor as 'irrelevant to decisions' and only seven as 'a major cause of rejection' (an AR of 1.77). In a similar manner those parent labs that had not actively considered overseas R&D were asked to assess 'the home country research environment, including skills of scientists, is fully adequate for our needs' as a possible influence precluding interest in dispersed R&D. A strong evaluation of the home country research capacity was in fact rated very decisively as a factor precluding contemplation of overseas R&D, with 42 (60 per cent) of

70 respondents rating this 'a major factor ruling out consideration of foreign R&D' and only nine (13 per cent) assessing it as 'of no influence' (an AR of 2.47).

The second supply-side influence that parent labs with overseas R&D were asked to evaluate was 'cost factors'. This, like distinctive capacity in overseas locations, was not generally rated as a major influence. Thus only 21 (18 per cent) of 119 respondents felt this was 'nearly always relevant' as an influence on the type of work done in overseas units, whilst 30 (25 per cent) considered it was 'never relevant' (an AR of 1.92).

It is possible to include amongst supply-side factors a number of characteristics of R&D work which have traditionally been expected to mitigate against its effective decentralisation. Thus it has often been suggested that in many industries decentralised R&D would be limited to unambitious adaptive activity, since more advanced work required such large facilities that the adequate realisation of economies of scale would restrict the number of units that could be used effectively. When those parent labs with overseas R&D were asked to assess 'only room for a small number of basic R&D laboratories' as an influence on their overseas R&D it emerged as of very little relevance. Thus only 27 (25 per cent) of 110 respondents felt it was 'nearly always relevant' and 53 (48 per cent) 'never relevant' (an AR of 1.76). UK firms (an AR of 2.04) seemed to feel particularly constrained by this influence.

However, when those parent labs that had considered overseas R&D before rejecting it were asked to evaluate 'research economies of scale (critical mass) requires centralised facilities', the relevance of this factor was somewhat enhanced. Thus 15 of the 34 respondents noted this as 'a major cause of rejection' and 12 more as 'of some influence on rejection' (an AR of 2.23). Similarly when those labs that had not actively considered overseas R&D were asked to evaluate 'scale factors must limit our research to one site' as a factor precluding possible dispersion, 30 of 64 respondents rated it as 'a major factor ruling out consideration of foreign R&D' and 21 more believed it to have been of some influence (an AR of 2.27). It thus seems that decision makers with actual experience of overseas R&D find less reason to be concerned about the influence of economies of scale than those seriously contemplating, or broadly speculating about, implementing such operations.[4]

Another factor which has often been argued to mitigate against international dispersion of R&D is the sensitivity of a firm's research. Our results in fact indicate that this is of little relevance. Where overseas R&D had been considered and rejected only four of 31 respondents believed that 'the sensitivity of our research requires close home country control' was a 'major cause of rejection' but 22 felt it was 'irrelevant to the decision' (an AR of 1.42). Similarly only eight of 61 labs that had not actively considered overseas R&D suggested that they felt 'sensitivity of our research' was a 'major factor ruling out consideration of foreign R&D', whilst 36 believed it was 'of no influence' (an AR of 1.54).[5]

The last of the factors which is traditionally believed to mitigate against the decentralisation of R&D is the possibility that communications problems could compromise the effectiveness of dispersed operations. Thus parent labs that had rejected overseas R&D were asked to evaluate 'communications problems with dispersed units would harm the type of R&D we do'. This was again of limited relevance, with 14 of 31 respondents rating it as 'irrelevant to the decision' and 11 as 'of some influence on rejection' (an AR of 1.74).

(iii) Competition factors

Results already discussed make it clear that overseas R&D provides significant support to overall group competitiveness, by adapting products to increase their competitiveness in distinctive host-country markets, by adjusting current production techniques to increase their efficiency under different operating conditions, and by creating new products suitable for the needs of particular host countries or to make the best use of the potential of competitive foreign production locations. However our results provide less support for the view that overseas R&D might play a role in oligopolistic technological competition, as part of the way in which firms respond to the R&D moves made by their main competitors.

Thus when parent labs were asked what influence the R&D work of rival firms was likely to have on the functioning of their unit, only 39 (17 per cent) of 226 respondents felt that it was 'likely to stimulate increased use of our overseas R&D units'. Similarly when parent labs that had considered, but not implemented, overseas R&D were asked to evaluate factors that may have stimulated such consideration of overseas operations, only 18 (41 per cent) of 44 respondents included 'increased internationalisation of R&D by our rivals', all except three of these combining this influence with at least one of the other options offered.

The logical momentum behind the growth of overseas R&D in MNEs is that it should increasingly play a role in the creation and development of group technology, and not merely be limited to assisting in its effective application. This would extend the evaluation of supply-side factors, and the more ambitious demand-side ones, in MNEs to overseas R&D. However this momentum may still be subject to some inertia with, for example, myopic centralised perspectives still dominating in the assessment of supply-side inputs into the more precompetitive phases of the innovation process. To investigate the division of specialisation between central and overseas labs, those parent units which possessed affiliated labs overseas were asked to assess five types of R&D (Table 4.2) according to whether they were perceived as being (i) relatively more important in the overseas R&D units than in the parent, (ii) equally important in the overseas and parent R&D units, (iii) relatively less important in the overseas R & D units than in the parent, or (iv) not carried out in either overseas or parent units.

Table 4.2 Relative position of different types of R&D in overseas and
home-country laboratories of MNEs[1]

	Types of research (relative importance in overseas laboratories)[2]				
	A	B	C	D	E
By industry					
Food, drink and tobacco	1.50	2.00	1.89	2.20	1.86
Aerospace	1.00	1.50	2.00	2.00	1.00
Industrial and agricultural chemicals	1.40	1.86	1.81	2.05	1.81
Petroleum	1.33	1.67	1.64	1.92	1.64
Electronics and electrical appliances	1.38	1.89	1.94	2.35	1.75
Industrial and farm equipment	1.50	1.86	2.13	1.88	1.43
Metal manufacture and products	2.00	1.75	2.00	1.75	1.75
Motor vehicles (including components)	1.33	1.89	1.56	2.11	1.89
Office equipment (incl. computers)	1.33	2.00	2.33	2.00	1.67
Photographic and scientific equipment	1.67	2.20	1.80	2.00	2.00
Pharmaceuticals and consumer chemicals	1.50	1.93	1.83	2.07	1.50
Other manufacturing	1.00	2.14	1.86	2.29	1.71
Total	1.40	1.89	1.85	2.09	1.71
By home country					
USA	1.24	1.80	1.80	2.04	1.63
UK	1.50	1.88	1.79	2.04	1.82
Other Europe	1.44	2.18	1.95	2.26	1.79
Japan	1.89	1.83	2.00	2.08	1.73
Total	1.40	1.89	1.85	2.09	1.71

Notes:

1. Responding parent R&D labs with affiliated overseas units were
   asked to assess each of the types of R&D as either (i) relatively
   more important in the overseas R&D units than in the parent, (ii)
   equally important in overseas and parent R&D units, (iii) relatively
   less important in the overseas R&D units than in the parent, (iv) not
   carried out in either overseas or parent R&D units.
2. An average response calculated (after omitting cases where the type
   of R&D was not performed at all) by allocating a value of 3 where
   it is more important in the overseas laboratory, a value of 2 where it

(Contd. overleaf)

is equally important in the overseas and parent laboratory, and a value of 1 where it is less important in the overseas laboratory.

Types of research

A – basic/original research.
B – research to derive new products in present industry.
C – research to derive new production technology in present industry.
D – improvement of existing products and/or techniques.
E – research to derive additional products in new areas of specialisation.
Source: Pearce and Singh survey.

———————

The first type of work covered here is basic research. This emerged as the type that firms were most likely to omit totally from their research portfolio, with 25 (22.7 per cent) of the 110 labs that assessed its position saying that it was not performed at all in their group. Basic research was also the type where centralised performance did still retain greatest prominence, with 57 (51.8 per cent) of respondents rating it as relatively less important in overseas R&D units, and only 6 (5.5 per cent) rating it as more important in these units than in the parent. Japanese MNEs seemed to have the most notably decentralised perspectives on basic research, and those from USA the least (Table 4.2). There is no clear indication that the tendency towards relative decentralisation of basic research is strongest in high-technology industries. Overall the response to this question may indicate that whereas basic research is emerging in overseas labs in response to the supply-side factors already discussed, the parent labs do still see themselves as the main custodians and arbiters of its position in their MNEs' technological evolution, so that this type of work is perceived as relatively more significant in their operations than in that of affiliated overseas units.

Only two of 115 parent labs that evaluated the position of 'research to derive new products in the present industry' felt that their group did not perform this type of work. It was also, by comparison with basic research, relatively more prominent in overseas labs. Thus 77 (67.0 per cent) of respondents felt product development was equally important in overseas and parent labs, 24 (20.9 per cent) rated it relatively more important in the parent and 12

(10.4 per cent) relatively more important overseas. Laboratories from Other European MNEs were most likely to be adopting a decentralised perspective on product development. The complementary type of 'research to derive new production technology in the present industry' was performed in all except eight of responding parent labs' MNE groups, with 29 (25.2 per cent) of these considering it to be relatively more prominent in the parent facilities compared with 13 (11.3 per cent) overseas and 65 (56.5 per cent) who rated it equally important in both types of unit. Process development was relatively most strongly decentralised in Japanese MNEs. It may be that these companies, with a long understanding of the competitive value of their often exceptional production techniques, believe that the best way to preserve this source of leadership during the international expansion of their production activity is to involve the overseas operations' perceptions and skills in the further evolution of their process technology.

All of 114 respondents who evaluated 'research to improve existing products and/or techniques' felt it was performed in their group. The widespread commitment to adaptation was also reflected in the fact that 80 (70.2 per cent) of the responding labs felt such work was of equal importance in parent and overseas facilities. Where some degree of specialisation was reported this adaptive work emerged as the only form of research with an overseas orientation. Thus 22 (19.3 per cent) of responding labs felt this work was relatively more important in overseas units compared with 12 (10.5 per cent) which considered it more important in the parent. Such adaptation research was notably relatively prevalent in electronics industry overseas labs and in those of Other European MNEs.

The final type of research evaluated is that aimed 'to derive additional products in new areas of specialisation'. All except seven of 111 respondents undertook such research, aimed at extending the product range into new areas of specialisation. However, with its focus relatively far from commercial implementation it is not surprising that such work most closely resembled basic research in its location. Thus 43 (38.7 per cent) of the 111 parent labs that evaluated this diversification research considered it to be relatively more important in their own operations than in those overseas, 48 (43.2 per cent) rated it equally important in both, and only 13 (11.7 per cent) felt it was more important in overseas labs. Again it seems that, within programmes of decentralised R&D in pursuit of global competitiveness, those types of research (here quite fundamental expansions of product scope) that are most likely to affect in quite radical ways the evolution of the MNEs' overall technological trajectories are the ones over which the home- country operations prefer to retain most precise responsibility.

4.3   COORDINATION AND INTERDEPENDENCE OF OVERSEAS R&D

As overseas R&D emerges into a more strategic role in support of MNEs' global competitiveness, its contribution depends increasingly on the reaping of synergistic potentials. Thus issues of coordination and interdependence become crucial to its effective use. Several questions in the survey of parent labs investigated such processes.

The first of these questions asked the parent unit if interaction with overseas affiliate labs took the form of (i) systematic coordination, (ii) ad hoc consultations, or (iii) infrequent interaction (Table 4.3). Of these alternatives systematic coordination clearly predominated, with 87 (72 per cent) of respondents indicating the relevance of this approach, though 11 of these indicated that one of the other approaches was also relevant. *Ad hoc* consultations were used by 35 (29 per cent) of respondents, though 12 of these also incorporated one of the other approaches. Infrequent interaction was believed to describe their approach by 12 (10 per cent) of the respondents, though four of them also perceived the relevance of other approaches. The quite common combination of systematic coordination and ad hoc consultations (10 cases) may indicate that in some cases where the parent wishes to use systematic coordination an informal basis may also exist for other units to have an early say in the policies that will ultimately be implemented through such formal central coordination.

Table 4.3   Parent laboratory evaluation of the nature of interaction between parent and overseas affiliate R&D units

By industry	Per cent[1] Systematic coordination	Ad hoc consultations	Infrequent interaction	Total
Food, drink and tobacco	72.7	36.4		100.0
Aerospace			100.0	100.0
Industrial and agricultural chemicals	64.0	36.0	16.0	100.0
Petroleum	75.0	25.0		100.0
Electronics and electrical appliances	72.2	27.8	11.1	100.0
Industrial and farm equipment	62.5	25.0	12.5	100.0
Metal manufacture and products	66.7	16.7	33.3	100.0
Motor vehicles (including components)	87.5	25.0		100.0
Office equipment (incl. computers)	50.0	50.0		100.0
Photographic and scientific equipment	20.0	60.0	20.0	100.0
Pharmaceuticals and consumer chemicals	100.0		6.7	100.0
Other manufacturing	77.8	44.4		100.0
Total	71.9	28.9	9.9	100.0
By home country				
USA	70.9	27.3	10.9	100.0
UK	76.0	32.0	8.0	100.0
Other Europe	72.0	32.0	12.0	100.0
Japan	64.2	28.6	7.1	100.0
Total	71.9	28.9	9.9	100.0

Note:
[1] Number of respondents that endorsed a particular form of interaction as relevant to their operations. Totals add to more than 100 per cent where one or more respondents endorsed more than one form of interaction as relevant.
Source: Pearce and Singh survey.

In another question respondents were asked what proportion of overseas R&D units they considered to be closely coordinated with the parent unit. The prevalence of a strong tendency towards coordination in global R&D was confirmed, with 35 (39 per cent) of 90 respondents indicating that they considered all their foreign units to be closely coordinated, and a further 27 (30 per cent) considering that 50 per cent or more were. Only 15 (17 per cent) of respondents believed none of their foreign units were closely coordinated. A complementary question indicated that only three of 69 respondents believed all their overseas facilities were autonomous from the parent, whilst 28 (41 per cent) considered they had no autonomous units abroad.

A particular aspect of intra-group R&D specialisation and coordination investigated was the possibility of project mobility. With various skills and perspectives available in a range of locations, projects initiated in one location may benefit from being moved to other labs to facilitate completion. Thus parent labs were asked 'are promising projects shifted from an affiliate to the parent at crucial stages of their development?' Of 116 respondents 19 (16 per cent) said this 'never' happened, 50 (43 per cent) that it happened 'rarely', with 18 (16 per cent) saying it occurred 'sometimes', 23 (20 per cent) 'frequently' and only six (5 per cent) that it happened 'automatically'.

Of the respondents who admitted to some project diversion from laboratories overseas to the parent, 81 answered a question relating to the motive behind such mobility. Of these 47 (58 per cent) considered that this project mobility was needed 'to better complete the research work', though some of these also indicated the relevance of the second motive. Overall 29 respondents (including four who also indicated the relevance of the first motive and another which had also responded to 'other reasons') believed projects had been centralised 'because the parent is the most likely market for innovation of a new product'. Ten respondents considered that 'other reasons' had brought about the movement of projects into the parent laboratory.

In a parallel pair of questions parent laboratories were first asked if 'promising projects were shifted from parent R&D units to a foreign R&D unit'. This seemed to happen to a slightly greater degree than the centralisation of projects. Thus nine (eight per cent) of 116 respondents said it 'never' happened, 38 (33 per cent) that it happened 'rarely', 19 (16 per cent) 'sometimes', 46 (40 per cent) 'frequently' and four (3 per cent) that it was 'automatic'. The motives for this outward movement of projects differed quite notably from those already described for migration in the opposite direction. Thus only 18 of 102 respondents (including three that also acknowledged another motive) suggested that projects were moved to overseas subsidiaries 'to better complete the research work'. However, outward project mobility aimed 'to ensure that the outcome is best directed to a particular market' was cited by 82 of the respondents (including five that indicated the relevance of another reason). Seven respondents acknowledged 'other reasons' for outward project mobility, though two of these also indicated the relevance of the second influence.

4.4 CONCLUSIONS

Overall the results of our survey support the view that in MNEs a foreign-located component in their R&D capacity is playing an increasingly important role in supporting their global strategy. Thus, by comparison with an established view that such overseas R&D as occurred in MNEs would be relatively autonomous operations focusing almost exclusively on providing product and/or process adaptation support to local-market-oriented subsidiaries, our results find that relatively few of MNEs' overseas labs are autonomous and that parent labs see the majority of such units as being subject to systematic coordination, often as component parts in integrated networks. An aspect of the possible types of behaviour that might emerge within such coordinated global R&D networks which received some verification in our survey results is project mobility, with different units carrying out different stages of projects, according either to their available specialised skills and abilities or to the requirements of inter-functional links. Thus there is evidence that projects initiated in overseas labs may be relocated to the parent if the need for special centrally-available capabilities becomes apparent, or that projects may be moved out to overseas units if these can contribute to the effective dispersed innovation of the commercial potentials of new knowledge (created centrally in the group) by linking with local marketing and/ or production facilities.

The pattern of motivations for project mobility in fact reflects our more detailed evidence on the roles played by overseas R&D in MNEs. Firstly it is clear, within the demand-side factors influencing overseas R&D, that whilst *adaptation* of existing products and processes remains very pervasive *development* work, creating new products for host-country markets or to be produced locally for wider markets (i.e. as part of world or regional product mandated operations) is now prevalent in the majority of such dispersed facilites. This strong role for development work indicates the way in which foreign-located R&D units are supporting a geographically-dispersed and differentiated approach to innovation in MNEs.

The suggestion that a second emerging role of overseas R&D units in MNEs might be to support the creation of new basic scientific knowledge by providing specialised high-quality sources of expertise to integrated programmes of original research, is somewhat less clearly supported by our evidence. Generally parent labs did not consider the availability of distinctive skills accessible to overseas labs to be a major influence in defining their roles, frequently holding the view that their own centralised capacity was adequate to provide for group needs in support of such research. However if supply-side attraction did not seem to be particularly influential in drawing R&D away from the centre, our evidence also tended to play down the relevance of a number of aspects of the research process that are alleged to pull such work into centralised locations. Thus, in the main, parent labs did not feel any strong force precluding overseas R&D to stem from economies of scale, the vulnerability of such work to security risks when dispersed, or from excessive problems of communications.

Finally competitive influences from within the area of R&D and technology itself seemed of little relevance to the initiation or the role of overseas units. Thus, though such units clearly support MNEs' overall global competitiveness through product adaptation and development, they were little motivated by the need of the group to respond to scientific moves made by rival MNEs.

Notes

1. The survey covered 560 major enterprises. These comprised the 500 largest industrial enterprises in the world in 1986, as derived from the *Fortune* listings, plus 30 more which Directories of R&D facilities revealed to have substantial numbers of overseas laboratories, plus 30 similar companies without overseas R&D (to match the 30 self-selecting overseas-R&D-oriented enterprises). Since several of these 560 companies were diversified their main divisions often had 'parent laboratories' so 623 were surveyed in total.

2. The questionnaire was originally sent out in February 1989, followed where necessary by a reminder in April 1989. Due to resource constraints it was not possible to send a second reminder at that stage. The first stage yielded a total of 163 responses. Later it became possible to send previous non- respondents a second reminder and an additional copy of the questionnaire in June 1990. This yielded a further 82 replies, to give our total response of 245.

3. The average response is obtained by giving a value of 1 to 'never relevant', 2 to 'sometimes relevant' and 3 to 'nearly always relevant'.

4. Reasons why economies of scale factors may become less influential on the evolution of overseas R&D when this is already well-established in a MNE's operations, compared with where this is only under consideration, have been suggested by Pearce (1989, pp. 38–40).

5. See Pearce (1989, p. 2) for reasons why the security argument against decentralised R&D may be exaggerated.

5 Overseas R&D Laboratories in MNEs: An Analysis of their Roles and Motivations

with Satwinder Singh

5.1 INTRODUCTION

To further investigate the position of decentralised R&D in MNEs the Pearce and Singh survey (see Chapter 4) supplemented the evaluation of the parent laboratory viewpoints through a complementary questionnaire that was sent to the overseas units themselves.[1] This chapter presents selected evidence from this subsidiary laboratory survey. The next section begins the review by providing broad perspectives on the positioning of these labs in their MNEs' global technological and competitive strategies through their evaluation of the relative importance of various roles in their operations. Following this, section 5.3 assesses in turn the manner in which those roles reflect the ways in which various factors are influencing the development of the labs. The next two sections investigate the possibility that such labs achieve their distinctive position through two different dimensions of integration, firstly into the technology strategy and programmes of their MNE group and secondly from collaboration with host-country scientific institutions. Finally section 5.6 draws some conclusions from this evidence.

5.2 TYPES OF OVERSEAS R&D LABORATORIES

Using the tripartite classification outlined in Chapter 2, the subsidiary R&D units were questioned with respect to their perception of their prevalent role. Thus these overseas units were requested to grade themselves by each of the three types of laboratory as being either 'predominantly this type of laboratory', 'partially this type of laboratory', or 'not this type of laboratory'. Table 5.1 summarises the results of this, by industry and by both *home* country of parent MNE and the *host* country of the subsidiary lab, in terms of average responses (AR).[2]

Table 5.1 Prevalence of particular types of overseas R&D laboratories[1]

	Type of laboratory (average response[2])		
	Support laboratory	Locally integrated laboratory	Internationally interdependent laboratory
By industry			
Food, drink and tobacco	1.91	2.73	1.64
Petroleum	2.20	2.00	2.40
Metal manufacture and products	1.73	2.30	1.46
Industrial and agricultural chemicals	2.06	2.06	2.11
Pharmaceuticals and consumer chemicals	1.46	1.62	2.69
Motor vehicles (incl.components)	1.25	2.50	1.75
Industrial and farm equipment	2.25	2.67	1.50
Electronics and electrical appliances	2.08	2.17	1.75
Office equipment (incl.computers)	1.25	1.63	2.38
Other manufacturing	1.75	2.20	1.80
Total	1.80	2.05	2.10
By host country			
USA	1.91	2.19	1.89
UK	1.62	1.88	2.32
Other Europe	1.96	1.96	2.22
Japan	1.50	2.00	3.00
Other countries	1.43	2.12	2.12
Total	1.80	2.05	2.10
By home country			
USA	1.67	2.02	2.12
UK	1.89	2.24	1.84
Other Europe	1.89	1.98	2.17
Japan	2.00	2.67	2.33
Total	1.80	2.05	2.10

Notes:

1 Respondents were asked to grade their facilities in terms of each type of unit as, 'predominantly' this type of laboratory; 'partially' this type of laboratory; 'not' this type of laboratory.

2 Average response calculated by allocating values to the responses of 3 for 'predominantly', 2 for 'partially', 1 for 'not'.

Source: Pearce and Singh survey.

(i) Support laboratories (SL)

As the classification introduced in Chapter 2 describes in greater detail the major function of an SL is to assist the production and marketing facilities in a host country to make the most efficient use of the MNE group's existing technology. In doing this an SL may provide limited, but quite distinctive, benefits to a host country. These emerge when the work of such a lab enhances the commercial effectiveness of a MNE's established products, by improving (through adaptation) their relevance to the needs of local consumers, and/or by improving the suitability of the complementary production process (conversion to local supply conditions) with its possible scope for permitting lower prices. These two benefits should in turn lead to increased output providing higher levels of employment and of tax revenues paid to the host government.

Of the respondents that evaluated themselves by SL criteria only 21.5 per cent considered that they were predominantly a SL, 37.2 per cent felt they partly were and 41.3 per cent said they were not SLs. This provides an overall AR for SL status of 1.80, rating it the least prevalent lab type, and suggesting that this traditional form of short-term adaptive work is a diminishing motivation in the expanding strategic positioning of overseas R&D. As Table 5.1 shows, SL work was reported as strongest in industrial and farm equipment, petroleum, electronics, and industrial and agricultural chemicals, and relatively rare in office equipment, motor vehicles and pharmaceuticals. Labs located in Other Europe and USA had a relatively strong commitment to this type of work, which was quite weak in those in UK and Other Countries. Labs with Japanese, UK and Other European parents were most likely to perform such support work, and those from US or Other Countries MNEs least likely.

(ii) Locally integrated laboratories (LIL)

As the earlier discussion (Chapter 2) of LILs described, these R&D units achieve close integration with a subsidiary's other key functions (management, marketing, engineering) in order to develop distinctive products for market areas that are likely to extend well beyond their host country. Compared with the short-term adaptive work of SLs the mode of operation of LILs takes on a medium-term dimension by building very distinctive creative competences into its associated subsidiary. Thus the subsidiary with a LIL helps expand the dynamic creative scope of the MNE, rather than merely marginally improving the current application of a rather static knowledge stock through a SL. In this way the host country may benefit more from LILs, in that the same range of benefits as accrue from SL work are likely to be available in a significantly enhanced degree but, more importantly, with the promise that these should extend further into the future and in a form which embodies a much more distinctively local element than is likely to be valued as such by the MNE and which thus can underpin a continued high-quality commitment to such local operations.

In the survey 29.4 per cent of respondents considered that they were predominantly LILs, 52.9 per cent partially LILs and 25.3 per cent felt they were not that type, giving an AR of 2.05. As Table 5.1 shows, LILs were notably prevalent in food, drink and tobacco, industrial and farm equipment (where SLs were also strong) and motor vehicles (where SLs were notably weak). LILs were relatively prevalent in the US, indicating a strong motivation to develop distinctive products for that large and individual market using local creative inputs. Subsidiaries of Japanese MNEs were most likely to incorporate LILs, perhaps reflecting a particular sensitivity to the need to develop their technology for specific market needs.

(iii)   Internationally interdependent laboratories (IILs)

IILs are considered to have very limited connection with any other functions of the same MNE in its host country (by clear contrast with LILs) and instead establish their most systematic and persistent links with other R&D facilities of the group in other countries (including presumably a very strong association with the home-country parent laboratory). We have assumed (Chapter 2) that the prevalent motive for this is to allow such labs to perform precompetitive (basic/original) research that embodies distinctive specialised capacities of the host-country science base. An integrated network of such specialised IILs then provides a MNE with access to a broad scope in basic science, maximising the likelihood that its precompetitive work can cover all the disciplines that can contribute to the new core technology needed to underwrite major new commercial innovations.

In the survey, 44.4 per cent of respondents considered themselves to be predominantly IILs, 21.0 per cent felt that they partially were, and 34.6 per cent said that they were not. IIL work was very clearly the predominant form of operation in pharmaceuticals, petroleum and office equipment, whilst metals, industrial and farm equipment, and food, drink and tobacco had little commitment to such activity. Labs in the UK and Other Europe were most likely to be involved in IIL work (perhaps in a regional context) and those in USA the least so. Labs of Japanese, Other European and US MNEs were most committed to IIL activity and those of UK parents least so.

The overall AR for IILs of 2.10 makes it the most prevalent of all three subsidiary lab types (Table 5.1). This may appear somewhat out of line with the viewpoints of parent labs, elaborated in Chapter 4. Those results indicated that the parent labs felt that responding to the types of high-quality specialised inputs that are likely to underpin the basic research of IILs was a relatively insignificant factor in the expansion of their overseas R&D. By contrast they placed more decisive emphasis on the types of product adaptation and development done by SLs and LILs. One factor that contributes to this, as supported by results to be discussed later, is that IILs in fact seem to apply their expertise in international inter-lab collaboration to areas of the product development and innovation process other than those relating to the creation of precompetitive knowledge. Thus the international networking of specialised creative competences in MNEs will be seen to extend into wider contexts than previously envisaged.

Nevertheless the particular association of IIL activity with basic research does, in a clear sense, still emerge from our results. Thus amongst respondents that both specified their predominant lab type and also the extent (regularly, occasionally, or never) to which they did basic research, 29.1 per cent of IILs performed basic research regularly, compared with 2.8 per cent of LILs and no SLs. Furthermore of the responding labs that did basic research regularly 94.1 per cent considered they were predominantly IILs. This does then suggest that where basic research is done in overseas subsidiary labs it is decisively oriented towards a role in wider group programmes. A plausible corollary of this is that where LILs develop products they are unlikely to do so by picking up in a vertically-integrated manner locally-generated IIL basic-research results, but instead apply other group knowledge. It can then be suggested that

> from the point of view of countries acting as hosts to MNE R&D facilities these results may be seen as having the doubly worrying implication that local resources applied to basic-original work produce results that leave the country, with no potential for generating direct benefits in local productive output, whilst the development and adaptation work remains dependent

on the assimilation of externally generated technology.
(Pearce and Singh 1992c, p. 149)

5.3 INFLUENCES ON DEVELOPMENT OF OVERSEAS R&D UNITS

To further elaborate the factors influencing the strategic positioning of geographically-decentralised R&D in MNEs, the overseas subsidiary labs were asked to evaluate the relevance of a number of conditions and circumstances to recent decisions relating to the development of their unit. As in the discussion of parent viewpoints on the evolution of R&D strategy (Chapter 4) it is possible to see the influences on overseas facilities as embodying supply-side, demand-side and competitive factors.

(i) Supply-side factors

The first supply-side factor was defined as 'a distinctive local scientific, educational or technological tradition conducive to certain types of research project'. This then seeks to define the presence of very distinctive elements of specialised research capacity in a country's science base, which are likely to be applicable to very specific areas within a MNE's wider research programme. The need for such idiosyncratic knowledge and research competences would therefore be expected to be most applicable to precompetitive basic work, and less necessary in subsequent development or adaptation activity.

Overall, the influence of this factor on subsidiary labs' decisions was relatively limited. Thus, only 22.6 per cent of respondents rated it as a 'major factor contributing to their decisions', whilst 33.1 per cent believed it had been of 'some influence' and 44.3 per cent felt it had been 'irrelevant'. This provides an AR of 1.78. Nevertheless the greatest influence for this supply-side factor does emerge where it would be predicted to contribute most to the performance of the lab's specific role. Thus, as Table 5.2 shows, the AR to this factor for labs that were predominantly IILs was 2.02, compared with 1.57 for LILs and 1.42 for SLs. Furthermore, labs that said they did basic/original research 'regularly' provided an AR for this factor of 2.10, compared with 1.77 for those that only did basic research 'occasionally' and 1.62 for those that 'never' did it. Thus it does seem that any moves towards incorporation of increased amounts of precompetitive research in overseas labs are likely to be strongly influenced by the presence in host countries of unique sources of particular types of specialised research competence.

The second supply-side factor was defined as the 'presence of a helpful local scientific environment and adequate technical infrastructure'. This is intended to indicate a broadly-based high level of technical competence in a host country, rather than reflect on specific elements of outstanding specialisation within it, as are delineated in the first factor. Though confidence in this general level of competence is clearly essential for basic and other precompetitive research it might be expected to be a less decisive influence than areas of specialised expertise. By contrast, labs involved in development and adaptation may have less need for specialised capacities but feel a need for the security of a reliable foundation in broad competences.

This factor was only considered to be a major influence by 18.3 per cent of respondents, with 35.9 per cent believing it of some influence and 45.8 per cent rating it as irrelevant. The overall AR of 1.73 is, therefore, somewhat below that for the first factor. However it again appears to be labs oriented to the earlier phases of the R&D process that have greatest concern with this element of their research environment. As Table 5.2 shows IILs again provide a much higher AR than do LILs or SLs. Furthermore labs that regularly did basic/original research gave an AR of 2.09 for this influence, compared with 1.75 for those doing it occasionally and 1.49 for those that never did it. Overall it seems that labs involved in the earlier phases of research do have quite extensive concern with the ability to access specific areas of scientific expertise, but within a wider technological environment that also guarantees general support of reliable quality. Labs involved in the later phases seem generally to be surprisingly little influenced by these supply-side characteristics, though there is some suggestion that those involved in development work (LILs) are somewhat more responsive than those limiting themselves to adaptation (SLs).

By contrast with their moderate evaluation of the two broadly defined supply-side characteristics, the responding subsidiary labs were somewhat more responsive to 'availability of research professionals' as a specific element within the scientific environment. Thus whilst 29.0 per cent considered this to be irrelevant, 28.2 per cent saw it as a major factor, giving an AR of 1.99. The more scientifically-committed elements of research still emerged as clearly most responsive to this characteristic of the host-country technological environment. Thus IILs are again the most decisively responsive (Table 5.2) whilst labs regularly doing basic research provided an AR of 2.46, compared with 1.95 for those doing it occasionally and 1.81 for those that never did it.

Whilst the previous result indicates that *availability* of research personnel of suitable ability is a key facet in the evaluation of a host-country's technological environment by MNE subsidiary labs it also emerges that the *wages* that they expect to pay is much less influential. Thus 62.3 per cent of respondents felt that 'favourable wage rates for research professionals' was irrelevant to their decisions, with only 6.2 per cent rating it as a major factor. This provides an AR of only 1.44. If labs performing the more sophisticated precompetitive phases of R&D expect to pay more for their scientists it could be that they also take a more careful view of wages to be paid. This is only supported to a very modest degree. Thus IILs are only slightly the most responsive to wage rates, whilst labs regularly doing basic research report an AR of 1.59, compared with 1.37 for those that do it occasionally and 1.45 for those that never do it.

Table 5.2 Conditions and circumstances considered to have most influenced recent decisions with regard to development of subsidiary R&D units[1]

	A	B	C	D	E	F	G	H	I	J	K	L
					Types of influence (average response[2])							
By industry												
Food, drink and tobacco	1.60	1.54	1.82	1.27	2.46	1.91	2.82	2.36	2.91	1.91	1.91	1.46
Petroleum	2.00	2.17	2.50	1.50	2.17	2.83	2.00	2.17	2.33	2.33	2.00	1.33
Metal manufacture and products	1.20	1.18	1.46	1.46	2.36	1.91	2.36	2.00	2.82	2.36	1.46	1.27
Industrial and agricultural chemicals	1.83	1.65	2.05	1.42	2.22	2.14	2.69	2.11	2.73	2.19	1.97	1.44
Pharmaceuticals and consumer chemicals	2.07	2.03	2.20	1.53	1.77	2.03	2.07	1.79	2.47	2.34	2.30	1.31
Motor vehicles (incl.components)	1.00	1.40	1.80	1.80	3.00	2.75	2.50	1.75	3.00	2.25	2.25	2.00
Industrial and farm equipment	1.50	1.50	1.50	1.75	2.50	1.75	2.25	2.00	2.50	2.25	1.50	1.50
Electronics and electrical appliances	1.83	1.77	1.92	1.31	2.21	1.77	2.38	2.00	2.31	2.15	1.92	1.67
Office equipment (incl. computers)	1.86	1.75	1.88	1.25	1.50	1.87	1.37	1.75	2.38	2.75	1.50	1.25
Other manufacturing	1.67	1.83	2.17	1.33	2.33	1.83	2.17	2.00	2.50	1.83	2.00	1.17
Total	1.78	1.73	1.99	1.44	2.14	2.05	2.34	1.97	2.60	2.24	1.96	1.41
By host country												
USA	1.76	1.67	1.90	1.38	2.27	1.85	2.51	1.79	2.76	2.03	1.96	1.57
UK	1.83	1.71	2.12	1.64	1.88	2.29	2.03	1.94	2.53	2.68	1.88	1.21
Other Europe	1.71	1.68	1.96	1.29	2.11	2.15	2.44	2.20	2.48	2.20	1.93	1.27
Japan	2.50	2.50	2.50	1.00	2.00	2.00	2.00	1.50	2.00	1.50	2.50	2.50
Other countries	1.78	2.11	2.11	1.67	2.33	2.11	2.22	2.33	2.33	2.22	2.22	1.33

	A	B	C	D	E	F	G	H	I	J	K	L
Total	1.78	1.73	1.99	1.44	2.14	2.05	2.34	1.97	2.60	2.24	1.96	1.41
By home country												
USA	1.71	1.64	2.02	1.45	2.08	2.21	2.25	2.14	2.56	2.44	1.92	1.21
UK	1.76	1.62	1.91	1.52	2.48	1.86	2.57	1.91	2.86	2.05	2.24	1.65
Other Europe	1.92	1.90	2.04	1.39	2.10	1.98	2.31	1.80	2.58	2.14	1.98	1.57
Japan	1.50	1.50	1.50	1.25	1.75	1.00	2.75	2.00	2.00	1.50	1.25	1.00
Total	1.78	1.73	1.99	1.44	2.14	2.05	2.34	1.97	2.60	2.24	1.96	1.41
By type of laboratory[3]												
SL	1.42	1.35	1.85	1.39	2.54	2.04	2.81	2.28	2.73	2.08	1.81	1.52
LIL	1.57	1.57	1.69	1.43	2.36	2.00	2.69	1.92	2.86	2.03	2.22	1.66
IIL	2.02	2.02	2.20	1.48	1.80	2.17	1.98	1.89	2.37	2.43	1.94	1.26

Notes:

[1] Respondents were asked to grade each condition or circumstance as either (i) irrelevant to decisions, (ii) of some influence on decisions, (iii) a major factor contributing to decisions.

[2] The average response is calculated by allocating the value of 1 to 'irrelevant', 2 to 'of some influence' and 3 to 'major factor'.

[3] The average response for subsidiary labs that evaluated themselves as 'predominantly' this type.

Types of influence

A – A distinctive local scientific, educational or technological tradition conducive to certain types of research.
B – Presence of a helpful local scientific environment and adequate technical infrastructure.
C – Availability of research professionals.
D – Favourable wage rates for research professionals.
E – Need to provide technical services to local production unit.
F – To provide technical support to other parts of the multinational group.
G – To help modify/standardise products for the local market.
H – To help modify/standardise products for overseas markets.
I – To help develop new products for the local market.
J – To help develop new products for overseas markets.
K – A large and growing local market where R & D is seen to play a critical role.
L – To match local R & D of competitor firms.

(ii)   Demand-side factors

We turn now to three demand-side influences on decision making with regard to the evolution of decentralised R&D labs in MNEs. These comprise ways in which the development of the labs responds to the nature of the services that are demanded of them in their support of various needs of their MNE group's evolving competitive strategies. With the emergence of globalised perspectives on production and marketing in MNEs it would be inappropriate to assume that the services provided by their decentralised R&D units inevitably focus uniquely on their local (host-country) market. Thus respondents were asked to evaluate each demand-side factor according to whether it was provided to local host-country operations or overseas (i.e. to parts of the MNE in other countries).

The first of these factors was the 'need to provide technical services to the local production unit'. The provision of such technical services, in the form of day-to-day problem solving and backup, to associated host-country operations is quite a strong influence on labs. Thus 45.0 per cent rated it a major factor, 23.9 per cent felt it was of some influence and 31.3 per cent thought it irrelevant, providing an AR of 2.14. As would be expected it was more relevant to labs whose main motivation lies in the commercial application of technology (SLs with an AR of 2.54 and LILs with one of 2.36) than in those that are mainly concerned with the creation of new knowledge (IILs with an AR of 1.80).

The complementary factor, 'to provide technical support to other parts of the multinational group', was also quite influential. Thus 31.6 per cent rated it a major factor and 26.9 per cent as irrelevant, to give an AR of 2.05. However it is IILs that react most strongly to the need to provide this type of support when it is required by MNE operations outside the lab's host country. Thus whereas IILs report an AR of 2.17 here (compared with only 1.80 for local support) both SLs and LILs now record much lower ARs (2.04 and 2.00 respectively compared with 2.54 and

2.36 for local support). The key element contributing to this role for IILs is their established expertise in international intra-group communications. It may also be that, to some extent, the problems that are not solved on site (perhaps by their own SL or LIL) in other countries need the higher levels of knowledge and expertise that exist in IILs.

The second demand-side factor investigated was 'to help modify/standardise products' either for 'the local market' or for 'overseas markets'. In terms of supplying this type of support for the host-country market (i.e. probably as an integral part of a local-market-focused subsidiary) 53.5 per cent of respondents felt this was a major factor contributing to decisions and only 19.4 per cent considered it to be irrelevant, giving an AR of 2.34. As would be expected, SLs provided the highest response to this factor and IILs decisively the lowest, with LILs also recognising it as a substantial element in their decision making (Table 5.2). Provision of this type of product adaptation for overseas markets was rated as a major factor by 32.3 per cent of responding labs and as irrelevant by 35.4 per cent, giving an AR of 1.97. Whilst the evaluation of this role by SLs and LILs for overseas markets was very much lower than their comparable assessment for local markets, the fall for IILs was much less substantial. This suggests that these units' expertise in intra-group communication again emerges as an attribute conducive to playing this role effectively.

The last pair of demand-side factors relate to the subsidiary labs' participation in product development. 'To help develop new products for the local market' was considered irrelevant by only 10.0 per cent of respondents, and with 70.0 per cent rating it a major factor the overall AR of 2.60 emerges as clearly the highest for any of the influences investigated. LILs provided an AR of 2.86 for this factor, but the AR of 2.73 for those that said they were predominantly SLs indicates the extensive presence of this as a secondary preoccupation, perhaps supporting the expectation of a natural evolution of SLs into LILs (Ronstadt 1977, 1978). Though the AR of 2.37 for IILs is clearly the lowest it is still considerably more prominent than the relative position of these labs in local-market product *adaptation*. This may reflect the fact that the more techno-logically ambitious work of product development can benefit from the higher level of expertise in IILs in a manner not relevant to adaptation.

'To help develop new products for overseas markets' was considered a major factor influencing decisions by 45.3 per cent of overseas labs, whilst only 21.1 per cent believed it to be irrelevant, providing an AR of 2.24. Performance of this role emerges as a very strong preoccupation of IILs. Thus whereas SLs only reported an AR of 2.08 (compared with 2.73 for local market development) and LILs one of 2.03 (compared with 2.86) that of IILs was 2.43 (compared with 2.37). Both of the distinguishing characteristics of IILs may contribute to this result. As was noted for both technologi-cal support and product adaptation the experience of intra-group international cooperation in IILs is again crucially relevant here. The high level of scientific competence embo-died in such labs may be of additional significance in this case if the task is to answer questions that have perhaps been defined but not resolved in LILs that are pursuing product development in other markets.

(iii) Competition factors

The first factor relating to the nature of the competitive environment was described as the presence of 'a large and growing market where R&D is seen to play a critical role'. Thus subsidiary labs were evaluating the extent to which they believed that the nature of their evolution was affected by the need for R&D to contribute to the ability of their group to underwrite its current and longer-term competitive position in an expanding market environment. Whilst 28.9 per cent of the labs considered this was a major factor, 32.8 per cent believed it to be irrelevant, giving an AR of 1.96. LILs emerge with the highest AR (2.22), which is likely to reflect the importance of the continual develop-ment of new product variants in order to retain a secure share of such a growing and technologically-evolving mar-

ket. The much lower AR for IILs (1.94) indicates the
longer-term objectives of these facilities and their relative
isolation from the immediate competitive environment,
whilst the low AR for SLs (1.81) suggests the relative
irrelevance of their mainly adaptive functions to the needs
of such a dynamic market situation.

The second competitive factor was 'to match local R&D
of competitor firms', which introduces an element of oligopolistic interaction into the ways in which globally-competing enterprises may be articulating the development of their
internationalised R&D programmes. However, only 7.9 per
cent of respondents felt this to be a major factor and with
66.9 per cent believing it to be irrelevant the AR was only
1.41. The influence was felt most strongly in LILs (an AR
of 1.66), suggesting that helping to establish a strong local
presence through the development of a distinctive product
could be considered a key oligopolistic tactic. The low AR
(1.26) for IILs may be somewhat surprising if global oligo-
polists are seeking to create internationally-integrated
R&D programmes that seek to build a strong technological
base for future product innovation.

5.4 INTEGRATION OF SUBSIDIARY LABORATORIES WITH OTHER GROUP R&D UNITS

To elaborate on the growing interdependence of the globalised R&D activities in MNEs the responding subsidiary
labs were asked to evaluate the extent to which parent (or
other sister) labs become involved in their projects. Four
types of such involvement were reviewed.

Firstly, labs were asked to assess the extent to which
'systematic coordination of projects into wider programmes' occurred. This formalised interdependence was
quite prevalent, with 41.2 per cent of respondents feeling it
occurred 'regularly', 48.9 per cent 'occasionally' and only
9.9 per cent believing it 'never' happened, giving an AR of
2.31 (Table 5.3). As would be expected, those labs that
considered themselves as predominantly IILs were most

likely to see their projects as subject to centralised influence (AR of 2.56). In a complementary manner this type of coordination was also most associated with the performance of basic/original research, with labs that did such work regularly providing an AR of 2.64 compared with 2.26 for those only doing it occasionally and 2.21 for those that never did it. The quite high AR of 2.23 for SLs may reflect the view of some such units that their role in adapting the MNE's existing technology in effect integrates them with the other group units from which they secure that knowledge. By contrast the lower AR of 1.97 for LILs reflects the greater autonomy of their development work and their feeling that their strongest integration is with other local functions (e.g. engineering and marketing).

Next, subsidiary labs were asked to assess the likelihood of external 'intervention to bring about a major change in the direction of a project'. With many of their projects more systematically embedded in externally directed programmes the respondents felt relatively immune from this more *ad hoc* type of intervention. Thus only 13.2 per cent rated such intervention as regular and 31.0 per cent believed it never happened, giving an AR of 1.82. Once again such externally imposed advice was more likely to be received by IILs than LILs or SLs (Table 5.3). The presence of basic/original work in such units contributes to this, with labs doing such work regularly providing an AR of 2.09 compared with 1.77 for those that did it occasionally or never.

The positioning of the overseas R&D labs is such that whilst they are relatively immune from external intervention to alter the direction of ongoing work they are more likely to have received 'advice on the development of a project'. Thus 27.9 per cent of respondents received such advice regularly and only 10.9 per cent never received it (an AR of 2.17). Such advice is most likely to be offered when the lab's work is in some way symbiotic with wider group aims and indeed IILs emerge as more often subject to it than LILs or SLs (Table 5.3). That such advice is more likely to be associated with precompetitive work is also indicated, with labs regularly doing basic/original research reporting an AR of 2.32 compared with 2.14 for those who did it either occasionally or never.

Table 5.3   Nature and frequency[1] of parent or sister affiliate laboratory involvement in the projects of subsidiary R&D units

	Types of involvement (average response[2])			
	A	B	C	D
By industry				
Food, drink and tobacco	1.91	1.64	2.18	2.55
Petroleum	2.50	2.40	2.40	2.60
Metal manufacture and products	1.91	1.55	1.73	2.09
Industrial and agricultural chemicals	2.28	1.78	2.11	2.08
Pharmaceuticals and consumer chemicals	2.60	2.00	2.47	2.33
Motor vehicles (incl.components)	2.50	1.25	2.25	2.00
Industrial and farm equipment	2.50	1.75	2.25	2.25
Electronics and electrical appliances	2.29	1.85	2.08	2.39
Office equipment (incl.computers)	2.22	1.78	1.89	2.11
Other manufacturing	2.33	2.00	2.17	2.00
Total	2.31	1.82	2.17	2.23
By host country				
USA	2.19	1.70	2.18	2.23
UK	2.43	2.09	2.18	2.21
Other Europe	2.33	1.67	2.11	2.33
Japan	3.00	3.00	2.50	2.00
Other countries	2.44	1.78	1.89	2.11
Total	2.31	1.82	2.17	2.23
By home country				
USA	2.36	1.83	2.17	2.23
UK	2.05	1.70	2.15	2.15
Other Europe	2.45	1.88	2.27	2.29
Japan	1.25	1.50	1.50	2.00
Total	2.31	1.82	2.17	2.23
By type of laboratory[3]				
SL	2.23	1.69	2.08	2.19
LIL	1.97	1.61	2.03	2.28
IIL	2.56	2.07	2.31	2.33

Notes:

[1]   Respondents were asked to grade frequency of the various types of involvement as (i) never, (ii) occasionally, (iii) regularly.

(*Contd. overleaf*)

2 The average response is calculated by allocating the value of 1 to 'never', 2 to 'occasionally' and 3 to 'regularly'.
3 The average response for subsidiaries that evaluated themselves as 'predominantly' this type.

Types of involvement

A – Systematic coordination of projects into wider programmes.
B – Intervention to bring about a major change in the direction of the project.
C – Advice on the development of the project.
D – Technical assistance at the request of the R&D unit.
Source: Pearce and Singh survey.

The last type of intervention investigated involved 'technical assistance at the request of the R&D unit'. Here the external advice is not involved in helping to determine the nature of the subsidiary labs work, but rather comprises detailed assistance offered in response to requests from the unit relating to problems in achieving their aims. This was quite a prominent procedure, with 28.7 per cent saying it happened regularly and only 5.4 per cent that they never sought such advice. It was rather more prevalent in the two lab types with higher levels of technical ambition (IILs and LILs) than in those involved with the more routine application of established technology (SLs). It was not, however, particularly associated with basic/original research as those labs never doing such work reported an AR of 2.32 compared with 2.18 for both those doing it occasionally or regularly.

5.5 COLLABORATION WITH HOST-COUNTRY SCIENTIFIC INSTITUTIONS

Earlier discussion in this chapter has demonstrated that the extensive commitment of MNE overseas R&D labs to product development or adaptation may provide substantial benefits to the host-country economy through improved service to consumers, higher levels of employment and additional revenue to the local government. As noted in Chapter 2 another form of potential benefit may reside in the ability of the interaction of such labs with the local scientific community to improve the quality of its longer-term evolution, by increasing its access to knowledge and widening the range of skills and experience available to its personnel and institutions. One way in which this enrichment of the local technological base could occur is if MNE labs collaborate with local institutions by providing them with contract research jobs. The questionnaire asked MNE subsidiary labs to evaluate the extent of such association with three types of local research institution. The results are summarised in Table 5.4.

Collaboration of MNE labs with host-country universities emerged as being widespread, though perhaps quite rarely comprising a major input into their research work. Thus whilst only 19.4 per cent of respondents rated such associations as 'frequent', a further 66.9 per cent did report that such collaborations occurred 'sometimes'. This gave an AR of 2.06. As Table 5.4 shows, IILs were clearly the most likely to establish links, with LILs also somewhat ahead of SLs. This suggests that to some degree such associations reflect the level of ambition of the subsidiary lab's work. In support of this it can be noted that the AR for such University collaborations was 2.32 for respondents that did basic/original research regularly, 2.13 for those that did it occasionally and 1.87 for those that never did it.

Provision of contract research opportunities to 'independent research laboratories' in the host country was considered to be frequent in 15.0 per cent of respondents, and occurred sometimes in 61.7 per cent more, to give an AR of 1.92. Unlike the case of Universities the pursuit of this type of collaboration with independent local labs varied little by type of MNE unit (Table 5.4). Nevertheless, subsidiary labs doing basic/original research were still somewhat the most likely to need such an association, with an AR of 2.05 for those that did this type of work regularly compared with 1.90 for those that did it occasionally or never.

Table 5.4   Extent to which MNE subsidiary laboratories give contract work to host-country scientific institutions[1]

	Institutions (average response[2])		
	Universities	Independent research labs	R&D labs of other firms
By industry			
Food, drink and tobacco	1.70	2.10	1.13
Petroleum	2.00	2.00	1.67
Metal manufacture and products	2.00	1.90	1.50
Industrial and agricultural chemicals	1.97	1.97	1.23
Pharmaceuticals and consumer chemicals	2.28	2.00	1.24
Motor vehicles (incl.components)	2.40	2.00	1.80
Industrial and farm equipment	2.00	1.50	1.33
Electronics and electrical appliances	1.92	1.64	1.33
Office equipment (incl.computers)	2.22	1.78	1.00
Other manufacturing	2.00	1.67	1.40
Total	2.06	1.92	1.29
By host country			
USA	1.98	1.83	1.36
UK	2.09	1.97	1.17
Other Europe	2.15	2.04	1.27
Japan	2.50	2.00	1.00
Other countries	2.00	1.88	1.25
Total	2.06	1.92	1.29
By home country			
USA	2.10	2.02	1.23
UK	1.84	1.84	1.36
Other Europe	2.13	1.89	1.34
Japan	1.50	1.00	1.00
Total	2.06	1.92	1.29
By type of laboratory[3]			
SL	1.83	1.96	1.29
LIL	1.94	2.00	1.36
IIL	2.17	1.92	1.24

Notes:

[1]   Respondents were asked to grade frequency of provision of work to the institutions as (i) never, (ii) sometimes, (iii) frequently.

2 The average response is calculated by allocating the value of 1 to 'never', 2 to 'sometimes', and 3 to 'frequently'.
3 The average response for subsidiaries that evaluated themselves as 'predominantly' this type.
Source: Pearce and Singh survey.

Finally, MNE subsidiary labs found very little reason to provide contract research work to the labs of host-country enterprises. Whilst only 1.9 per cent did this frequently, 72.6 per cent said that they never did (an AR of only 1.24). This type of association tended to be most prevalent in LILs, maybe suggesting that the specialised input of host-country companies' labs could be related to knowledge of local market conditions. Perhaps in line with this labs that never did basic/original research had the highest AR for such links with local firms' labs (1.36), though there was little difference for those that occasionally did it (1.24) and those that did it regularly (1.27).

Another way in which the operations of MNE subsidiary labs may contribute to positive knowledge spillovers into the host-country economy could be through the provision of technical support or assistance to local suppliers to their associated production subsidiary. Such collaboration may benefit the host economy directly if the knowledge improves the efficiency of the local firms, and indirectly if engineers in the local enterprises gain constructive insights into R&D processes and procedures through their participation in the technology transfer. Though only 18.3 per cent of responding labs provided such support 'frequently' a further 57.3 per cent did so 'sometimes' and only 24.4 per cent 'never' supplied such assistance. As would be expected, IILs were least likely to provide such advice to local suppliers (an AR[3] of 1.78), with LILs quite strongly ahead of SLs (2.09 compared with 1.85). This could suggest a quite creative element in the relationship with local suppliers if LILs work with them to help in the development of a new component that is then integral to the MNE subsidiary's own product development operations.

5.6 CONCLUSIONS

The evidence provided by the overseas R&D laboratories themselves is broadly compatible with the view of the positioning of such units as part of an international group-level strategy for the creation and commercial application of technology. Three perspectives emerging from these results may be perceived as providing support for this new dimension in MNEs' approach to knowledge-based competitiveness.

Firstly, the prominence of LILs and the prevalence of product development work in such labs is in line with the suggestion that a competitive response to key segments of the global market requires more than peripheral adaptation of established products. Instead the commercial application of *new* knowledge has to be carried out in the light of the needs of separate and distinctive regional markets. Secondly, quite a strong element in the work of many subsidiary labs involves interdependence with MNE-group operations outside of their host country. This not only includes IILs' participation in internationally-networked programmes of pre-competitive research but also various types of support for market-related activities in other countries. Reflecting this few subsidiary labs felt their decision making in the articulation and progress of their programmes of work was immune from external coordination or advice. Thirdly, it does seem that, whilst still secondary to market-related roles, participation in group-level programmes of precompetitive research is emerging as a preoccupation of many such labs in MNEs. In addition, where this is occurring, the quality and distinctiveness of host-country research inputs (especially personnel) seems to be a relevant factor in determining the location of such work.

Notes

1. The questionnaire was sent to 405 overseas subsidiary laboratories from 560 of the world's leading enterprises (see note 1 to Chapter 4), and 133 replies were received.
2. Average responses were derived by allocating values to the responses of 1 for 'not', 2 for 'partially', and 3 for 'predominantly'.
3. Average response derived by allocating values to the responses of 1 for 'never', 2 for 'sometimes' and 3 for 'frequently'.

6 Global-Innovation Strategies of MNEs and European Integration: The Role of Regional R&D Facilities

with Marina Papanastassiou

6.1 INTRODUCTION

It is now widely accepted that most leading MNEs compete through the implementation of a global strategy. However it may also be argued that, in many cases, the effective application of such a *global* approach requires the full and active recognition of the distinctive market needs and productive potentials of the world's major *regional* markets. Thus the European operations of a globally-competing firm need to develop special characteristics, within the company's basic technological and managerial background, that optimise its competitive potential in that market. It is one central argument of this chapter that in the context of the priorities of contemporary international competition MNEs are more likely to use their European operations to *develop* distinctive new products for the region's markets than to merely *adapt* to local characteristics a well-established product that (with similar minor adaptations) is also marketed in other key areas. This follows from the likelihood that MNEs can perceive that not only do European markets have particular aspects that require a unique response, but that subsidiaries in several European countries can access quality scientific inputs that facilitate such effective development work.

The underlying premise of the chapter is that MNEs are moving towards the adoption of a global-innovation strategy (see Chapter 2.1), and that decentralised R&D facilities in a range of countries contribute to the implementation of such an approach. In the European context this view of a global- innovation strategy suggests that MNEs may use local R&D facilities for one of two aims. Firstly, they may do basic or applied research aimed to provide knowledge to the programme seeking to create a new product concept. This aim, therefore, does not respond to any particular problem of current European operations, and is motivated more by the quality of the European science base. The second aim of MNE R&D laboratories in Europe *is* to react to current European conditions, by helping to develop the new concept in the ways that most meet the region's needs and thus derive a specifically European variant of the new outline idea. It can now be seen that the roles of overseas R&D in MNEs have moved on from the relatively unambitious adaptation of existing products that was once seen as the predominant function of subsidiary labs, to incorporate precompetitive basic and applied research and extensive product and process development. A further implication of this is that location decisions relating to overseas laboratories in MNEs may no longer be dominated by demand-side influences (i.e. in important and distinctive markets), but may increasingly respond to supply-side factors (i.e. quality of host-country science). Thus the precompetitive laboratories in a global-innovation strategy clearly seek the best inputs in terms of individual scientific personnel and the wider technological infrastructure. Also, whereas the product development labs do obviously need to be in touch with the relevant market, when this is a large regional one several possible locations may be available and the choice between them may again be determined by input influences. The relevance of such supply-side factors is one of the questions investigated in our analysis of MNEs' R&D in supporting their European operations.

In this chapter we investigate selected aspects of the application of a global-innovation strategy by MNEs through their European operations. The increasing integration of the European market encourages MNEs to see it as one of the key distinctive segments in their global market with, therefore, an increasingly important supporting role for European-based R&D operations.

6.2 THE SURVEY

The survey analysed in this study covers 119 subsidiaries of MNEs operating in Europe.[1] Sixty-two of these subsidiaries belonged to US parent MNEs, 13 to Japanese parents, 40 were subsidiaries of a European MNE operating in a country other than its home country, and four had Canadian parents. The survey covers subsidiaries in four countries, the UK (85 subsidiaries), Belgium (16), Greece (11) and Portugal (7). Though the total rows in tables presenting data from this survey covers all observations, the detailed focus is on four relatively technologically-dynamic industries, i.e. electronics and electrical appliances (20 cases), industrial and agricultural chemicals (22), pharmaceuticals and consumer chemicals (13) and automobiles (11).

Evidence from this survey supports our underlying view that MNEs now mainly tend to integrate their individual operations in European countries into an overall European strategy, seeking to allow each subsidiary to contribute to an optimally effective supply of the whole regional market. Thus only 36 (30.5 per cent) of 118 respondents to a question on market orientation said that their host-country market was their only one. Generally the target markets of these subsidiaries seemed very extensive, with 79 of the 82 subsidiaries that did not focus on their host country including other EU countries as part of their market, 74 including non-EU European countries and 70 of them markets outside of Europe. Subsidiaries of Japanese MNEs were least likely to focus exclusively on host-country markets, with only 15.4 per cent saying this was their sole market. Their relatively recent arrival in Europe has allowed these subsidiaries to predominantly set up with a regional perspective. US MNEs' subsidiaries have also extensively adopted the regional approach, with only 23.0 per cent focusing exclusively on the national market. Whereas the more recent US subsidiaries may have been established with this viewpoint, others may have needed to restructure their approach to meet the new competitive environment. By contrast, 47.5 per cent of European MNEs' subsidiaries in European countries other than the group's home country said the host-country market was their only one. Two factors may contribute to this result. Firstly, it may be that European companies are more able to perceive important differences between national markets in the region than US or Japanese enterprises, and are more willing to allow their individual subsidiaries to focus on responding to the particular needs of the markets of the countries they operate in. The second factor is that whilst US and Japanese MNEs may be less responsive to differences in national markets in Europe, they may be more responsive to differences in production conditions. Thus, having opted to supply a product range aimed at the overall European market, these MNEs can choose a limited number of specialised, export-oriented, production sites to supply it from. They can then make this production choice through a quite subtle evaluation of a range of relevant factors reflecting on different potential supply locations. By contrast with this optimising approach European MNEs may adopt a more satisficing view of the location of export-oriented plants to supply wider markets. Thus there may be a historically- and culturally-derived tendency to keep such operations in the group's home country until very strong evidence emerges that a plant elsewhere in Europe could supply the products more efficiently. This may then tend to limit the number of export-oriented subsidiaries European MNEs have set up outside their home country.

Another interesting contrast emerges at the industry level. Here a well-above-average 38.5 per cent of pharmaceuticals subsidiaries said the host country represented their only market, compared with a well-below-average 19.0 per cent for chemicals. Thus chemical products aimed at industrial and agricultural markets are sufficiently standardised to allow for centralised specialised production facilities to realise economies of scale and supply the wider European market. The distinctive nature of consumer tastes and national regulatory conditions for pharmaceuticals, however, leads to a much greater prevalence of subsidiaries concentrating on responding to the unique needs of their host countries. Within electronics there is a contrast between US subsidiaries, where a high 42.9 per cent of subsidiaries focused on only their local markets, and Japanese and European subsidiaries where the figures were below average at 12.5 per cent and 20.0 per cent respectively. Finally 36.4 per cent of automobile subsidiaries supplied only the host-country market.

To obtain an indication of the types of scientific support received by the subsidiaries a question in the survey asked if any technological work was carried out by them in (a) a properly constituted R&D laboratory with a permanent staff, (b) less formally by members of the engineering unit during the process of production. Overall 97 of the subsidiaries replied to the question, with only one of them saying it received neither type of support (though this may be more common amongst non-respondents). The results are summarised in Table 6.1 (omitting the respondent with neither type of work). Clearly formal R&D laboratories play a relatively important role in supporting those subsidiaries' operations, with 70.8 per cent of respondents either depending exclusively on this source or combining it with less formal work. As would be expected three of the four technologically-dynamic industries we focus on had an above average inclination to use the more ambitious type of R&D support, with automobiles being the notable exception. Generally both US and European subsidiaries were very close to the average in terms of their use of formal R&D laboratories.

6.3 ROLES OF R&D SUBSIDIARIES

The survey enables us to investigate in more detail the roles of MNEs' decentralised R&D facilities in support of their

Table 6.1 Sources of technological work carried out for MNE subsidiaries[1]

per cent

Parent country of MNE

	USA			Japan			Europe[2]			Total[3]		
	a	b	a+b	a	b	a+b	a	b	a+b	a	b	a+b
Automobiles	37.5	50.0	12.5					100.0		30.0	60.0	10.0
Industrial and agricultural chemicals	33.3	33.3	33.3				60.0	10.0	30.0	50.0	20.0	30.0
Pharmaceuticals and consumer chemicals	71.4		28.6				66.7	33.3		70.0	10.0	20.0
Electronics and electrical appliances	80.0		20.0	60.0	40.0	40.0	20.0	40.0	40.0	53.3	26.7	20.0
Total[4]	45.3	28.3	26.4	50.0	50.0	50.0	50.0	28.1	21.9	47.9	29.2	22.9

Notes:

[1] Respondents were asked 'is any technological work carried out for your subsidiary
(a) in a properly constituted R & D laboratory with a permanent staff of scientists,
(b) less formally by members of the engineering unit during the process of production'.

[2] Covers subsidiaries of European MNEs in countries other than the home country.

[3] Includes subsidiaries of Canadian MNEs.

[4] Includes other industries.

Source: Marina Papanastassiou database.

European operations. Table 6.2 reports the results of a question which asked those production subsidiaries that had supporting R&D laboratories to evaluate various types of work that they might carry out.[2] For US respondents the strongest role was 'development of a new product', this predominating in each of the four industries. This fits in with our view that the implementation of a global-innovation strategy requires the explicit application of important new technology to the distinctive needs of key markets. In three of the industries a prominent role also exists for 'adaptation of product or production processes', suggesting that modified versions of established US products may be derived to supplement the newly-developed 'European' products. This is much rarer in electronics, which indicates that European technical characteristics (e.g. TV transmissions standards) are so widely different from those of the US as to almost always impose the need for distinctive new product development. The US MNEs seem to differentiate to only a limited degree in their allocation of these two roles between their European operations. Thus adaptation is a little less prevalent in the UK (an average response [AR] of 2.38) than the three other countries (2.64), whilst development is very slightly more important in the UK (2.84) than in the others (2.73). Generally the Japanese subsidiaries' balance between development and adaptation work in their R&D facilities is similar to that of US subsidiaries.

Though European MNEs also find extensive roles for both adaptation and development in their decentralised R&D units, the overall AR for development in Table 6.2 reflects quite distinctive behaviour. Thus whereas the European companies' subsidiaries in the UK recorded an AR of 2.73 for development work, those in the other three countries only recorded 1.83. A downgrading in the position of development in decentralised R&D units would have been quite predictable in reflecting a degree of intuitive preference to do the core product development in the MNE's home country. The pervasive role of adaptation (AR of 2.64 in UK and 2.63 in the other countries) may

Table 6.2 MNE subsidiaries' evaluation of the importance of various types of work[1] in their research laboratories (average response[2])

	USA			Japan			Europe[3]			Total[4]		
	a	b	c	a	b	c	a	b	c	a	b	c
Automobiles	2.25	2.50	1.67							2.25	2.50	1.67
Industrial and agricultural chemicals	2.86	3.00	1.57				2.71	3.00	2.00	2.80	3.00	1.75
Pharmaceuticals and consumer chemicals	2.33	2.43	2.33				3.00	1.00	1.00	2.43	2.25	2.14
Electronics and electrical appliances	1.25	3.00	1.25	2.40	3.00	1.40	2.80	2.33	2.00	2.21	2.83	1.54
Total[5]	2.46	2.81	1.79	2.50	3.00	1.50	2.64	2.48	1.68	2.54	2.71	1.71

Notes:

[1] Types of research are: (a) adaptation of the product or production process
(b) development of a new product
(c) provision of scientific knowledge to a broader research project organised by the MNE group

[2] Respondents were asked to evaluate each type of work as either important; relatively important; not important. The average response was then calculated by allocating responses of important the value 3, relatively important 2 and not important 1.

[3] Covers subsidiaries of European MNEs in countries other than the home country.

[4] Includes subsidiaries of Canadian MNEs.

[5] Includes other industries.

reflect the European MNEs' stronger reaction to individual national markets that we surmised earlier, with this perhaps adding a further element of adaptation to a more centrally-derived new product.

It is clear from Table 6.2 that so far MNEs have been rather less inclined to use their European R&D facilities as part of the precompetitive phase of a global-innovation strategy. Thus 'provision of scientific knowledge to a broader research project organised by the MNE group' is usually clearly the least prominent type of work done in the decentralised laboratories. The notable exceptions are US labs in pharmaceuticals which do find European scientific expertise in this industry an important input to their wider research programmes.

Another question in the survey of MNE subsidiaries asked those that created and supplied a new product to evaluate the reasons for doing so. Overall 73 per cent of the subsidiaries surveyed responded to the question, confirming the widespread nature of this creative role amongst MNEs' subsidiaries in Europe. Furthermore the results (see Table 6.3) again confirm the view that such subsidiaries develop products to maximise their MNE group's competitiveness in the European market, within the context of a global-innovation strategy.

6.4   SOURCES OF TECHNOLOGY IN SUBSIDIARIES

Further evidence on the technological independence or interdependence of MNEs' European subsidiaries can be obtained in a question which investigated the sources of technology used in their operations. As reported in Table 6.4 it is clear that technology imported from elsewhere in the MNE group plays a pervasive role in the operations of the European subsidiaries. However, as we have already suggested, this imported group technology may be *adapted* locally if it takes a form embodied in current products and production processes, or *developed* for the European market if it takes the form of a newly-derived product concept

Table 6.3 MNE subsidiaries that create and supply a new product: evaluation of reasons[1] for doing so (average response[2])

	USA			Japan			Europe[3]			Total[4]		
	a	b	c	a	b	c	a	b	c	a	b	c
Automobiles	2.14	2.57	2.25							2.14	2.57	2.25
Industrial and agricultural chemicals	1.50	3.00	2.25				2.63	2.78	2.33	2.23	2.86	2.29
Pharmaceuticals and consumer chemicals	1.89	2.67	2.25				2.50	2.33	2.00	2.00	2.58	2.18
Electronics and electrical appliances	2.33	2.33	2.00	2.29	2.57	1.86	2.40	2.50	2.25	2.33	2.50	2.00
Total[5]	1.93	2.68	2.37	2.12	2.44	2.00	2.15	2.41	2.36	2.03	2.58	2.29

Notes:
[1] Reasons are: (a) to make full use of distinctive scientific abilities available to the subsidiary.
(b) to increase the competitiveness of the subsidiary in the European market.
(c) as part of our parent group strategy for a global approach to innovation.
[2] Respondents were asked to evaluate each type of work as either important; relatively important; not important. The average response was then calculated by allocating responses of important the value 3, relatively important 2 and not important 1.
[3] Covers subsidiaries of European MNEs in countries other than the home country.
[4] Includes subsidiaries of Canadian MNEs
[5] Includes other industries.

Source: Marina Papanastassiou database.

Table 6.4 Sources of technology[1] used by MNE subsidiaries (average response[2])

| | Parent country of MNE | | | | | | | | | | | |
| | USA | | | Japan | | | Europe[3] | | | Total[4] | | |
	a	b	c	a	b	c	a	b	c	a	b	c
Automobiles	2.00	2.14	2.00				3.00	2.00		2.20	2.12	2.00
Industrial and agricultural chemicals	2.44	1.89	2.13	3.00	3.00	1.00	2.10	1.90	2.00	2.29	1.95	2.05
Pharmaceuticals and consumer chemicals	2.33	1.86	2.12				2.67	2.00	1.33	2.42	1.90	1.91
Electronics and electrical appliances	2.40	1.25	2.00	2.50	1.43	2.12	2.40	1.75	2.25	2.44	1.47	2.13
Total[5]	2.43	1.96	1.96	2.69	1.67	1.83	2.56	1.67	1.78	2.49	1.83	1.89

Notes:
[1] Sources of technology are: (a) technology imported from elsewhere in the MNE group.
(b) established host-country technology.
(c) results of R & D carried out by the subsidiary.

[2] Respondents were asked to evaluate each source of technology as either the main source; a secondary source; not a source. The average response was then calculated by allocating the responses of main source the value of 3, secondary source a value of 2, and not a source a value of 1.

[3] Covers subsidiaries of European MNEs in countries other than the home country.
[4] Includes subsidiaries of Canadian MNEs.
[5] Includes other industries.
Source: Marina Papanastassiou database

(i.e. it is the output of the precompetitive phase one in a global-innovation strategy). The results in Table 6.4 indicate that there is at least a slight tendency for the subsidiaries in the four high-technology industries analysed separately to be somewhat less dependent on such imported technology than is the case for the whole sample. It can also be reported that subsidiaries in the UK are rather less reliant on this source of technology (AR of 2.42) than those in the other three countries (AR of 2.67). Generally established host-country technology does not seem to be a major input into the subsidiaries' operations, though it is somewhat more important for US subsidiaries (especially in automobiles) than in other cases. Subsidiaries in the UK (AR of 1.96) were rather more inclined to utilise established host-country technology than those in the other countries (AR of 1.52). Taken with the result for imported technology just noted this indicates that subsidiaries in the UK seem to have the strongest degree of technological independence.

The third source of technology analysed, the results of R&D carried out by the subsidiary, is generally of moderate relevance throughout the sample. For the US MNEs' subsidiaries each of the four industries covered in Table 6.4 has a somewhat above average tendency to incorporate this source. Since, apart from automobiles,[3] they are all also quite strongly inclined to incorporate imported group technology, the results can be interpreted as compatible with a global approach to technology in US MNEs in these high-technology industries. Thus it is plausible to suggest that the subsidiary R&D efforts are developing new imported group technology in ways that meet the needs of European markets. This interpretation could also, quite convincingly, be extended to the results for Japanese MNEs' subsidiaries in electronics and electrical appliances, where important centrally-created new technology needs substantial further development by local research before it can be effectively applied to European markets.

In European MNEs, their subsidiaries in the region outside the home country are most notably dependent on their own R&D in electronics and chemicals. This may either reflect work to respond to particular national market needs in the host-country-focused subsidiaries that we have seen are rather more prevalent in European MNEs, or an independent mandate allocated to a subsidiary to play a strong role in developing a part of the product range for the European market. In pharmaceuticals it seems that the strong capacity of the European MNEs' home countries in relevant areas of science limits the R&D done in other subsidiaries, which are instead particularly strongly inclined to import the technology.

Overall, subsidiaries in the four high-tech industries tend to be more reliant on their own R&D than the rest of the sample. Taken with their tendency to be somewhat less oriented to imported technology, it may seem that the needs of global technological competitiveness in these dynamic industries does require a strong creative input from their overseas subsidiaries. Amongst the subsidiaries in Europe the relatively independent position of those in UK is further emphasised in respect of their own R&D, with an AR of 1.99 compared with 1.67 in the other countries. Alongside the comparison for imported technology previously noted, this suggests that UK-based subsidiaries are believed to have access to scientific inputs (including established host-country technology) that endow them with the capacity to make a strong individual contribution to group technological competitiveness.

As we have now clearly emphasised, one way that MNEs' subsidiaries often contribute to the overall competitiveness of their group is by applying existing technology in a way that responds optimally to their own segment of the global market, which here can be the individual host country but is more often a wider area in Europe. In the survey the question reported in Table 6.5 investigated one dimension of this process, by analysing the degree to which the subsidiaries adapted technology. Overall only 24.0 per cent of respondents said they adapted technology extensively, though a further 66.3 per cent did so to some extent.

In the light of our view of the importance of local (including regional) market responsiveness in the MNEs' global strategy, an interpretation of this result is that where established technology would need more than moderate adaptation to meet distinctive conditions, the firms usually opt for a more substantial step in technological progress. This then involves the subsidiaries developing a new product from recently created group technology (a new outline product concept) rather than limited evolution of an older generation of products.

For US subsidiaries, Table 6.5 suggests that the choice of development is especially prevalent in electronics and electrical appliances, where adaptation of US products to European conditions would need to be so extensive that an independent development from the relevant underlying technology is usually a preferred option. Interestingly, US subsidiaries in the other three high-tech industries covered do have an above average tendency to include adaptation in their operations. This suggests that the nature of competition in these dynamic industries requires that, alongside the development of uniquely European product variants, adapted versions of other parts of the groups' product ranges can also make a contribution.

Two contrasting factors may lead to the moderate levels of adaptation reported by the subsidiaries of European MNEs. The first is that since the core product development activity is likely to be based in European operations in these companies it is likely to have an initial orientation towards the region's market in a way that the new basic product concepts of US and Japanese MNEs would not. Against this, however, the greater prevalence of subsidiaries strongly oriented to their national markets in European MNEs, and the possibility that these companies are better able to discern relevant differences between national markets in Europe, may lead to a greater propensity for them to carry out adaptation for individual host-country conditions.

Table 6.5   Extent of technological adaptation of MNE subsidiaries
(average response[1])

	Parent country of MNE			
	USA	Japan	Europe[2]	Total[3]
Automobiles	2.29		1.50	2.11
Industrial and agricultural chemicals	2.22	2.00	2.22	2.20
Pharmaceuticals and consumer chemicals	2.25		2.33	2.27
Electronics and electrical appliances	1.60	2.50	2.40	2.22
Total[4]	2.11	2.23	2.17	2.14

Notes:
[1] Subsidiaries that used imported MNE technology and/or established host-country technology were asked if they adapted this to suit their current needs extensively, to some extent, or not at all. The average response was then calculated by allocating responses of extensively the value 3, to some extent 2 and not at all 1.
[2] Covers subsidiaries of European MNEs in countries other than the home country.
[3] Includes subsidiaries of Canadian MNEs.
[4] Includes other industries.
Source: Marina Papanastassiou database.

Evidence from the survey confirms the expectation that the strongest motivation for adaptation of technology by the subsidiaries in Europe lies in the need to make products fully responsive to distinctive market needs. Thus when respondents that performed adaptation were asked to assess three possible reasons as important, relatively important or not important, the overall average response[4] for 'to make the product more suitable for our market' was 2.66. Though this was highest for subsidiaries of US (AR of 2.71) and Japanese (2.75) MNEs and the fact that it was also strong for those of European MNEs (2.58) further confirms the view that *within* Europe market differences between countries are often sufficient to require adaptation in response. Amongst the industries covered product adaptation was especially prevalent in automobiles (2.90) and electronics (2.79). Of two motives for adaptation relating to aspects of production, marginally the more prominant (an overall AR of 1.77) was 'to achieve a more suitable scale of production'. This was a notably prevalent influence on adaptation in pharmaceuticals (2.56) and also relatively prominent in automobiles (2.13). Production-scale adaptation was marginally more relevant in US (1.84) and European (1.80) subsidiaries than in those of Japanese MNEs (1.50). The somewhat less relevant motive for adaptation of production technology was 'to make more suitable use of local factor proportions', with an overall AR of 1.67. Pharmaceuticals (2.00) was again the industry most influenced by this factor.

6.5 SUBSIDIARIES' HOST-COUNTRY SCIENTIFIC LINKS

As the discussion of the previous section has emphasised it is one clear theme of our analysis that overseas subsidiaries of MNEs play an interactive role in the creative activity of the overall group. Thus a global-competitive MNE is likely to have a pervasive dominant technological trajectory which is likely to influence the evolution in the operations of each of its subsidiaries. These subsidiaries, however, often pick up this underlying technology and apply their own resources (managerial and marketing, as well as scientific) to it, in order to complete the implementation of a global-innovation strategy as competitively as possible in their own market area. Though this clearly implies a very strong demand-side (i.e. market-based) influence on the decision to set up R&D facilities targeted at a local market we have also seen that where in a large regional market, such as Europe, such a facility is located may depend to some extent on supply-side factors, notably the quality of the local science base. Where these R&D subsidiaries play a role in the supply of basic research to the precompetitive phase of a MNE's global-innovation programme, the availability of quality scientific inputs is likely to be an even more influential factor. Thus alongside their integration into the wider operations of their MNE these R&D laboratories are also likely to interact significantly with other elements of the scientific community in their host countries.

Some aspects of this interaction were investigated in the survey of MNE subsidiaries, through a question reported in Table 6.6. The subsidiaries' links with host-country universities are found to be quite widespread, but relatively few of the respondents felt they were very strong. Thus overall 59.0 per cent of respondents said they did collaborative research with universities, but of those only 28.6 per cent described such links as extensive. US pharmaceutical industry subsidiaries were particularly prone to establish links with host-country universities. This reflects a particularly strong evaluation by US pharmaceutical MNEs of the relevant areas of basic science in certain European countries, with this being coupled into the precompetitive basic research phase of a global-innovation strategy. If this strong base is in the home countries of European pharmaceutical MNEs (as is a logical expectation) then this would also explain the limited need of their subsidiaries elsewhere in Europe to establish collaborative links with host-country universities.

Research collaborations of the MNE subsidiaries with independent research laboratories were limited in number (only 34.1 per cent of respondents said they existed at all) and rarely strong (only 13.8 per cent of such links were considered to be extensive). As Table 6.6 shows, such collaborations were again relatively prominent for US pharmaceutical subsidiaries and also for European chemical subsidiaries (whose university links were also relatively strong). Associations with industry research laboratories are slightly less sparse, with 41.2 per cent of respondents reporting their existence though, again, they tend to be quite weak with only 11.4 per cent of them considered to be extensive. Research collaborations with industry laboratories were relatively common in chemicals (for

Table 6.6 MNE subsidiaries' evaluation of their collaborative research with local organisations[1] (average response[2])

| | Parent country of MNE | | | | | | | | | | | | | | | |
| | USA | | | | Japan | | | | Europe[3] | | | | Total[4] | | | |
	a	b	c	d	a	b	c	d	a	b	c	d	a	b	c	d
Automobiles	1.89	1.14	1.43	1.17					1.50	1.00	1.00	1.50	1.82	1.13	1.38	1.25
Industrial and agricultural chemicals	1.75	1.38	1.63	1.83	1.00	1.00	1.00	1.00	1.90	1.63	1.71	1.75	1.85	1.50	1.65	1.81
Pharmaceuticals and consumer chemicals	2.00	1.60	1.33	1.13					1.50	1.00	1.00	1.33	1.92	1.50	1.27	1.18
Electronics and electrical appliances	1.50	1.00	1.00	1.83	1.67	1.00	1.33	1.80	1.75	1.33	1.75	1.25	1.63	1.07	1.31	1.67
Total[5]	1.82	1.40	1.43	1.48	1.40	1.22	1.30	1.44	1.71	1.44	1.54	1.44	1.76	1.39	1.46	1.48

Notes:
1 Covers collaborative research with: (a) Universities
                                       (b) Independent research laboratories.
                                       (c) Industry research laboratories
                                       (d) Other firms.

2 Respondents were asked to evaluate each type of collaboration as extensive, moderate, or non-existent. The average response was then calculated by allocating responses of extensive the value 3, moderate 2 and non-existent 1.
3 Covers subsidiaries of European MNEs in countries other than the home country.
4 Includes subsidiaries of Canadian MNEs.
5 Includes other industries.
Source: Marina Papanastassiou database.

subsidiaries of both US and European MNEs) and for European electronics subsidiaries. Overall, 40.0 per cent of respondents took part in research collaborations with other firms, with 18.8 per cent of these links being considered as extensive. Both US and European MNEs' subsidiaries in chemicals were relatively strongly committed to interfirm research collaborations, as were US and Japanese subsidiaries in electronics.

6.6 FUNDING OF SUBSIDIARY R&D

Since the R&D carried out by MNEs' foreign subsidiaries is seen as frequently playing a role within wider group-level programmes for the creation and implementation of technology, and since this often involves some degree of collaboration with host-country scientific institutions, the potential sources of funding for this work can be quite diverse. Nevertheless, as the survey evidence quoted in Table 6.7 shows, 39.8 per cent of the subsidiaries felt that their own funds represented their only source of funding and, in addition, the same proportion felt that this was their major source of finance even when not the sole one. Only 6.8 per cent of subsidiaries did not play some role in financing their research. Subsidiaries of European MNEs tend to be most likely to finance their own R&D which to some extent probably reflects their higher propensity to focus on the supply of their host-country market. Apart from automobiles the high-tech industries covered separately have a below-average tendency to see their own finance as either their only or major source of funding, indicating that it is in these industries that involvement in wider research roles is most likely to involve diversified sources of support.

Though 52.4 per cent of respondents said that funds from the parent company supported their R&D to some degree this source was the major or sole one in only 26.8 per cent of cases. US MNEs were most likely to be the major or unique source of funding for their European subsidiaries' R&D, and though Japanese R&D subsidiaries

Table 6.7   Sources of funding for MNE subsidiaries' R&D laboratories[1]

	Our own funds				Per cent Funds from parent company				Funds from host-country government				Funds from EU budget			
	1	2	3	4	1	2	3	4	1	2	3	4	1	2	3	4
By MNE parent country																
USA	33.3	42.2	13.3	11.1	7.0	27.9	25.6	39.5	2.3		23.4	74.4		2.4	9.5	88.1
Japan	27.3	45.5	18.2	9.1		18.2	45.5	36.3			27.3	72.7			27.3	72.7
Europe[2]	53.6	32.1	14.3		4.7	17.9	14.3	67.8	1.2		23.1	76.9			22.2	77.8
Total[3]	39.8	39.8	13.6	6.8	4.7	22.1	25.6	47.6	1.2		23.8	75.0		1.2	16.9	81.9
By industry																
Automobiles	57.1	28.6	14.3			14.3	42.9	42.9			28.6	71.4				100.0
Chemicals	50.0	22.2	22.2	5.6		17.7	35.3	47.0			6.7	93.3			12.5	87.5
Pharmaceuticals	12.5	62.5	12.5	12.5		75.0	12.5	12.5			25.0	75.0		12.5		87.5
Electronics	23.5	47.1	17.7	11.8	5.9	11.8	35.3	47.1	5.9		35.3	58.8			31.3	68.7
Total[4]	39.8	39.8	13.6	6.8	4.7	22.1	25.6	47.6	1.2		23.8	75.0		1.2	16.9	81.9
By host country																
UK	43.1	35.6	15.4	6.2	6.4	22.2	25.4	46.0	1.6		17.7	80.7		4.6	11.5	88.5
Other[5]	30.4	52.2	8.7	8.7		21.7	26.1	52.2			40.9	59.1		1.2	31.8	63.6
Total	39.8	39.8	13.6	6.8	4.7	22.1	25.6	47.6	1.2		23.8	75.0		1.2	16.9	81.9

Notes:
[1] Respondents were asked to evaluate each potential source as either:
  1 the only source of funding.
  2 the major source of funding.
  3 a supporting source of funding.
  4 not a source of funding.
[2] Covers subsidiaries of European MNEs in countries other than the home country.
[3] Includes subsidiaries of Canadian MNEs.
[4] Includes other industries.
[5] In Belgium, Greece and Portugal.

were least likely to be totally excluded from parent funding this rarely went beyond being a supplementary source. Pharmaceuticals is the industry in which the subsidiaries' R&D is most likely to receive major parent company funding, a fact which is highly compatible with the position of US MNEs' European labs in this industry being strongly oriented towards basic research, supporting group-level technical progress rather than the immediate needs of European operations.

Only 25.0 per cent of respondents indicated that their research received funding support from the host-country government, with this almost never going beyond being a supplementary source. Electronics was the industry most likely to receive government research funding, and chemicals least so. Subsidiaries were considerably less able to secure government research funds in the UK than in the other three European countries. Use of funds from EU budget was limited to 18.1 per cent of responding subsidiary laboratories. European and Japanese subsidiaries were more inclined to seek, or be successful in securing, such EU funds (compared with those of US MNEs), as were subsidiaries in electronics and those in Belgium, Portugal and Greece by comparison with those in UK.

6.7   CASE STUDIES

In this section our analysis of broad patterns in the earlier discussion is given a detailed focus by using information from the Marina Papanastassiou database to scrutinise the approach to European markets of particular MNEs. This is given richness in the cases covered where replies were received from several subsidiaries of the same MNE operating in more than one of the countries covered.

Case A

This is a European electronics MNE for which we have information on two UK subsidiaries and one each in Belgium and Portugal. All the subsidiaries are serving their national markets, but for the Portuguese subsidiary this is its main market indicating import- substituting behaviour. The other three subsidiaries have a definite export-oriented focus, covering a wide range of international markets but mainly European. However, export orientation doesn't mean identically-motivated subsidiaries as they can be either regional or world product mandates (RPM/WPM) if we deal with those creating their own autonomous products, or rationalised product subsidiaries (RPS) supplying established products or intermediate goods (inputs), or even truncated miniature replicas (TMRs) in a creative transition towards becoming RPMs or RPSs.

Thus export orientation, although it is normally a more dynamic attitude compared to that of import substitution, can itself be characterised by different forms that can be perceived as stages that are relatively static (RPS) or dynamic/evolutionary (RPM or WPM). Overall market orientation is an important characteristic that can help us not only understand the activity of individual subsidiaries within the MNE group but also their importance to the evolution of industry of the host country.

An important element in this is the preference of most subsidiaries (as noted earlier) to possess an R&D lab. The R&D lab is associated with the dynamism of a subsidiary and is expressed through the creation of new products or the adaptation of existing ones or alterations in the production process. All four of the subsidiaries in this case possessed R&D facilities, with three of the units being established as fresh installations and the other (Belgian) acquired as part of a takeover. The export-oriented behaviour of company A's Belgian and UK subsidiaries can be a sign of their labs' serious adaptation of existing products, or creation of new products, for regional markets. The R&D lab in the case of the Portuguese subsidiary indicates alterations in production processes in response to the available cheap labour.

The main point here is that in all four subsidiaries the parent company has provided for their support by an R&D lab. This can be easily explained by the fact that electronics is a very dynamic and 'daily evolving' sector, with strong European, US and, of course, Japanese competitors. This is further reflected in the fact that in all the subsidiaries the labs interact with other sources of technology.

For the Belgian subsidiary the R&D lab's own results act as the major source of technology, with the secondary support of imported technology and host-country technology. We must recall here that this R&D lab was acquired, and as a matter of strategy it would not be wise to underestimate the importance of the acquired lab or perceive its acquisition as a sideline. Also host-country results may be inherited from the previous ownership of the laboratory. The UK subsidiaries involve all possible sources of technology but sometimes attribute varying relative importance to them, indicating that subsidiaries can have independent managerial attitudes especially where they involve different product lines. Generally, differing significance is given to the grade of importance (priority) of each source not only for the UK subsidiaries but for all those of the group, indicating different views on efficiency of supply of technology as the role of each subsidiary differs and as each host country possesses different characteristics which influence the shaping of technology use.

Regarding the extent of adaptation, the Belgian subsidiary makes full use of its R&D personnel by extensively adapting the external technology supply. The other subsidiaries in the other two countries also adapt, but only to a more moderate degree. The extent of adaptation also gives us an indication of the sort of export orientation, and of the gravity of the role of each subsidiary and its R&D lab in the host-country industry and the MNE group. The main purpose of adaptation for all the subsidiaries is to make their products suitable for their markets. This is in line with the fact that most of the subsidiaries export and each one plays a specialised role in the group. Thus their production covers needs beyond the national and represent the flag of the company in wider markets, which makes the role of the subsidiaries very complicated, with wider responsibilities. However, even in the case where the national market plays the major role we see that the parent company takes this market seriously, despite its size, as its subsidiary may later serve other markets and must be dedicated to international standards. Further, even if the subsidiary serves only its national market, in an interrelated world a wrong attitude in one market can undermine the reputation of the company in other countries (via the media).

The responsibilities of the subsidiaries also often extend to creation of new products. In all our examined subsidiaries a major influence on the creation of a new product is the availability of scientific personnel. Capable scientists are an important asset to each company. Companies may accumulate them, if they can afford it, in order to be prepared for future competition. Also, as every company is interested in future markets, for three of the four subsidiaries its increased competitiveness in the European market is also reported as an important factor in creating a new product.

We noted earlier the character of each subsidiary and although all of them have some sort of export orientation we can classify that of the Portuguese as an RPS as its exports are limited to intermediate products supplied to other parts of the MNE group. This can explain why the other three subsidiaries, who are variants of the RPM type, view their role of deriving new products more as part of the global vision of their parent strategy. The Portuguese RPS, with its main clients in the national market and the MNE itself, does not see increased competitiveness and a global view on innovation as part of its existence, as the nature of this subsidiary is more or less externally defined. This indicates its position in a sort of hierarchy, but without underestimating the contribution of its role.

In examining the spillovers to the host-country economy via subsidiaries' links with local suppliers and any sort of scientific exchange, at first glance we must say that they are mixed. The Portuguese and Belgian subsidiaries have very strong links with local suppliers as they provide them with technical advice. The UK ones seem to have the least possible links with their local surroundings, with just one collaboration with a university. The Belgian subsidiary has the strongest links with local research factors, which it inherited from its previous ownership.

The position of any subsidiary in an MNE group may be subject to tensions and change, and the potential for this may be discerned amongst the subsidiaries described here. So it seems that the Belgian subsidiary, through its previous local ownership, still benefits the local market as it would not be wise for the parent company to diminish the role of this newly acquired subsidiary as a matter of policy towards the host-country. Maybe after a certain time has passed, in a process of rationalisation of its activities, the subsidiary will go through a more substantive adjustment process. The Portuguese subsidiary's role is mainly to supply the host-country market efficiently with a high-quality standardised product, but it also supplies inputs to other parts of the MNE group. Although its role in the group seems therefore very stable it does not mean that the management would not tend to seek a different role now, especially as it has a large research laboratory. Finally the UK subsidiaries, although they differ between themselves in some respects, both seem to be playing an increased role in the MNE group, despite which neither seems to have a deep relationship with local factors, either subcontractors or research institutions.

So from this point of view the Portuguese subsidiary offers more to the host country in the form of help for creative infrastructure, but takes a less fundamental role in the MNE group. Frustration, however, may be felt by the two UK subsidiaries as the personnel of an MNE wants to see itself participating in more challenging roles. The Belgian subsidiary may need to protect its traditional local links and develop a new role around them to establish its position in the group hierarchy.

Case B

Here we deal with the UK and Portuguese subsidiaries of a Japanese electronics company. We note that the UK subsidiary has a more dynamic attitude, with a larger share of exports, wider market orientation and a large R&D lab. On the other hand the Portuguese company focuses mainly on the national market with minor exports to other non-European markets and does not possess an R&D lab. Although these characteristics could prohibit us from comparing the companies which only seem to have as a common factor their Japanese parent, by proceeding with the analysis we can also see that the subsidiaries do have things in common.

Both import parent company technology and both adapt it extensively. The Portuguese subsidiary also uses host-country established technology, whilst the UK one uses results from its own laboratory. So for the Portuguese subsidiary other host-country labs seem to do the work its own R&D unit would do. Regardless of the role of technology, adaptation is extensive for both companies. So a question is posed. How can two outwardly so different subsidiaries show such similarities in attitude?

The answer to that question starting from the Portuguese one, which definitely lacks the robustness (physical in terms of size – employment and financial), is that the Portuguese management nevertheless recognises that its company belongs to a major competitor internationally and thus gains from a spirit of confidence. However, as there are certain hierarchies in the MNE, the Portuguese subsidiary does not perform the range of activities of the UK one and maybe will not evolve to do so. But as the Portuguese market is an emerging one, and as other companies are accumulating there, this subsidiary is, in relative terms, as much involved competitively as the UK one. As the parent company is a leading name internationally it is a big name nationally as well. This is more pointed in the Portuguese case where despite the small role the subsidiary plays in the MNE group (in terms of sales and employment) it does play a major role in the host-country economy. It would then not reflect well on the parent company if it had established a subsidiary without important dynamic characteristics, as the subsidiary in the Portuguese economy can be a pioneer in the field and an aristocrat among other competitors. Thus this subsidiary has the same close relationships with local subcontractors and local research institutions as does the UK subsidiary.

We can thus see how, as in the previous case study, the national market is treated with significant seriousness despite its size. This is in line with the fact that host-country governments must use their national market dynamically as an especially important location advantage for MNEs.

Case C

Our last case study deals with the operations in Belgium, Greece, and Portugal of a well-established American pharmaceutical company. For the Belgian subsidiary the national market is the only market, whilst the company exports from Portugal and Greece. However, their export markets differ as the Portuguese exports only to EU markets while the Greek sells to other European markets, probably eastern European due to the geographical position, and also other markets, which may well be Middle Eastern markets, again for geographical reasons as well as possibly political (the friendly Greek relationship with Arab countries). So we can see that the peripheral subsidiaries of the company act as exporters, indicating the distinct role subsidiaries play.

However, the export operations of the Greek company are not formally supported by an R&D lab, though they may be through the work of their qualified engineers. On the other hand the Portuguese activities are supported by a lab as are those of the Belgian subsidiary despite the fact that its operations concentrate on the national market. Both these labs were fresh installations. All the subsidiaries make use of imported technology, but as would be expected those with laboratories also use results derived in these labs and also home-country technology. All of the subsidiaries adapt their external sources of technology. For the Greek subsidiary the basic influence behind adaptations are cost factors, for the Belgian the main reason is product suitability and for the Portuguese a combination of both is relevant.

So we see that the peripheral countries are used as export sites, for cost reasons, in a manner that may resemble an upgraded and developed form of an import substitution operation. For the Belgian subsidiary, although the signs point to a more pure import-substituting behaviour, the case is not so. The fact that the Belgian market is in the heart of Europe and comprises different consumer tastes may indicate that the subsidiary may play a specialised role in the group where products are tested within its national market. The size of the laboratory supports that view and also justifies the fact that Belgium is seen as a site of international scientific recruitment and that the lab plays a supporting role to other parts of the group. All the subsidiaries said they were involved in the creation of new products, with this seen as both aimed at increasing their competitiveness in Europe and as part of the group's global- innovation strategy.

The cost orientation of the Portuguese and Greek subsidiaries is seen through the close relationship they establish with local subcontractors, which is, of course, a very important spillover effect. On the other hand only the Belgian subsidiary has established local scientific links. Again in this case it would not be wise to make rough comparisons and underrate the type of spillovers to others because we need to see things in relative terms – different roles, different approaches, different markets, different goals. The comparison of the three small European markets reveal some importance for the host-country market and its peculiarities and how the parent company views it. In all cases trade within Europe takes predominantly the form of intra-firm trade, while the extent of intra-firm trade diminishes when non-European markets have importance and classic trade occurs.

6.8 CONCLUSION

The case studies indicate that whereas Europe plays a role in MNEs' *global* strategies, national markets still often play particular roles in their *European* strategy. Countries like Belgium, Greece and Portugal do not possess a lot of traditional market advantages (current size), but are still treated with particular respect. This respect is certainly relevant to the type of industry we examined. Both pharmaceuticals and electronics are highly competitive industries and a small disorder in one market may influence consumer behaviour in others. Proximity in the case of the European markets justifies that. Although we deal with quite homogenised products, this homogeneity may appear at the core of the product but in order to market it particular consumer tastes should be taken into consideration. European integration can or should provide similar standards that secure consumer safety, but cannot standardise tastes and resources. The evidence shows that European MNEs are highly sensitive to the characteristics of national markets, as often are long-established American and other companies.

Another important issue (illustrated in the case studies) is the commitment of the management, not only to its subsidiary but also to the other parts of the group. All companies look forward to a better role in the future. It seems that European integration is often perceived by companies only as legislative and financial procedures, which in some cases can facilitate their work but in others contradict it as they want to preserve and develop their individual subsidiaries' character within the group. The equilibria are fragile, but this should be the role of EU, preserve, integrate and promote.

Notes

1. The study was carried out by Marina Papanastassiou in 1992/93.
2. Sixty-six of the 68 subsidiaries that said they had such R&D units replied to the question.
3. In automobiles, subsidiary R&D may perhaps be applied rather more to established host-country technology in order to derive a specific source of distinctive competitiveness from it.
4. Important was allocated a value of 3, relatively important a value of 2 and not important 1.

7 Firm-Strategies and the Research-Intensity of US MNEs' Overseas Operations: An Analysis of Host-Country Determinants

with Marina Papanastassiou

7.1 INTRODUCTION

Previous studies of the determinants of overseas R&D in MNEs have analysed the differences, between firms or industries, in the proportion of total R&D that is carried out in subsidiaries abroad.[1] In particular, these studies have approached consensus in suggesting that internationalisation of R&D has very broadly reflected the internationalisation of sales and production. However it has also been very persuasively argued[2] that, within this general picture of market-supporting overseas R&D, the nature and intensity of the work carried out in a particular country will differ considerably according to the role played by the operations it is required to support. This chapter seeks to analyse the determinants of the R&D–intensity of US subsidiaries in particular host countries, in order to investigate the relation between the strategic role of these subsidiaries' operations and their need for technological support.

In the context of import-substitution subsidiaries, focusing their activity on the supply of their host-country market, it has long been accepted that a role exists for relatively small-scale R&D-backup, this obtained from Support Laboratories (SLs) which aim to adapt existing product and process technology to local needs.[3] Where the subsidiaries are predominantly export-oriented it may be suggested that the need for R&D support depends on which of two types of operations are most important. Where the subsidiaries simply play an externally-determined role in a globally-coordinated network of supply facilities, producing an existing product in predetermined ways, there is only a very limited role for even SL operations (to assist the effective implementation of the established production process). However, if the subsidiary is given a mandate to take wider responsibility for not only the production of a product, but also its creation, development and innovation, a role exists for much more ambitious Locally Integrated Laboratories (LILs). These integrate the laboratory's work much more thoroughly with subsidiary management, marketing and engineering in order to implement the more dynamic role of the subsidiary in fulfilling its exclusive responsibility for the mandated product.

Beyond these demand-side forces there may also be a role for supply-side influences. Thus whatever the discerned *need* for local R&D-support in overseas subsidiaries, the *ability* of the host-country science-base to provide the resources to fulfil the role efficiently, and cost competitively, may also be relevant. An extension of this supply-side perspective may occur where the strength of the local technological capacity that is accessible to a MNE exceeds the needs of its subsidiary's immediate activities. Under such circumstances an Internationally Interdependent Laboratory (IIL) may be set up, to play a role, alongside similar laboratories in other countries, in the longer-term basic-research programmes of the MNE group. Such an IIL would have no systematic direct supporting relationship with host-country production facilities.

The independent variable tested, to investigate hypotheses developed in the light of the broad views outlined above, is the R&D-intensity (RAD) of the operations of US MNEs' subsidiaries in particular countries. This is defined as 'expenditure for R&D performed for affiliates in a particular country, divided by their sales in that country'.[4] It was possible to calculate this variable, and thus perform separate tests, for all industries (including petroleum and services, as well as manufacturing), for total manufacturing and for five separate manufacturing industries.[5] As will be elaborated in section 7.2.vi, the tests of RAD include a measure of royalty payments for licensed technology as an independent variable, in order to investigate the effect on subsidiaries' R&D of their access to existing knowledge (either elsewhere in the MNE group or from independent sources). However, as a supplement to our main analysis we also use this royalty measure as a dependent variable and test it, for comparative purposes, against the same independent variables as RAD. This variable (ROY) is defined as 'payments of royalties and license fees by affiliates in a particular country divided by their sales in that country'.[6]

7.2 HYPOTHESES AND INDEPENDENT VARIABLES

(i) GDP

In line with the well-established view of support for host-country markets as a likely role for R&D in MNE subsidiaries we include the country's GDP as an indicator of the relative size of such markets. GDP is then hypothesised as being positively related to the research intensity of US firms' operations (RAD). The first reason for this view is that, other things being equal,[7] the larger is the host-country market the more competition firms are likely to face in it, and the greater the rewards for competing successfully. Local R&D to adapt and develop products, or revise production processes to make local output more cost competitive, is central to such competition and is likely to be implemented more intensively the higher is GDP. A second facet of the hypothesised positive relationship between GDP and RAD is that as the R&D effort expands in a particular country the additional increments implemented may represent more expensive operations, involving a qualitative upgrading of the overall activity. Thus when the research commitment reaches certain levels further expansion may, for the first time, merit the acquisition of certain pieces of expensive machinery or instrumentation, whilst the research teams may reach sizes where the incorporation of personnel with especially specialised, but expensive, skills can be justified.

Turning to the tests of licensing payments it is not possible to extend either the adaptation or indivisibilities arguments to support a positive relationship between GDP and ROY, in a way that would complement that predicted between GDP and RAD. If the factor considered most likely to underlie variation in ROY is the quality of technology licensed (i.e. sophistication compared with standardisation) then average income levels (i.e. GNP per capita) are much more likely to influence the intensity of royalty payments than aggregate income (i.e. GDP). Therefore there is no *a priori* expectation with regard to the relationship between GDP and ROY.[8]

(ii) GNP per capita

We may discern two opposing influences of a host-country's GNP per capita on the research intensity of US subsidiaries' operations. Firstly it may be suggested that generally the lower is a country's GNP per capita the greater the difference of its average income level from that of the USA, and therefore the greater the range and strength of influences (both relating to product characteristics and the requirements of optimum production processes) likely to make adaptive R&D desirable. However, for resources to be committed to such work an adequate return in terms of boosted profitability would be required and, with other factors such as, in particular, the potential aggregate market (i.e. GDP) held constant, this is more likely to occur with higher GNP per capita. Thus whilst the first influence suggests a negative relationship between GNP per capita and RAD the second indicates a positive one, so that our overall prediction is indeterminate.

With regard to the relationship between GNP per capita and the intensity of commitment to licensing technology (i.e. ROY) we are rather more decisive in predicting a positive result. As previously indicated it is expected that the factor most likely to influence inter-country differences in the value of ROY is the quality of technology licensed. The higher is a host-country's GNP per capita the more likely is a subsidiary of a US MNE to be able to utilise effectively the most recent (i.e. high-quality) technology implemented by the parent (or another high-income-country subsidiary) in a manner that supports the ability to pay the higher levels of royalty fees that may be required. By contrast subsidiaries in lower-income countries may use standardised technology that does not involve royalty payments at all, or more accessible middle-range technology for which fees are lower.[9]

(iii) Education

Whereas the previous variables broadly relate to the extent to which US MNEs may perceive the need to carry out adaptive or development work in particular host countries (i.e. demand-side factors) it is also plausible that the degree to which such activity is actually implemented may be influenced by supply-side factors relating to the capability of the host-country's science-base. Whilst there are familiar arguments that suggest that, other things being equal, work aimed to adapt or develop products and processes is best carried out within the environment that determines its nature and aims, this is not immutable and other locations could be chosen for this R&D if the local science-base cannot accommodate it.

The first aspect of the local technological capability that it would be desirable to investigate is the relative availability of scientists and allied support personnel. As a proxy for this we incorporate in our tests an education variable (EDUC), which is formulated as the 'number enrolled in higher education as a percentage of population aged 20-24'.[10] Inter-country differences in this variable are believed to reflect the relative availability of those scientists and administrative personnel needed to facilitate the effective implementation of local R&D by MNEs. The obvious positive relationship between EDUC and R&D implied above is enhanced by the view that this supply-side factor can not only influence the willingness to implement the adaptive (i.e. SL) and development (i.e. LIL) work required in support of host-country production, but also may attract those laboratories which play a wider role in the creation of new group-level technology (i.e. IILs).

Turning to the relation between EDUC and ROY (as the dependent variable) it might be suggested that, with the inclusion of RAD as an independent variable to control for the level of commitment to *adapting* technology, the higher the capacity of the host-country science-base (i.e. EDUC) the higher the quality of technology (and thus value of ROY) that MNE subsidiaries would be willing to license. A factor that might mitigate against this positive relationship could be the occurence of the 'not invented here' syndrome within MNE subsidiaries. Thus the stronger is the local science-base the greater the pressure that might arise from scientists and allied personnel within the subsidiary to reject the assimilation of licensed technology and move towards a greater commitment to an independent creativity.[11]

(iv) Scientific-wages

A second supply-side factor that may influence a US MNE's willingness to implement R&D in a country is the cost of doing so. In an attempt to distinguish wage costs as a key element of this we formulated a proxy variable (WAGE) as 'the average compensation paid to non-production workers by US subsidiaries in manufacturing'.[12] If such costs are indeed an important element in decisions with regard to the location of overseas R&D by US MNEs then WAGE would clearly be expected to be negatively related to RAD. However, where cost considerations play a relatively minor role in making such decisions, with the need and ability to carry out R&D the more central influences, WAGE might be rather more strongly interpreted as an indicator of quality. Under these conditions high values of WAGE might tend to encourage the implementation of R&D, with the enhanced confidence that the quality of scientific and allied labour would ensure satisfactory outcomes then overriding the higher implied cost. This suggests an alternative positive relationship between WAGE and RAD.

Of the two contrary influences that may affect the relationship between WAGE and RAD, the second seems most likely to prevail in that between WAGE and ROY, here providing a less equivocal prediction of a positive result. Thus, once the commitment to actively adapting technology is covered by the inclusion of RAD as an independent variable, it is hard to envisage a way in which host-country scientific labour-costs could affect the quality of technology licensed. However, where WAGE is seen as reflecting the ability of local scientific and administrative labour to assimilate and implement licensed technology it would be expected to be positively related to ROY (bearing in mind that ROY is believed to rise with the quality, and therefore probably complexity and unfamiliarity, of the technology).

(v) Market orientation

Though the first two variables discussed dealt with ways in which characteristics of a subsidiary's host-country market might influence its commitment to R&D, it needs to be acknowledged that many US subsidiaries have a wider market orientation and that exports may have different implications for their R&D-intensity. To test this we calculated a variable (LOCAL) which is 'the share of US subsidiaries' production in a particular country which is supplied to the local (i.e. host-country) market'.[13] It was possible to calculate this variable for all industries, for total manufacturing, and for each of the industries tested separately.

It is our view that the relationship between LOCAL and RAD depends on the nature of any exports that occur, and that export orientation in US subsidiaries may respond to two very different motivations which have notably different implications for the subsidiaries' R&D-intensity. One export-oriented role that a subsidiary might play is that of the Rationalised Product Subsidiary (RPS), in which it specialises in the cost-effective production of a product or component as part of a centrally- coordinated network of MNE facilities linked through intra-group trade. Since this role involves the supply of established products, at predetermined specification and quality levels, to other parts of the MNE group, very little scope for local adaptation exists. Certainly product adaptation would be ruled out, and though it would be possible to envisage some process adaptation to make more effective use of local conditions it is likely that MNEs would in fact select production locations to suit their established technology in a way that would limit the need for this. Thus the more important are RPS-type exports in the operations of US subsidiaries in a country, the lower we would expect their R&D-intensity to be. This provides the prediction of a positive relationship between LOCAL and RAD.

The second type of export-oriented operation we consider is the World (or Regional) Product Mandate (WPM) subsidiary. This is given quite a degree of autonomous responsibility for the development of a distinctive product in the MNE's range, for its production, and for its marketing in the global (or at least an extensive regional) market. By contrast with RPS operations, where we considered export sales to require less R&D-support than would local market sales, WPM activity is considered to involve a much stronger commitment to product development (i.e. LIL work) demanding a much enhanced R&D input. Therefore the more important are WPM operations in the overall production of US subsidiaries in a country the higher we would expect their R&D-intensity to be, providing the anticipation of a negative relationship between LOCAL and RAD.

Turning to the relationship between LOCAL and ROY it is not easy to derive strong views with regard to any distinctively different need to license technology in support of local-market operations, or either type of exports. Since RPS operations are, as already noted, committed to the use of technology well established in the group they may be required to make some royalty payments for this, making their value of ROY distinctively higher than that for RAD and perhaps more in line with the value of ROY for host-country-market operations. Though we have argued for particularly high values of RAD in support of the effort to derive distinctive export goods in WPM operations, this may well be complementary with quite high values of ROY in these subsidiaries. This would follow from the likelihood that the original product-development efforts in WPM subsidiaries would occur within the context of the group's staple background stock of knowledge, and payments may be made for access to the relevant parts of this. There is, however, no *a priori* reason to expect such payments to differ strongly from those required to support RPS or local-market production. These lines of argument do not preclude the emergence of a significant relationship between LOCAL and ROY, but do make it difficult to predict the likely form it might take.

A further elaboration of these lines of argument relating to market orientation was possible from the aggregate data for all industries. Here it was possible to formulate a variable (INTRA) as 'the proportion of US subsidiaries' exports from a particular country which were supplied to other parts of the same MNE group; i.e. were intra-group trade'.[14] Since this is effectively the share of RPS exports in total exports (where the other part is WPM) the views underlying the hypotheses developed for LOCAL would clearly extend to the prediction of a negative relationship between INTRA and RAD. However, our perception of a much less clear distinction between the likely involvement of licensed technology in RPS and WPM operations excludes a clearcut prediction for the relationship between INTRA and ROY.

(vi) R&D and licensing

We also test the relationship between the R&D-intensity of US-firms' operations in a particular country and their propensity to license technology. This test is incorporated in both equations; i.e. by including ROY as an independent variable when RAD is the dependent variable and by reversing this.[15] Intuitively two broad possibilities may exist for this relationship. The first of these is that the two means of access to technology may be *substitutes*. One way of looking at this possibility would be to suggest that the higher is ROY the more likely licensed technology is to fulfil the needs of a subsidiary and the less it therefore has to implement its own research effort (i.e., lower RAD). An alternative perspective on the substitution relationship would be that the higher is RAD the wider is likely to be the scope of such subsidiary creativity and therefore the less its dependence on licensed technology inputs (i.e. lower ROY).

The second broad possibility, however, is that local research work and the licensing of technology may be *complements*. Indeed most of our earlier discussion of the other independent variables has developed hypotheses from the viewpoint of subsidiary R&D doing adaptive or development work and therefore being to some degree dependent on externally (i.e. outside the subsidiary, though often internal to the MNE group) acquired technology inputs. Elaboration of this general perspective of complementarity into a hypothesis of a positive relationship between ROY and RAD requires that the higher are payments for acquired technology the greater the need to commit subsidiary resources to support its effective implementation.

Certain aspects of these possibilities may be elaborated in the light of some of the perspectives on the roles of overseas R&D already invoked in our earlier discussion.

Under circumstances where RAD tends to be generally relatively high we may consider that an important component of the role of such work is likely to be the creation of quite distinctive product variants as part of a fairly autonomous responsibility undertaken by host-country operations (i.e. the work of LILs supporting a WPM subsidiary). Frequently such a role may be secured by subsidiaries seeking to obtain the greatest scope to fully develop the potential of entrepreneurial management backing up particularly capable and creative local scientific personnel. Where the motivation of such subsidiaries incorporates a strong drive towards autonomy it may be that certain elements in the expansion of research work (i.e. upward pressure on RAD) does seek to achieve the independent performance of facets of the research programme which could have been met by licensed inputs (i.e. downward pressure on ROY). Alternatively, however, recent perspectives on global innovation by MNEs[16] may suggest a complementary relationship, even where subsidiaries are undertaking the introduction of distinctive products. One view on this might suggest that global competitiveness in high-technology industries requires an essentially centralised effort to create new background technology combined with a more dispersed programme for the innovation of distinctive product variants derived from this technology, in order to fully meet the idiosyncratic needs of major markets. If the royalty payments made by an overseas subsidiary for access to new technology reflect its newness and unrealised innovative potential (i.e. higher ROY), its own research inputs may need to be greater to fully achieve its competitive embodyment in distinctive products for its particular markets (i.e. higher RAD).

These alternative possibilities may also persist at the other end of the technology scale, where standardised production techniques and familiar mass market products have emerged, so that local-market or RP subsidiaries prevail, requiring only limited support from SLs. One interpretation of this environment is that the more the operations of US subsidiaries in a country depend on such standardised technology the lower would be the royalty payments required (i.e. low ROY) and the less problem there would be in assimilating it to local conditions (i.e. low RAD). Another possibility, however, might be that the lower the value of RAD the more completely are the operations of the US subsidiaries likely to be committed to playing a (RPS) role strongly dependent on the use of imposed group technology, with an implication of higher royalty payments (albeit at levels well below those that prevail in more high-technology industries).

(vii) Technology transfer requirements

Since the ability to create and transfer technology is recognised as a factor central to the competitiveness of MNEs, and as a key component of their possible contribution to host countries, governments have often sought to adopt policies to influence behaviour in this respect. From the US Department of Commerce data[17] we formulate a variable (TECH REQ) as 'the proportion of US affiliates in a host country that had been required to transfer technology to it'. Other things being equal, it would be our expectation that where such pressures for the transfer of technology existed MNEs would tend to respond positively to them to some extent. It might be suggested that this type of performance requirement serves to alienate MNEs and lessen their commitment to the host country in question. Though this may be so it seems likely that often the reaction to any specific performance requirement (such as the one at issue here) may be rather more generalised, holding back the wider development of operations in a country, rather than altering in a specific way detailed aspects of their implementation. Thus we would not expect strict technology transfer requirements to actually lessen royalty payments per unit of sales (i.e. provoke a negative relationship between TECH REQ and ROY) though, if they contribute to a wider view of an unsatisfactory, perhaps overregulated, environment, they may have helped make sales themselves lower than they would otherwise have been.

Invoking once again the lines of argument just outlined, we would expect that if there is any relationship betwen RAD and TECH REQ it would tend to be positive. It seems reasonable that most host countries interested in seeking to stimulate the technological contribution of MNEs would see local R&D in the same favourable light as technology transfer. Therefore countries where TECH REQ is high would be expected to be countries where, other things being equal, RAD would be high also.[18]

(viii) Industry composition controls

In the tests of the two aggregate samples (i.e. all industries and total manufacturing) we include variables that control for the influence on the value of RAD and ROY (as dependent variables) of the industry composition of US subsidiaries' operations in a particular country. Since manufacturing sales are generally much more technology intensive than those in other sectors, the values of RAD and ROY in the all industries sample would be affected by the share of sales accounted for by manufacturing. We include a variable (MANU), defined as 'the share of total US subsidiary sales in a country accounted for by manufacturing industries', to control for this. Similarly the value of RAD in the total manufacturing sample may be influenced by the share of sales in three industries where subsidiaries' operations are especially R&D-intensive (i.e. chemicals, electrical engineering, transport). The variable HIGH TECH is defined as 'the share of the total US subsidiary sales in manufacturing in a country accounted for by the three high-R&D industries', and controls for their influence in the two aggregate samples.

Multiple regressions using these independent variables were run, with RAD and ROY as the dependent variables. Since both the dependent variables were constrained (to take non-negative values), and since both included several observations at the limit (i.e. zero), the regressions were run using the tobit technique rather than OLS. The results for RAD are given in Table 7.1 and those for ROY in Table 7.2.

7.3 RESULTS

(i) GDP

In the aggregate samples significant support for the hypothesised positive relationship between GDP and RAD is obtained for both all industries (i.e. including petroleum and various services) and for total manufacturing. Of the five manufacturing industries tested separately the significant positive result persists for chemicals, transport equipment and the miscellaneous sector. Thus our hypotheses for GDP appear to be not only supported for two of the more technology-intensive industries, but also for the grouping that includes a range of industries using much more staple technology.

The two industries for which no relationship emerged between GDP and RAD in fact differ very notably with regard to their approach to overseas subsidiaries' access to technology. In the first of these, electrical equipment, the average value of RAD for all overseas operations of US MNEs is (at 2.06) the highest of any industry, whilst royalty payments for licensed technology (a value of 0.87 for ROY) are relatively low. Thus in this industry it seems that the foreign operations of US MNEs have established a notable level of independence from centralised technology creation, but that potential size of host-country markets does not play its usual role in determining the location of the overseas R&D activity. By contrast the second case of an insignficant relationship between GDP and RAD, mechanical engineering, occurs under circumstances where very high dependence on licensed technology (a ROY of 3.13) is combined with low levels of overseas R&D (a RAD of 0.64). Initially this result may contrast with an *a priori* expectation that high levels of customisation of mechanical equipment to distinctive host-country produ-

Table 7.1 Multiple regressions with RAD as dependent variable

	All industries	Total manufac-turing	Chemicals and allied products	Machinery except electrical	Electric and electronic equipment	Transportation equipment	Other manu-facturing
GDP	0.6724D-3**	0.1157D-2**	0.3519D-2***	-0.9458D-3	0.6145D-3	0.5569D-2***	0.1786D-2*
	(2.1566)	(1.9771)	(3.5955)	(-0.9209)	(0.2918)	(2.9747)	(1.8262)
GNP per capita	0.0198	0.1383***	0.1077	0.0822	-0.3456	0.0746	-0.8364D-3
	(0.7694)	(2.8893)	(1.4458)	(0.7876)	(-1.4183)	(0.4177)	(-0.0096)
EDUC	0.9537D-2	-0.4037D-2	0.0108	-0.0292	-0.0685	-0.0325	-0.3859D-2
	(1.1752)	(-0.2962)	(0.4823)	(-0.7136)	(-1.0534)	(-0.6728)	(-1.1168)
WAGE	0.3976D-3	-0.0334	-0.0274	-0.1214D-2	0.3443**	0.0293	0.0198
	(0.0373)	(-1.5893)	(-0.8689)	(-0.0212)	(2.5740)	(0.4920)	(0.4449)
LOCAL	-0.5349D-2*	-0.0101**	-0.4520D-2	-0.5645D-2	-0.0372D-2**	0.0299*	-0.5330D-2
	(-1.8101)	(-2.1379)	(-0.6175)	(-0.8235)	(-2.0878)	(1.7822)	(-0.7120)
INTRA	-0.4438D-2						
	(-1.4246)						
ROY	-0.0914	-0.2049	-0.2261	0.2938**	-0.3524	0.4755*	0.0747
	(-0.5061)	(-1.6066)	(-0.9237)	(2.1086)	(-0.6074)	(1.7600)	(0.2219)
TECH REQ	-0.4176D-2	-0.0221	0.0112	0.1151	-0.4813**	0.1025	-0.0907
	(-0.3733)	(-1.2068)	(0.3921)	(1.3847)	(-2.1470)	(0.7280)	(-1.1267)
MANU	0.9400D-2***						
	(3.5330)						
HIGH TECH	0.3791D-3	-0.4382D-2					
	(0.1106)	(-0.8619)					
R²	0.4684	0.6474	0.5865	0.3788	0.4769	0.5259	0.3693
n	44	43	37	23	30	24	33

Notes: In the notation D-X: X is the number of 0 to be inserted after the decimal point.
Figures in ( ) are t values; n is number of observations.   * Significant at 10%   ** Significant at 5% *** Significant at 1%.

168

Table 7.2 Multiple Regressions with ROY as Dependent Variable

	All industries	Total manufac-turing	Chemicals and allied products	Machinery except electrical	Electric and electronic equipment	Transportation equipment	Other Manu-facturing
GDP	0.1605D-3 (0.5213)	0.2468D-2*** (3.0837)	0.2655D-2** (2.3842)	0.5696D-2*** (3.4905)	0.3216D-2*** (3.4496)	-0.2590D-2 (-0.6117)	0.1832D-2** (2.2894)
GNP per capita	0.0150 (0.5911)	0.0128 (0.1711)	0.0561 (0.7370)	-0.2209 (-0.9892)	-0.2422** (-2.5133)	0.2724 (0.6574)	-0.0712 (-0.9168)
EDUC	0.0117 (1.5768)	0.0293 (1.0966)	-0.0366* (-1.7083)	0.2524*** (2.9471)	0.0148 (0.4903)	0.0533 (0.6170)	-0.0469* (-1.6804)
WAGE	-0.8015D-2 (-0.7839)	0.3850D-3 (0.0127)	-0.0333 (-1.0991)	-0.1009 (-0.8751)	0.1108* (1.8436)	-0.1954 (-1.2172)	0.0795** (2.0357)
LOCAL	-0.1723D-4 (0.0107)	-0.0107 (-1.5960)	-0.0175*** (-2.7631)	0.3565D-2 (0.2747)	-0.9281D-2 (-1.2505)	-0.7302D-2 (-0.4179)	-0.8038D-2 (-1.2656)
INTRA	0.7976D-2*** (2.8519)						
RAD	-0.1257 (-0.7240)	-0.3822 (-1.4043)	-0.2058 (-0.7313)	2.1406*** (2.9284)	0.0543 (0.4725)	1.1999* (1.6693)	0.0401 (0.1727)
TECH REQ	-0.0172 (-1.5781)	-0.0141 (-0.5350)	-0.4803 (-0.1795)	-0.1166 (-0.6395)	-0.6025 (-0.1926)	0.2131 (0.6079)	-0.1205* (-1.8321)
MANU	0.3939D-2 (1.4823)						
HIGH TECH	-0.6370D-2** (-2.1790)	-0.3586D-2 (-0.5247)					
R2	0.5158	0.3403	0.3445	0.6902	0.4761	0.1672	0.4982
n	44	43	37	23	30	24	33

NB. In the notation D-X: X is the number of 0 to be inserted after the decimal point. Figures in ( ) are t values. * Significant at 10% ** Significant at 5% *** Significant at 1%.

cing (or market) situations would lead to an especially high commitment to local adaptive work.

The prevalent relationship of GDP with respect to the dependent variable ROY is that of a significant positive one in manufacturing industries, though not in other sectors (as is indicated by the insignificance for the all industries sample). To explain this pervasive result we may extend the view, underlying our initial hypotheses, that rises in ROY would reflect the licensing of higher qualities of existing technology. In fact where such intra-group royalties reach particularly high levels they may reflect an increasing component of payments for original R&D carried out by the parent (or elsewhere in the group) to support distinctive host-country needs. The willingness of subsidiaries to commission such work may be expected to respond to the size of the anticipated host-country market (indicated by GDP). In several industries, as already observed, this relationship parallels a similar one between GDP and RAD, with electrical equipment and mechanical engineering as the notable exceptions. Though GDP is positively related to ROY in electrical equipment this occurs at levels of ROY which suggest that this plays a secondary role to overseas R&D (i.e. high levels of RAD), though this in turn has been seen to be quite distinctive in not being related to GDP. By contrast the result for mechanical engineering indicates a strong centralised support for the technical needs of overseas operations, in a manner which does seem compatible with customisation of such equipment. Thus it may be that it is a key skill of central technology to derive effective product variants to meet the specific needs of customers of overseas subsidiaries.

(ii) GNP per capita

The relationship between GNP per capita and RAD is not significant for the all industries sample but becomes significantly positive for total manufacturing. This indicates that local R&D is more pervasively positively responsive to GNP per capita in manufacturing industries than in petroleum[19] and the service industries. However, within individual manufacturing industries the positive relationship never achieves significance.[20] By contrast, one of the strongest relationships (matched in significance only by chemicals amongst the positive signs) is the negative one for electrical equipment. In line with one aspect of our hypothesising this result may reflect a quite widespread acceptance of homogeneous but sophisticated electrical products amongst high-income countries (i.e. relatively low need for adaptive R&D), but a notable willingness to allow local R&D work (i.e. higher RAD) to derive more acceptable product varieties for low GNP per capita countries.

Generally, GNP per capita seems to have little influence on ROY, with no strong evidence in support of our hypothesis of a positive relationship. Interestingly the only significant result is a negative one for the electrical appliance industry, paralleling the similar distinctive negative relationship of GNP per capita with RAD in that industry. In fact, bearing in mind the generally low level of ROY in the electrical industry, it seems likely that the relatively high royalty payments by low-income-country operations may reflect access to central technology as part of the previously suggested adaptation (simplification) programmes that also involve a relatively strong commitment to local R&D.

(iii) Education

There is no sign of any strong or sustained relationship between EDUC and RAD. Thus this evidence suggests that the relative availability of adequately trained local scientific and organisational personnel has not been a factor significantly influencing the location of overseas R&D by US MNEs. For ROY as dependent variable the EDUC variable becomes strongly significantly positive in the mechanical engineering industry. We have already suggested that a key characteristic of this industry seems to be a strong commitment to the centralised derivation of customised product variants for implementation by overseas subsidiaries, with the extent of this being reflected in ROY. Other things being equal, the host countries most able to benefit from taking part in this strategy should be those where an adequate supply of trained personnel allow the effective definition and communication of needs to central facilities, and also permit the assimilation and commercial use of the response received. This viewpoint should, indeed, then be reflected in a positive relationship between EDUC and ROY. By contrast the relationship is marginally significantly negative for the chemicals and miscellaneous sectors. Our hypothesised basis for such a result was that a strong availability of such personnel would create a mood of independence in subsidiaries, so that access to licensed technology would be resisted, with a compensating emphasis on the creation of an autonomous capability.

(iv) Scientific wages

There is no evidence from any industry[21] of a strong tendency for low scientific (and allied) wages to act as a factor attracting US MNEs' overseas R&D operations. However WAGE is significantly positively related to RAD in the electrical industry. We have previously interpreted this industry as being one where overseas R&D in general has an unusually high level of apparent autonomy, but where its strength in any particular country is not influenced by host-country demand factors to the usual degree. Extending this perspective, and the possibility that in this industry WAGE is primarily interpreted as an indicator of personnel quality, it seems that overseas R&D plays a role in support of an integrated strategy in a way that opens up a range of potential locations for such facilities, with supply-side factors (here quality rather than cost) then able to move into greater prominence as determinants of the choice.[22]

Generally, the relationship between WAGE and ROY is rather variable. However the two significant results do support our positive hypothesis, these being for electricals (again confirming the view which treats WAGE as an indicator of quality) and miscellaneous.

(v) Market orientation

The variable LOCAL is negatively significant in both the all industries sample and the total manufacturing sample when RAD is the dependent variable. The relationship between LOCAL and RAD is also negatively signed for each of the manufacturing industries separately tested, except transport equipment, though this is only significant for electrical appliances. This result for electricals reinforces that industry's distinctive position, already discerned in our earlier discussion, as one where overseas R&D plays a particularly autonomous role in technology creation (low values of ROY), but one where the location of such facilities is unusually immune to host-country demand influences (GDP; GNP per capita), with support for competitiveness throughout a wider market area thus emerging as a priority motivation.

Though in a form that involves less clear-cut independence from central technology, or from the host-country market, than is implied for electricals, the pervasive negative result may similarly be interpreted, in the light of our hypotheses for LOCAL, as suggesting a strong role for LILs supporting WPM subsidiaries in US MNEs' overseas R&D. Thus the implication of the predominant result appears to be that overseas subsidiaries of US MNEs frequently carry out R&D in particular countries to derive new products to be manufactured in that country, but exported to a wider range of regional (or global) markets. Though this retains the view that a key role of overseas R&D is to work in an integrated way with local marketing and production (i.e. as LILs) to derive a distinctive competitiveness, it in effect also redefines these subsidiaries' concept of their 'local market' as one larger than the national market of the R&D and production facilities. This redefinition of 'local strategy' still leaves the question of the determinants of where, in the relevant wider market, the operations are located. Our earlier results indicate that, apart from selective relevance for supply-side factors, it is still national market influences (i.e. size [GDP] or income characteristics [GNP per capita]) that affect location[23] within this wider context for operations. One possible interpretation of this could be that, in a way compatible with the first stage of the original product cycle (Vernon 1966), US MNEs may choose large and profitable (high-income) markets to pioneer the new products ultimately aimed at wider regional markets.[24] However, since the negative result for LOCAL specifically implies that export sales receive more R&D support than host-country sales, it is also clear that the needs of the other parts of the target-market are addressed immediately within the LIL's work in a manner more in line with more recent perspectives on innovation in MNEs.[25]

The significant positive relationship between LOCAL and RAD for transport equipment can, in line with our hypotheses, be interpreted as suggesting that, since exports in this case receive less intensive R&D-support than host-country sales, RP subsidiaries (with their limited SL-type R&D-support) predominate, with their orientation to the production of standardised goods for intra-group trade. Finally, in the all industries sample, the negative result for INTRA (though not achieving significance) is compatible with the premise underlying our interpretation of the results for LOCAL, i.e. that intra-group exports require much less R&D support (i.e. the work of SLs) than exports to independent foreign customers (where the latter type are assumed to be the result of more ambitious LIL work implemented by WPM subsidiaries).

The relationship between LOCAL and ROY is weakly negative for the all industries sample, with this approaching significance for total manufacturing. At the level of individual industries the negative signs again clearly predominate, but the relationship is only significant for chemicals. Though our *a priori* hypothesising was neutral with regard to possible degrees of licensing support for the different types of exporting strategies, we may now perceive the negative results as being compatible with the particularly high levels of support from central technology for the more ambitious innovation programmes implemented by WPM subsidiaries that other results have suggested. This could involve the supply of particularly high-quality results from recent central research work, or the commissioning of specific work there to complement the programmes initiated by the LILs that are supporting the innovation plans of the WPM subsidiaries. Though the significant positive relationship between INTRA and ROY in the all industries sample runs against the view of stronger support from licensed technology for WPM compared with RP subsidiaries, this may reflect behaviour in the non-manufacturing sectors. The strengthening of the negative result for LOCAL in the manufacturing sample (compared with all industries) is certainly compatible with this.

(vi) R&D and licensing

Though the relationship between RAD and ROY is weak in the all industries sample it approaches negative significance for total manufacturing. This result, however, seems likely to reflect inter-industry effects,[26] since the prevalent relationship within the individual industry samples is the positive one, suggesting that the two sources of technology available to overseas subsidiaries frequently work as complements. In particular it may be noted that the fact that the positive relationship between RAD and ROY is strongest in mechanical engineering is clearly in line with our perception, from results discussed earlier, that in this industry central R&D plays a key role in deriving customised product variants for production by overseas subsidiaries (for which royalty payments are made), whilst the subsidiaries own R&D is strongly focused in facilitating the implementation of this approach.

(vii) Technology transfer requirements

Our results for the TECH REQ variable in the equations with ROY as dependent variable show no sustained evidence that such requirements for technology transfer actually result in increased knowledge flows, at least as reflected in higher royalty payments. Only the transport equipment industry even produces (in a very insignificant way) the positive sign hypothesised. Though the negative sign is only statistically significant in the miscellaneous group, this is clearly the prevalent relationship. This implies that tough specific performance requirements of this type may alter, in a negative way, the detailed *behaviour* of the foreign direct investment that takes place, rather than, as we hypothesised, mainly working through a contribution to a more general perception of the environment which would be more likely to affect the overall *level* of foreign direct investment.

The relationship between TECH REQ and RAD is significantly negative in electricals, which may again indicate that a tough host-country attitude with regard to technology induces a distinctively negative response in technology behaviour in this industry. However, in several other industries (especially mechanical engineering) there are slightly clearer indications of a positive relationship between TECH REQ and RAD than occurred with ROY. Very tentatively this may suggest that where a host country takes a positive line on technology generally (proxied by TECH REQ) MNEs may prefer to respond with local R&D than extra transfers of technology.

7.4 CONCLUSIONS

The primary conclusion of the results for the dependent variable RAD is the continued importance of market factors in determining the location of R&D facilities. Here aggregate market size (i.e. GDP) appears to be somewhat more influential than average income levels (i.e. GNP per capita). However it also appears that, as illustrated by the negative result for the variable LOCAL, export sales receive more R&D support than host-country-market sales. As we have already suggested, this indicates that there is a strong tendency for the R&D work of US overseas subsidiary laboratories to be oriented to the derivation of products for markets wider than those of their immediate host country. Thus it may appear that R&D activity in US MNE subsidiaries often supports world or regional product mandate operations, by deriving products aimed at clearly defined, but wider, geographical areas.

This perspective then leads to the subsequent question that if R&D work in one country is targeted at the derivation of products aimed at a larger group of countries, what factors determined that that particular country (amongst the group) was selected as the location for this facility. Our positive results for GDP and GNP per capita may have a role here, suggesting that even when the R&D work is targeted at markets beyond that of the host country, the size and characteristics of markets of individual countries could still influence the location decision. However, given a choice of countries for such operations, supply-side factors might well have been expected to play an important role. In fact neither the EDUC nor WAGE variables emerge as having any persistant explanatory power.

Following from this our interpretation of the role of WPM or RPM subsidiaries may suggest the relevance of less easily defined 'localisation' influences. Thus it has been argued (Pearce 1992) that the emergence within a MNE's global operations of such mandated subsidiaries reflects the initiative taken by individual entrepreneurial local-subsidiary managers in conjunction with allied creative marketing and technological personnel. In this way the dynamic subsidiaries stake their claim to supply wider markets. This distinctive subsidiary-level ability would be likely to have emerged in US MNEs where their well-established familiarity with the local technological and marketing environment permits the emergence of a unique local capacity, reflecting a localised identity.

Notes

1. For a survey see Pearce (1989, pp. 37–70).
2. See Behrman and Fischer (1980a; 1980b).
3. For an elaboration of the laboratory types introduced in this section see Chapter 2.
4. The source of data used to calculate RAD was US Department of Commerce, Bureau of Economic Analysis, *US Direct Investment Abroad: 1982 Benchmark Survey Data*, Tables III.H.3; III.E.3; III.E.4; III.E.5.
5. Initially the data covered seven separate manufacturing industries. However two of these (food and kindred products; primary and fabricated metals) had sales in too few countries for sufficient cases of RAD to be available for statistical analysis to be viable. Separate analysis of petroleum was also precluded for the same reason.
6. The source of the data used to calculate ROY was US Department of Commerce (*op. cit.*), Tables III.H.12; III.E.3; III.E.4; III.E.5.
7. In particular, GNP per capita is held constant in the regression equations, so that the result for GDP reflects the effect on RAD of different *aggregate* income levels for countries of the same *average* income levels.
8. The source for GDP was The World Bank, *World Development Report, 1984*, Table 3.
9. The source for GNP per capita was The World Bank, *World Development Report, 1984*, Table 1.
10. The source for EDUC was The World Bank, *World Development Report, 1985*, Table 25.
11. This is the type of factor which has been suggested to often lead to the pursuit of world (or regional) product mandates by subsidiaries (see Pearce 1992). One implication of this is a move from SL work to LIL work and thus probable rises in RAD. However, with RAD controlled in this test, this influence would probably imply a negative relationship between EDUC and ROY.
12. This measure is deficient in that its coverage is limited to manufacturing industries and includes a range of occupations beyond the purely scientific. Nevertheless it does seem plausible to expect that it is likely to serve as an effective indicator of inter-country differences in the type of costs relevant to the implementation of R&D work. The source of data for WAGE was US Department of Commerce (*op. cit.*), Tables III.F.3; III.F.6; III.F.13.
13. The source for LOCAL was US Department of Commerce (*op. cit.*), Tables III.E.3; III.E.4; III.E.5.
14. The source for INTRA was US Department of Commerce (*op. cit.*), Table III.E.1.
15. Minor differences would be expected in this result, between the two equations, if there is any difference in any collinearity between

RAD or ROY and the other independent variables. However the broad nature and strength of the relationship should be common to both tests.

16. See Bartlett and Ghoshal (1989; 1990) and Pearce and Singh (1992a).

17. The source for TECH REQ was US Department of Commerce (*op. cit.*), Table II.I.3.

18. It should be recalled that when RAD is the dependent variable ROY is included as an independent variable. This should control for the possibility that requirements for technology transfer might increase the licensing of technology at the expense of local R&D that might otherwise have occurred (i.e. provide the mechanism for a negative relationship between TECH REQ and RAD).

19. There is, in fact, a generally low commitment to overseas R&D in the petroleum industry, with an overall RAD of only 0.09. A possible explanation for this is that where climatic or other conditions may affect the effective use of petroleum the vehicle industry is more likely to take responsibility for relevant local adaptation. Alongside this it has been observed elsewhere (Pearce and Singh, 1992a, pp. 100–1) that even adaptive R&D does tend to be centralised in petroleum.

20. It may be that an inter-industry effect may reinforce the relatively weak intra-industry effects to generate the stronger total manufacturing relationship. This could occur if certain industries had above average proportions of their sales in high per capita income countries and an above average overall value of RAD (without a particularly strong relationship between GNP per capita and RAD within the industry sample) whilst others had an above average proportion of sales in low per capita income countries and below average overall industry value of RAD (again without a particularly strong relationship within the industry sample).

21. The rather stronger result for total manufacturing may owe something to inter-industry effects.

22. An interesting contrast may be implied here. Thus it is a common assumption that where an electrical industry MNE has an integrated network of operations (on a regional or global basis) one aim of this strategy is to pursue production-cost minimisation. However, in the pursuit of the ideal location for technology facilities to support such a network, our results suggest that pursuit of quality strongly overrides cost factors.

23. Generally the results suggest that for a given level of export orientation a country's operations will be more R&D-intensive the higher its GDP and/or its GNP per capita.

24. Another relevant factor may be the influence of US firms' familiarity with host-country conditions, such that R&D (and production) may be most likely to occur in countries where subsidiaries

have been in place longest. If size (or income levels) of markets determine the countries entered first, and the relative levels of these have not altered greatly over the years, GDP and/or GNP per capita may proxy this experience factor.

25. See Bartlett and Ghoshal (1989, 1990); Pearce (1989); Pearce and Singh (1992a); Vernon (1979).

26. Thus it may be that in some countries US subsidiaries are strongest in industries where, on average, RAD is high and ROY low, whilst in other countries industries with high ROY and low RAD predominate.

Part III
Industry and Country Cases

8 The Potential Role of Romania's Technological and Scientific Capacity in Attracting FDI: An Exploratory Analysis of its National System of Innovation

with Julia Manea

8.1 INTRODUCTION

Technological change and innovation are becoming more and more a central topic in economic analysis and policy making all over the world. This growing interest is a reflection of relatively new directions in the modern economy, which consider the main driving force in economic growth to derive from technical progress rather than capital accumulation. Both advances outside mainstream and neoclassical economics and an increasing number of industrial case studies have highlighted the importance of technological factors for industrial competitiveness and economic growth.

As Lundvall (1988, 1992) emphasises, in the modern economy the most fundamental resource is knowledge, and accordingly the most important processes are interactive learning and innovation-related phenomena.

In the modern marketplace, knowledge is the critical asset. It is as important a commodity as the access to natural resources or to low-skilled labour markets was in the past. Knowledge has given birth to vast new industries, particularly those based on computers, semiconductors, biotechnology and designed materials.

(Erich Bloch, quoted in Acs and Audretsch 1991)

On them modern industry is now built, and the ability of mastering them is affecting the pattern of competition, growth and of trade between countries.

In the science-based industries of our time science and technology are becoming intertwined, and in an economy that is increasingly knowledge-based their role is perceived as central to economic development and future national prosperity. Within this context of dynamically-changing technologies and increased global competition, when the pace of technological innovation is faster than ever and product life cycles are being dramatically compressed, multinational enterprises (MNEs) are forced to adopt a global approach to the creation and application of knowledge in order to enhance or preserve their global competitiveness. Thus the factors involved in the process of determining the best locations for MNEs' overseas production facilities increase the importance of a country's science and technology availability and cost.

The competitiveness of MNEs now stems from their ability to make the best use of research and development (R&D) and human capital located in different parts of the world and to integrate them into its international R&D network, from which new technological capabilities and, accordingly, future generations of products will emerge. There is a strong belief that the process of growth and transformation of a country's economy is increasingly dependent on its national system of innovation, which is closely connected with the R&D system, its resources, competencies and organisation. With the idea in mind that Romania, which following the communist pattern invested highly in education and training systems, as well as in research institutes and organisations in the process of building up cumulative technological capabilities, is therefore faced with a credible and sound R&D system, but by contrast by an industry with outdated technology and low productivity, the authors determined to ask themselves how this gap could be closed most effectively in the short term.

One of the most plausible and pertinent answers is that this knowledge, which has been developed through the scientific community but has never been properly used commercially because the communist industrial society in Romania had no commercial dynamism and no entrepreneurial ability, could be turned into commercial possibilities by foreign MNEs. These firms could therefore make a significant contribution to closing this damaging gap in the Romanian innovation system between knowledge potentials and the commercial realities of its domestic industry. It is, of course, highly desirable that such knowledge would become embodied in the commercial activities of Romanian firms, but this process could take a long time to emerge and we think that it could be assisted in a beneficial way, that would also provide short-term growth opportunities for Romanian industry, by MNEs that undertake high-value-added activities in their overseas operations.

The way that MNEs are developing strategically suggests that they can actually help the positive development of resources in a country which wants to move its industrial sector up the ladder of comparative advantage if they involve in their operations the host-country's creative resources and scientific potential and not just exploit its low-costs assets. This type of behaviour could allow MNEs to play a key role in the mid-term restructuring of Romanian industry and in its increased integration into the world economy. It could improve the efficiency and speed of the process of transfer of technology from research to industry, thereby stimulating domestic firms also to develop independently around the country's scientific capacity. In addition it could also underpin further developments in Romania's science and technology, in ways that are more coherently allied to commercial needs, and qualitatively enhanced through access to the MNE group's background research. We believe that this study could bring out useful insights both in identifying the nature of the 'innovation problem' and in setting out the grounds for successful policy making at the national level, and will act as a useful guide for foreign investors, especially MNEs which play the crucial role as transplanters of international best-practice technology and organisational practices and provide access to the world market.

The lesson is clear. The capacity of Romania's own economic system to generate and diffuse technical innovation was extremely limited due to the very nature of the communist system, which could not provide the domestic firms with the incentives and appetite for innovation and change. The key factor in technological advance is competition as a dynamic system in which firms seek to differentiate themselves and gain competitive advantages by introducing new products and processes. The more profitable it is to supply the market with new products and processes, the more quickly and efficiently the process of innovation and diffusion will take place in the economy. In fact it is already proved in various economic studies that the scientific and technological tradition (amount of resources allocated to it, the number of qualified personnel, the value that society places on science and research) causes the science-push type of innovation, while market and competition works considerably well as a stimulator for the diffusion of innovation, representing the market-pull side which sometimes can have a greater weight in the actual process of innovating. Why? Because invention (as a patent examiner would define it) is just a first stage in a complex system characterised by interdependencies and powerful feedbacks between its elements, where ultimately the designing and developing of a product or process, which has to achieve a number of performance characteristics subject to certain costs constraints, is dependent very much on the economic environment. The inventions emerge into the economic sphere first in immature forms, and then evolve very considerably in directions that accord to the incentives to development which arise in their application. This in turn is dependent on how the economic environment evaluates them in terms of profits and costs. The role of science and technology in the modern knowledge-based industries is fundamental. The organisation, resources and competencies of the R&D system is very important too in the process of innovation and modernisation of industry, but it seems that here the key role is played by the entrepreneur and entrepreneurial profits in the process by which technologies acquire economic weight (Schumpeter 1969). At least the argument rests on the indisputable empirical evidence on the innovation performance of the advanced capitalist countries and also of newly industrialised countries compared with that of the former communist countries, even though other factors could be assumed that have also played a crucial role.

However, major restructuring and adaptation of the economic circumstances in order to create a competitive environment which provides the basis for efficient allocation of resources and for stimulating investment in innovation and, most of all, an environment conducive to entrepreneurship, are urgently needed if all the efforts towards a market-orientated economy are going to be successful and rewarding. This restructuring can be facilitated and speeded up by investment, big investment. It is already acknowledged by many concerned with the economic restructuring and recovery of the economies in transition of Eastern Europe that if such investment is achieved it could trigger the entire socio-economic machinery. Much of this big investment would have to come from foreign sources, either in the form of pure capital (loans or the purchase of securities) or through FDI in production operations (joint ventures, wholly-owned subsidiaries). The importance of FDI may be the better addressed in the current situation where what is lacking, and is most needed, is an entrepreneurial and work culture, organisational capabilities, management and marketing expertise and access to foreign markets. Foreign MNEs are uniquely able to supply all of these, being recognised as ideal vehicles for spearheading industrial restructuring. Through their ability to transfer technology and management skills; through their introduction to up-to-date industrial practices and quality control techniques; through their example and their spill-over affects on local entrepreneurship, suppliers and competitors; and through their network of international linkages – with both large and small firms – they can provide much of the competencies and initiatives for economic growth.

(Dunning 1994)

Since foreign investment is so much needed, governments have an imperative to establish the conditions favourable to it and to create a climate favourable for the transfer by MNEs – and the absorption by local enterprises – of all these assets which are the *sine qua non* for structural upgrading of their economies.

There are a number of factors that are going to influence the injections of foreign capital, and not just macroeconomic factors, but also political, socio-historical and conjectural factors. But even in the most favourable situation, governments will need to design medium- and long-term policies for their economic strategy for development, and to identify both sectors and projects for investment and the conditions under which, and the ways in which, foreign MNEs are likely to benefit national competitiveness. The evidence that comes from comparing the experience of various countries which followed different development models brings out that industrial success has been associated with selective intervention rather than with policies of complete openness. The key example is of Japan and of 'South-East Asia's Four Tigers', which succeeded in the move from low-cost production of low-value-added products to high-value-added products, and which were all economies in which the state played an important role in the process by pursuing created comparative advantages and by focusing on managed competition and managed trade, including different forms of protectionism (see Pitelis 1994). Exposing promising infant industries too early to international competition, instead of encouraging them to grow up could, by contrast, accelerate their decline. But there is also the danger of the other face of the coin, when protecting them too much from foreign competition, instead of helping them to mature into competitive industries, can cause their retreat into a sheltered and lethargic state .

All these complicated issues again bring into the picture the role of the entrepreneur, this time from another perspective. Being a fundamental and scarce resource in an economy it would be essential for successful industrial policy making, and for society in general at this particular stage, to make the most of its limited supply of entrepreneurial talent, selectively recruiting talented entrepreneurs and concentrating them where all the big strategic decisions are to be made (see Casson 1994). The potential benefit from such a view has been achieved in other economies (see the example of the high-performing East-Asian economies, where documented intervention had accelerated growth and structural upgrading). This augments the speculation that where honest, talented and efficient public bureaucracies exist, in countries that want to speed up the process of catching-up with the advanced industrialised countries, a reconciliation between markets and government activism could help to more effectively create an environment that will encourage economic agents to react to competitive pressures in a way that would favour innovation rather than exit as the response to competition.

This perspective suggests that their policy makers have to clearly comprehend that host countries need not be passive recipients of investment and that their strategy towards attracting foreign investments should be grounded on careful study and analysis of the findings of a vast area of research on the economic impact of foreign investments on the domestic economy. It should also fully comprehend the new developments in international business, with particular attention paid to the likely impact of internationalisation on local technological development and industrial growth.

With an eye on developments in the international economic environment, where not only markets, products, finance and production are increasingly globalised but also technology and the process of innovation itself, policy makers will realise that MNEs are moving to a more dynamic strategy, upgrading overseas subsidiaries' roles within their operations, allowing them to use a wider range of creative local resources and to take full responsibility for development, production and international marketing of products. These strategic developments in the MNEs' attitudes, behaviour and organisational structure, towards decentralisation and dynamic creativity within the operations of its subsidiaries, may relate better to the need of a host country to achieve a more individual and dynamic basis for its evolving comparative advantage through continually changing structures of national specialisation and enhancing the level of local value-added in production and exports.

MNEs now adopt two approaches in setting up subsidiaries in individual host countries. One choice involves setting up import-substitution subsidiaries, and its role is to produce the group's established mass-market goods using its mature standardised technology in a cost-effective manner. The subsidiary is called Truncated Miniature Replica (TMR) because in a sense it is reproducing the behaviour of the parent company, being totally dependent on the MNE group and without room for innovative behaviour. Here the attractions of the host economies lie in low-cost labour and other inputs, such as government subsidies, a market protected from external competition, etc., but they lack any dynamic scope to enhance the growth of national competitiveness.

The other choice involves the decision to set up specialised cost-effective export-oriented subsidiaries that supply international markets. This latter approach can involve host-country resources much more profoundly in the creation of technology and in its original application to distinctive commercial situations. There are, however, two different types of export-oriented subsidiary. One is called Rationalised Product Subsidiary (RPS) and is focused on producing a limited part of the MNE's established product range (or selected component parts or a separate stage in a vertically-integrated production process). Even though this is more efficient than a TMR and also more specialised, its role is still defined within the existing product and process technology of the MNE group and its position in the network is allocated on the basis of its host-country's current resource base considered merely as a static comparative advantage. There is still no scope for technology creation, marketing or creative management, it just has to execute the production of current products for supply in externally-determined quantities. As for the TMR, the RPS approach is also unlikely to provide the basis for a creative transition to enhanced value-added potential around local creativity and distinctive attributes, and is going to bring only short-term benefits such as employment and balance of payments effects.

The other form of export-oriented subsidiary is the most progressive and creative type of MNE overseas facilities in which, coordinated and motivated by much more entrepreneurial subsidiary-level management, it takes full responsibility for the creation, production and marketing worldwide of new products. It is called World (or Regional) Product Mandate Subsidiary (WPM/RPM) because this subsidiary is mandated by the MNE parent to produce and market a product and, if circumstances allow, to undertake the necessary R&D activity. The mandated subsidiary then becomes the international (regional) centre for a product, with responsibilities for all key inputs relating to its creation, production and marketing. This forward-looking phase in MNEs' strategic response to increased global competition, which enables them to tap into a worldwide range of creative inputs through the use of higher-value-added operations in its overseas subsidiaries along with the decentralisation of its network of R&D laboratories, supports the idea that MNE subsidiaries and a host country can go through a mutually supportive period of creative transition, from which both can achieve dynamic comparative advantage.[1]

The conclusion derived from the previous analysis of the strategic behaviour of contemporary MNEs suggests that Romania should try to attract Product Mandate Subsidiary type of operations, which look for host-country scientific and knowledge capacity as well as for its cost-effective production resources. Only involving high-quality local inputs in a product-development role can help the host-country economy to enhance its value-added potential around its more creative and skilled local inputs.

The ability of Romania to attract such high-value-added subsidiaries might then depend on its scientific potential as much as on its production capacity, or the size of its market, the cost of its industrial labour force, etc. In these circumstances the authors were interested to assess the extent to which the existing scientific capacity and technological knowledge of Romania can be a factor relevant to attracting MNEs to operate in the country in terms of RPM type of operations and locally-integrated laboratory activity, that would bring together production, marketing and technology creation. The hypothesis underpinning our study is that many economies in Eastern Europe had, during the communist era, a substantial commitment to R&D (especially basic/applied research) and thus created a strong scientific community, but that little of this scientific fertility had been related clearly to comparable areas of competitive industrial activity in terms of product innovation or improved engineering efficiency. Furthermore we argue that in the short-run it is the MNEs that have the best prospects to discover these hidden assets of, for our case, Romania's economy, and to build them into its industrial sector in the most efficient and progressive way.

The chapter then attempts to analyse the national system of innovation of Romania, both because on its development and improvement ultimately depend its industrial competitiveness and productivity growth, and also because its quite well-developed system of national scientific institutions (that might not yet amount to a national system of innovation, since in the past innovation was not a strong attribute of centrally-planned state-owned Romanian

firms), can be a factor to attract the type of creative subsidiaries that have been introduced earlier in the paper.
These could in turn well help to convert the national
R&D system into a key part of a more effective overall
national system of innovation.

8.2   THE NATIONAL SYSTEM OF INNOVATION OF ROMANIA

The broad concept of a National Innovation System (NIS)
encompasses all the elements and relationships that interact in the creation, diffusion and use of new knowledge in a
national economy, i.e. not just the actors doing R&D, but
all the factors influencing national technological capabilities of a country. Lundvall (1992) suggests that practically
all the economic structure and the institutional set-up of a
country are involved in on-going processes of learning,
searching and exploring which finally result in innovations.
Therefore they are all part of the NIS.

These factors need to include the national R&D system;
its resources, competencies and organisation, its public and
private science and technology programmes; the national
education and training system; the functioning of labour
markets and financial systems; the production system; the
marketing system; monetary, fiscal and trade policies; policies on investment, competition and intellectual property
and so on, if you want to tell a comprehensive and coherent story about innovation.

The importance of studying innovation in a broad sense
is indisputable, especially if the interest is tied to concern
about economic performance. But for the interest of this
study we will focus mainly on the national system of
innovation in the narrow sense which encompasses just
that set of institutions which are more directly concerned
with scientific and technical activities. Thus the design of
this study of the NIS of Romania focuses mainly on the
following elements: the allocation of R&D activity and the
sources of its funding (the R&D system; resources,

competencies and organisation), the education and training system, the science and technology areas of government policies, the characteristics of the firms.

8.3   THE INSTITUTIONAL NETWORK SUPPORTING SCIENCE AND TECHNOLOGY FROM 1948 TO 1989

During this period, as Romania became part of the communist block, the Soviet model of the organisation of the
R&D system was adopted. In this research and development activities were directed administratively by the central state authority, through full-cycle planning of research,
and were subordinated to centrally-defined economic
goals.

The strong determination to create and develop a wide
national network of institutions and organisations supporting science and technology (S&T) was essentially
determined by the imperative to keep up with world developments in science and to support the country's industrial policies at a time when ties with the international
scientific community, and with foreign sources of technology, were seriously severed. Also the Marxist ideology's
belief in the virtues of S&T played a crucial role. Thus
there were a multitude of factors that determined the
structure of the Romanian R&D system, with its S&T
institutions and practices reflecting the demands placed
on the R&D system by the economic and political regime
of the time.

Most important was a strong desire to build a valid
national R&D system capable of creating endogenous
technology in the attempt to escape from its past industrial
experience, which had relied mainly on external sources for
technology. There was an awareness that mere acquisition
of foreign technology does not ensure the emergence of
national innovative capabilities and long-term industrial
development, which combined with the necessity to reduce
the technological dependence on traditionally advanced
industrial countries (which were all capitalist economies

and therefore adversaries) in a time of a very unfavourable international climate. This was an international climate in which trading with communist countries was extremely restrictive and politicised (the 'coldest' period of the Cold War) as notably reflected, for example, by the creation of the CoCom committee, which had the role to coordinate Western export policies toward communist countries and to administer the strategic embargo against the Soviet bloc in the 1950s (Young 1977; Stent 1980). The scheme was intended to restrict significantly the export of advanced technology to the East (any advanced technology and not just military technology), and of course it could not provide any special treatment for Romania (or for any other individual Eastern European country within the CoCom agreement) because any technology exported there would find its way to Moscow, due to the strong dependence on the USSR. The perceived Soviet military threat, combined with a more subtle ideological threat, reinforced the argued need for CoCom's existence, seeking to slow down Soviet countries' technological development and prevent them from becoming economic competitors.

Another important factor in building up the vast R&D system in Romania, with its peculiar organisation, was the belief that science is the foundation of the socialist system, and that on the funding and exploitation of scientific knowledge depends the ultimate economic development of a nation. Moreover supporting science and technological progress served the belief that it would help socialism to win the economic race with the most advanced capitalist countries, and thus prove its superiority as both a social and economic system. Therefore the communist authorities thought that it would speed up the process of technological change if a well-designed network of research institutes with separate functions conceived in the rationale of specialisation, rationalisation and centralisation (representative attributes of the communist ideology) could be set up under the overall control of central authorities that were able to select, and to concentrate resources on, the technologically most propulsive sectors.

In spite of this rhetoric, and the communist propaganda of the political leaders of the time, there was a genuine awareness that rapid economic development and swift technological progress had to be achieved if Romania were to succeed in breaking with the still-fresh memories of its economic past when, even under a free-market economy and with rich natural resources, it had been just a backward economy, overwhelmingly dependent on agriculture, supplying cheap food and raw materials for the industrialised Western countries and serving as a dumping ground for their manufacturers.

The evolution and development of the Romanian network of institutions and organisations supporting science and technology was a consequence and a reflection of the changes that occurred in the needs of national industry, and of the implementation of economic reforms that were aimed at improving the effectiveness of the operation of the national economy, which on reaching higher stages of development had become dependent to a very large extent on its capacity for stimulating technological change. Falling, after the second war, under the Soviet influence, Romania had embarked on a programme of forced industrialisation, in an effort to transform its background economy into a progressive one. This pursued a solid and viable industrial base and a well-educated labour force, through a process of economic development that inevitably had to borrow extensively from the experience, goals, values and norms diffused from the Soviet Union. The Romanian economy, characterised by a highly hierarchical structure of planning and management (decision making about all aspects of economic life was highly centralised, and all the elements of the economy were just executive organisations, implementing their part of the current plan) and an autarchy-based industrial strategy, had enforced similar structures and attitudes in the organisation and behaviour of the R&D network in the 1950s.

On that account research institutes performing basic research were established for each scientific discipline under the overall control of the Academy of Sciences, and for each branch of the economy an institute was set up for conducting applied research and development under the authority of the relevant branch ministries. Thus, on one side scientific research and development activities were divorced from all production activities, and on the other side the research institutes were clearly grouped, those devoted to basic research at the Academy, and those devoted to applied research at the branch ministries.

The Romanian economy in the 1950s and early 1960s was still in an early stage of development, when its strategy was based on extensive growth rather than intensive growth. Therefore as long as maximising the growth of national income could be achieved by continually adding extensive factors of production (investment capital, labour and raw materials) the need for technological change was underestimated, so that science had a more ideological role, pursuing its own self-interest and having little impact on the economy. The main task of research and development was to catch up with the scientific discoveries of the developed world by producing similar results in an autarkic manner.

By the creation of the network of independent institutes research was divorced from production activities, and the central authorities had to endeavour to force innovations upon enterprises through administrative methods. In fact technological progress was mostly introduced via the construction of new projects or plants, rather than through cumulative and incremental innovations and continuous modernisation. During the first stage of construction and development of the R&D system all research institutes were financed from the state budget and administrated by the Academy of Sciences, along with branch ministries and other central organisations, as budget-running organisations. This type of increased subsidy from the central state budget for research favoured the idea of science-lead technical development, and encouraged the creation of a high level of scientific research and professional commitment within the scientific community, which had its own life and pursued its own self-interest. This meant that scientific development evolved under a logic that was internal to the discipline itself, separated from the needs of the economy, which in any case did not have the infrastructure to absorb and master the technology produced within the research institutes.

Starting with the late 1960s, when the economy became more sophisticated and the view emerged of the critical importance of intensive sources of growth at this higher stage of development, the authorities increasingly realised that there was a need for a more radical approach in order to speed up technological progress. Therefore measures were undertaken to reform and restructure the R&D system, in parallel with the implementation of the New Economic Mechanism in the economic system.

A high-level body, the National Council for Scientific and Technical Development (NCSTD), responsible for the promotion of technical and scientific progress, was set up in the late 1960s, together with a new financial mechanism for funding research. These enforced a more economy-oriented science policy. A Central Technological Development Fund was also created to promote a competitive participation of the R&D institutes in the centrally-prioritised development programs, and also every enterprise had to set up an Enterprise Technical Development Plan to support R&D within the firms. The R&D projects undertaken by the firms could also ask, if supplementary resources were needed, for further subsidies from the NCSTD or from ministries.

This period is characterised by much more than a central planning of basic and applied research, with technological development itself becoming a centrally-managed activity. The national economic plan now had a counterpart R&D plan for every one-year and five-year period for each level of economic administration, i.e. the State Plan for Technological Development, sector and branch plans and the enterprise-level plans. The State Plan for Technological Development (or the National Plan for Research and Development) consisted of a listing of individual projects, where each project contained specification of all the research problems from basic research to the development of the technology, with targets for completion of all individual stages. This ran from conception to full application in the economic environment, with full specification of financial aspects and the personnel concerned for the execution of the project, along with the expected technical and economic effects.

In general the research institutes were granted a greater administrative and financial independence from central authorities, so that they could enter into contracts with, and perform work for, companies and other institutions. To improve the efficiency of the innovation process and to push science into the economic environment, further attempts were made to strengthen the independent status of research institutes and to advance the commercialisation of their R&D. Thus they began to function as commercial accounting entities, and to rely mostly on income earned through research contracts with enterprises and other customers. Therefore they were carrying out research, tests, experiments, consultancy activities, development, design, and even production. Closer links were thus established between research and production, with these measures aimed at creating a more market-oriented science policy and a more purpose-oriented research funding and thus also at the provision of scientific research that was more related to the real needs of the economy.

Moreover, to speed the pace of technological change and to accelerate the application of new products and processes in production, attempts were made to incorporate the independent research institutes into established economic production units. Integrating research institutes either with individual large enterprises, or with associations of enterprises producing similar products (these merged organisations were called scientific-production associations), was expected to bring many benefits, from the elimination of duplicative work to a wide and rapid diffusion in the economy of the invention itself.

Reforms were also introduced in the patent system and licensing policy. These were in clear opposition to the preceding period (until the late 1960s) when the protection of inventions was totally neglected (in line with the socialist view that science is a public good and therefore it is to the advantage of the economy, and the society in general, that everybody, or every domestic company, could have access to it without any charges). Now legislation was introduced to allow some exclusivity rights to the enterprises making the inventions and to provide them with the ability to charge other potential users of the technology. In fact, however, only limited charges were permitted, and in practice once the technology was developed other domestic firms would still have largely unhampered and costless access to such technology, because in fact the ultimate owner of the invention was the State (which retained the exclusive right to own and exploit a patent and hold responsibility for its costs, application and marketing abroad). But nevertheless there was a degree of progress in the treatment accorded to the inventors, mostly because of the increases in the royalties payable to them which were now linked to the economic benefits gained from patents applied domestically. As a result the number of patents applied for increased substantially, which also reflected a specific index that was introduced at the enterprise level with the purpose of controlling its economic efficiency by measuring the number of patents and their economic effects within an enterprise.

Planning and management at the central level had by the 1980s therefore become more flexible (comparative to the previous periods) and focused more on long-term structural changes. The details of the plan were now formulated on the basis of the reports of the capacities and proposals submitted by enterprises, the scientific and research community and other ministries, of course in accordance with the broad economic development programs laid down by the central authorities. Also a more subtle system of incentives and penalties was put into place to substitute (at least in part) for the former central directives.

In any case all the reforms undertaken did not have the expected economic benefits and did not improve the efficiency or the speed of the innovation process. Industrial enterprises did not actively seek R&D-based products, due to a variety of reasons that still derived from the fundamental nature of the communist economic system (on the fundamental principles that govern the allocation and use of productive resources in such types of economy). Therefore that is why, in spite of the phenomenal effort and big sacrifices undertaken in pursuing technological progress with fervour and persistence, Romania continued to be faced with low productivity and to lag behind the West in its technology. The professional skill and dedication of its scientists and engineers was not enough to stimulate an innovation-oriented attitude on the part of industry. Moreover the absence of a competitive environment in the hierarchical and centralised economy, along with a very fragmented approach to technological change which was seen by the central authorities more as a linear evolution between three stages (invention, innovation and diffusion) than a system of complex interdependencies (see the chain-link model proposed by Kline and Rosenberg 1986), generally blocked the implementation and diffusion of innovation and in particular increased the gap between invention and innovation.

The process of innovation is not a one-off matter, or a simple progression, it is a permanent interaction involving positive feedback between all parts of the process. The key element in a successful innovation is to maintain effective links between different phases of the process. Therefore research has to be viewed not simply as a source of inventions but rather as a form of problem solving, to be called upon every time that problems or new opportunities (either technological or indicated by the market) arise. 'Innovation consists of all those scientific, technical, commercial and financial steps necessary for the successful development and marketing of new or improved manufactured products, the commercial use of new or improved processes or equipment or the introduction of a new approach to a social service. *R&D is only one of these steps*' (OECD 1981, 'Frascati Manual 1980'; emphasis in original).

Innovations are sometimes incremental and sometimes radical. Sometimes the incremental type of innovation, those gradual, small and cumulative type of improvements undertaken within the firm could in fact have the greater impact on the efficiency and profitability of a product or process. Thus most of the existing products were themselves realised through subsequent improvements undertaken on product concepts that have long been in existence. In the Romanian economy such a type of gradual and cumulative innovation could not have taken place due to the structure and organisation of the R&D system, and of the economy as a whole. Other factors impeding the efficiency of its research potential were: the excessively long time-lag between invention and innovation, or slow diffusion once an implemented technology is in production in one particular enterprise, a lack of resources for the implementation of research findings, insufficient interest and ability of the enterprises to master the invention and to appreciate its potential benefits, lack of material incentives, etc.

In any case Romania succeeded in developing in a short time a comprehensive system of education and vocational training with a sound R&D system, in addition to a solid industrial base which, though it did not surmount the performance of advanced industrialised countries (particularly OECD countries), had been transformed successfully (more or less) from a backward and stagnant agricultural country to an essentially industrialised economy. This was achieved without investment, economic aid or technological assistance from West Europe or USA, and even more did so subject to trade and technology restrictions (by comparison with the NICs which benefited from free trade and access to external sources of key inputs).

The importance of R&D in the Romanian strategy for development and industrial modernisation can be seen in the growth of investment in R&D. Thus the share of R&D in the total government budget rose from 1.5 per cent in 1960 to 3.4 per cent in 1987, and remained at 3.0 per cent in 1989 (Table 8.1). Similarly the commitment to R&D is also reflected in the high ratio of Gross Expenditure on R&D (GERD) as percentage of GDP which, even in the period when the obsession with debt repayment became a principal policy objective of the economy, rose from 1.5 per cent in 1980 to 2.6 per cent in 1989. This GERD/GDP ratio is very high and is comparable with the OECD median of 1.5, or moreover even with the more R&D intensive OECD countries such as France 2.4 per cent, Sweden 2.5 per cent or USA 2.8 per cent in 1990. Of course this is not reflected in absolute terms because of the differences in the GDP values between these countries, but still the indicator of GERD/GDP is a good measure to compare the R&D intensity between countries and their commitment to undertake R&D.

In terms of R&D personnel its share in the total labour force increased from 0.2 per cent in 1950 to 1.5 per cent in 1985, or if we take it in absolute terms it increased from 16 754 in 1960 to 158 613 in 1985, and continued to rise to 169 964 in 1989.

Table 8.1   Expenditure on education and R&D as a percentage of the total Romanian government budget, 1960–1989

Year	R&D expenditure as percentage of budget	Education expenditure as percentage of budget
1960	1.5	6.3
1970	1.5	7.0
1980	1.6	5.9
1985	3.4	5.8
1986	3.2	5.1
1987	3.4	4.8
1988	3.3	4.8
1989	3.0	4.8

Source: Authors' calculations based on Romania's Statistical Yearbooks, 1960–1990.

Table 8.2 reflects a dramatic rising trend in the proportion of the working population engaged in R&D activities during the period 1950 to 1989, and also suggests other significant changes that occurred in the distribution of employment in different economic sectors in that period; for example, the percentage of industry, construction and services is rising substantially and that in agriculture is declining, which is the natural trend in a growing economy.

Table 8.2   The distribution of employment by principal economic sector, 1960–89

	Employment index (1950 = 100)							
	1960	*1970*	*1980*	*1985*	*1986*	*1987*	*1988*	*1989*
Total labour force	114	118	124	126	127	128	129	131
Sector of economy								
Industry	144	228	368	393	398	401	406	417
Construction	253	412	460	423	423	425	414	412
Agriculture	100	78	49	49	49	49	49	49
Forestry	98	112	224	220	242	236	243	250
Transportation	141	214	378	383	390	391	402	405
Communications	179	259	367	374	372	369	368	375
Distributive Trades	157	208	301	300	301	308	309	315
Science and Research	198	242	515	706	719	733	734	735
Education, Culture, Arts	132	191	225	216	209	193	194	195
Health and Social Services	172	248	310	315	321	320	318	322
Local authorities	251	522	668	733	767	819	861	912
Housing, Services, Public administration	78	49	46	40	40	40	40	38
Others	113	161	193	228	228	228	230	228

Source: National Commission of Statistics.

A high share of the total R&D personnel has been concentrated in the industrial sector, with an almost constant 66 per cent during 1985–89, and industry also accounted for 61 per cent of total R&D expenditure in the economy in 1989. In 1989, 152 of each 10 000 active persons in Romania were employed in R&D activities, of which 50 per cent were university graduates which indicates a proper quality level. The analysis of human research resources per science field reveals that about 10 per cent of such personnel were employed in basic research concentrated in the Academy of Science's institutes, and 90 per cent were in applied research and technological development. Almost two-thirds of the R&D personnel (researchers, technicians and support personnel) were concentrated in the engineering and technology fields, while natural, agricultural, medical and social and humanistic sciences shared 35 per cent. The high share of the personnel employed in engineering and technology was the direct result of the special attention paid to these fields before 1990.

The importance of education in the Romanian government's development strategy can be seen in the immense efforts undertaken to build up a well-developed system of general education and vocational training, free and available for everybody according to their potential, both to improve the quality of labour demanded by the technical progress achieved and to meet the future needs of a growing economy. It also was seen as a matter of social ethics. Education was perceived as the most important means of social reform and as the cornerstone of permanent economic development. As a result of the high commitment to education held by the communist authorities, the number of educational establishments, the number of teachers, and the enrolment rates in the various levels of the formal education system had all increased rapidly since 1950. Thus the number in the basic education system rose from 1779 thousands in 1950 to 2892 in 1989, in vocational and apprenticeship schools from 99 000 to 305 000, and in the high-school education system from 93 000 to 305 000. In the higher education system, student enrolment increased from 53 000 to 165 000. Now speaking in terms of teaching staff, the numbers increased as follows: in the basic education system from 67 100 to 141 700; in the high-school education system from 5 100 to 42 500; and in the higher education system from 8 500 to 11 700. Also the number of students in the engineering and technological sciences rose from 13 244 in 1950 to 106 299 in 1989, and in natural sciences from 7 783 to 13 482. Romania also ranks high among European countries for high-schooling rates with 24 per cent of the total population in 1989 (Romanian Human Development Report, 1995).

Concerning the quality of human capital, we can say that the economic evolution of the last 20 years and its deep structural changes influenced the labour resources both quantitatively and qualitatively. Remarkably significant changes occurred in the structure of labour resources, in terms of the social and professional structure of the working population this reflecting changes in the structure of the economy, the technical progress demanded in a labour force with complex skills and high qualifications, and the emergence of a pool of new diversified and complex professions. Within the adult population a major increase in the number and share of university and high-school graduates took place, at the same time as a decrease in number and share of primary graduates and non-graduates, due to an extensive system of adult training. The most significant increase was associated with university graduates and secondary school graduates, which rose from 2.2 per cent of total adult population in 1966 to 5.0 per cent in 1989 in the former case, and from 22.5 per cent to 66.0 per cent in the latter. The number of illiterates decreased sharply from 25 per cent in 1950 to 2 per cent in 1989. Over three-quarters of all illiterates are women, mostly in the rural area and concentrated in the older age groups.

According to the last census, the youth proved to have a higher education level than the aged. For instance over 70 per cent of the youth aged 20–24 had a university degree or secondary school degree (secondary school degree means 12 years in school, i.e. from first form when 7 years old to twelfth form when 18 years old), while the ratio for the population aged 65 and over was only 14 per cent.

Until 1989 the number of students in universities, and their share by scientific sector, was strictly regulated and centrally planned in concordance with the expected and foreseen needs of the economy in each subject (as a consequence of the policies adopted by the regime, i.e. full employment, a system of job assignments for young graduates, and a policy of centrally-managed technological change and rapid industrialisation). Therefore, due to the free access in terms of payment for education and restriction in terms of limited number of places in universities, the bar on entry was enforced by means of particularly difficult entrance examinations, which could only be passed with the help of many years extra tuition by private teachers, or otherwise through exceptional intellectual abilities. Moreover this emphasises that high quality-people are emerging from the higher education system, and also a similar conclusion can be formulated that from this high-quality base of graduates there will emerge high-quality scientists and engineers to produce a competitive and viable R&D system. In consequence, due to the emphasis placed on engineering and technology sciences, their share in the total number of university graduates has been particularly high, at almost 50 per cent of total, and constant over a long period of time.

Despite following the right path to industrial development through investing in education and training systems and allocating high levels of resources for R&D activities, Romania, like the other Eastern European countries, did not yet succeed in emulating the economic performance of the Newly Industrialised Countries (for example Korea and Taiwan). It is said their phenomenal economic success was a remarkable example of education led growth and technical progress; that the availability of a young domestic workforce with high skills made it possible for their national industry to move from simple goods to complex and technologically-sophisticated products in a very short period of time (from 1960 to 1980). In the case of Romania, we can speak only about the success in creating a large supply of literate and numerically-competent people, a pool of well-trained scientists and engineers, a wide network of institutes and organisations supporting science and technology, etc. There thus exists the infrastructure and the people with requisite knowledge and skills to provide sustained technological change, but it has not been able to do so.

We think that the answer to the problem is that the availability of an educated workforce is not enough by itself if it is not matched by economic measures to create a competitive and flexible system that is opened to the international economy, in terms of international transfer of technology, foreign trade, capital import and import of foreign ideas and experts. The superiority of a free market over the planned economy consists most of all in its capacity to allow its economic agents the freedom to exploit their own creative resources, to provide the incentives and space for economic experimentation. A competitive environment increases the innovation effort undertaken by firms and spurs the innovation more efficiently into the economy, and also compels them to watch the market carefully and to take advantage of the skilled labour force present in the economy.

8.4 CHANGES IN THE NATIONAL SYSTEM OF INNOVATION AFTER 1989

With respect to innovation, the combination of liberalisation, stabilisation and privatisation programmes being presently undertaken by the Romanian government will not be enough to generate a rapid improvement in performance of its industry in the short term. Nevertheless, these measures will gradually create a more competitive environment as new firms and imports enter various markets. As a result of competition and tougher financial conditions, domestic firms will be forced to operate more efficiently and to increasingly innovate in order to diversify and increase the quality of their products. The way that firms will innovate will be determined to a great extent by the industrial structures that emerge. But in any case these presumed and hoped-for positive developments are likely to operate rather slowly in the short-term, when the thinking of many businesses will be dominated by survival considerations.

The government will still have to play, for the next few years (decades), a significant role in promoting and supporting innovation in areas important for the country's longer-term economic success. The simplistic assumptions that just pure economic measures such as pricing, taxation, incentives and the liberalisation of trade will improve the innovative behaviour of the domestic firms, and that technological change will occur at a faster rate without any specific measures to influence technological progress and the investment behaviour associated with it, is refuted by the new evidence in the world economy. In this era of rapid technological change, *laissez-faire* does not work. Active worldwide technology sourcing strategies are required, together with efforts to redesign the national system of innovation both in order to respond to the changes in the economic environment and to sustain the country's economic growth by building up and strengthening capabilities in the key technologies that Romania needs for industrial transformation.

After 1989, for a period of time, little attention was paid to the S&T sector and little was said about innovation in most of the government's reform proposals. Faced with acute problems of short-term survival the government had no interest in innovation, and possessed a very limited amount of resources available for financing R&D, due to the deep economic recession, budgetary uncertainty and hyperinflation, the characteristic ingredients of an economy in crisis.

In consequence the ratio GERD/GDP fell from 2.6 per cent in 1989 to 1.5 per cent in 1992, and also the share of capital R&D investment in total R&D expenditure (GERD) fell from 11.5 per cent in 1989 to 2.7 per cent in 1992. All these trends in R&D funding characterise a period of crisis in the R&D system, a period of great challenge; to adapt and to restructure to the requirements of an economic system in transition from a centrally-planned economy to a market economy, while surviving the transition; and an attempt to preserve the valuable resources existing in the S&T sector in a time when dramatic changes are taking place in the political and economic system and when everybody (government and industry) is questioning what science can contribute to a system in such profound crisis.

Understanding that the failure to build up a sound and effective R&D system, properly matched to the requirements of a dynamic market economy, can impede a successful change and erode the human capital needed to sustain technological progress, the Government had started by the end of 1992 to again design a series of measures oriented to revitalise and enhance the development of science and technology in Romania. As part of this program, in December 1992, the Ministry of Research and Technology (MCT) was created as the central authority enforcing the government development strategy and policy in the field of scientific research and technological development. The Ministry of Research and Technology is responsible for coordinating, in cooperation with the Romanian Academy of Sciences and other ministries and authorities in public administration, the elaboration of government programs in scientific research and technological development for prioritised strategic purposes, preparing legislative norms, and managing and financing public funds for the national S&T programmes.

The Ministry of Research and Technology had elaborated 'The Romanian Research and Development Program' aimed at preserving, improving, supporting and stimulating R&D activity in Romania and to extend Romanian scientific research's contribution to the modernising and integration of the national economy into the world economy on a competitive basis (Government Decree/Report on the organisation and functioning of MCT). Thus the goals promoted by the Reform are: in the short term to strengthen the relationship between research and the economy; in the medium term to integrate Romania into international technology flows; and in the long term, to reach the stage of technological independence in some high-technologies. In general, the Reform intends to link the S&T policy more closely to the domestic industrial capabilities and national industrial policy, in the context of a small country that cannot afford financially to put into production all the research results created within the R&D system.

Other institutions have been created in the R&D public administration since 1992. Firstly, the Advisory College for R&D, which now encompasses the R&D Interdisciplinary Commissions and the Specialised Commissions and has the following responsibilities; to make proposals and recommendations on how to draw up and implement the national R&D policies, and to help the transfer of R&D results to the economic agents concerned. Secondly, in order to improve the exploitation of the R&D system and to speed up the process of innovation, the following institutions are also presently being designed: National Agency for Technology Transfer, Technology Transfer Centres Territorial Network, Innovation and Business, Technology and Business Incubators, Consultancy Centres, Science and Technology Parks, Small and Medium Enterprises based on advanced technologies (Romanian Ministry of Research and Technology 1994).

In response to the policy of decentralisation, the number of R&D units rose from 334 in 1989 to 520 in 1994. The R&D personnel also rose from 102 601 in 1989 to 126 820 in 1994 as a consequence of the decentralisation and increased autonomy of institutes; now they could employ new graduates, in contrast with the past period when the institutes were not allowed to employ above the number set out for them by the centre through the plan requirements.

Another increase was recorded in the number of students in higher education, due to the emergence of private universities and the weakening of the previous enrolment restrictions. This thus grew by 135 per cent from 1989 to 1994, i.e. from 164 000 to 385 000, of which 130 000 were in private universities. Big changes occurred in the number of students enrolled in the major scientific fields in the higher education system; the share of the total number of students in engineering and technology sciences declined from 68 per cent in 1989 to 40 per cent in 1994; in economics it rose from 9.4 per cent to 20 per cent, and in law from 1.4 per cent to 6.0 per cent (Ministry of Education Statistics).

The primary sources of R&D expenditure are the business enterprise sector (primarily state enterprises), a Special

R&D Fund created from a 1 per cent tax on economic agents, and the state budget. In 1993, the largest share of R&D financing was provided by the Special R&D Fund, 60.4 per cent of the total; the business enterprise sector accounted for 16.8 per cent; and the state budget only for 14.5 per cent. The need to design this new type of financial resource for R&D was due to the decline of both business and state funding after 1990, as a result of the transitional processes that were taking place in the economy, which were accompanied by high budgetary uncertainty, and uncertainties concerning the business enterprise sector both in terms of changes in ownership (privatisation) and the continuing existence of the enterprises themselves.

In terms of R&D expenditures by type of research activity, we acknowledge the following trends: the share of experimental development in R&D funding is increasing from 5.5 per cent in 1991 to 8.2 per cent in 1993, applied research remains constant around 70 per cent (in 1991 its share of the total was 69.6 per cent and in 1993 it was 70.7 per cent) and basic research is slightly decreasing from 24.9 per cent to 21.1 per cent.

The structure of the R&D personnel by level of training, was characterised by an increase in the proportion with a higher degree, from 45.9 per cent in 1991 to 51.1 per cent in 1993. Of these certified scientific researchers were respectively 26.7 per cent in 1991 and 23.8 per cent in 1993. An increase occurred in the number of technicians from 18.5 per cent to 23.9 per cent, and there was a significant decrease in the number of support personnel, from 35.5 per cent to 22.0 per cent.

An analysis of the structure of the R&D personnel with a higher degree per science field, and by age groups, reveals that in 1993 the highest share was concentrated in engineering sciences and technologies, which accounted for 65.7 per cent of total. Regarding the distribution per age group, the statistics show that most of them are in the 40–49 years age group, with 36.0 per cent, followed by the 30–39 years age group with 31.7 per cent, the 50–59 group accounts for 15.5 per cent, and the up to 30 years group accounts for

12.7 per cent. Over the period a slight decrease was encountered in the number of young researchers (up to 39) due to phenomena such as brain drain and internal emigration to other sectors of the economy (Ministry of Research and Technology statistics).

8.5 CONCLUSIONS

The argument of this paper has suggested that contemporary patterns in the strategic evolution of MNEs, as they seek new ways to implement dynamic responses to the new forms of globalised competition, may enable them to play an unexpectedly progressive and high-value-added role in the emergence of Central and Eastern European transition economies into the international economy.

In fact MNEs may assist these economies in a creative transition. It is increasingly understood that as MNEs expand their global supply networks to support their worldwide competitiveness, the subsidiaries in these networks can (to varying degrees) play two roles. Firstly to simply supply existing products in the most effective manner, and secondly to play a substantial role in the creation of new products, either to meet particular regional needs and characteristics or to supply the full world market (when the product is very distinctive).

Thus once a subsidiary is established in a country to supply established products (to use the country's static comparative advantage in terms of cost-effective inputs) it may detect the presence of under-utilised creative potential (a quality science base and well-educated labour). If the subsidiary managers themselves also reflect underdeveloped creative potential, in the form of an entrepreneurial aspiration, they may seek to encompass the more dynamic host-country scope into their activity by seeking a product-development role. As a subsidiary goes through such a creative transition (from supply of established goods to developing original products) they can lead an underachieving host-economy through the same dynamic

procedure. The ongoing research that this chapter introduces suggests that a transition economy such as Romania
can provide a classic potential for such a scenario. We have
documented a strong institutional and policy commitment
to R&D and technical education in Romania during the
communist period. It is also indicated that this substantial
resource played a relatively small role in determining the
nature of the development of Romanian industry. There
was, in fact, a particularly severe gap between Romanian
science and Romanian industry. Though institutionalised
attempts were made to close this gap the lack of commercial motivation in industry (probably coupled with the fact
that many scientists considered the decisions taken on the
part of political power as conservative, and too ideological,
and in general irrational or irrelevant for the development
of science) meant this had very limited success.

As MNEs increasingly encourage the development of
heterogeneous competences and scope amongst their subsidiaries, with a knowledge-seeking role a priority in many
cases, it becomes increasingly plausible that subsidiaries
that pioneer a company's entry into a new environment
may look beyond the cost of routine production inputs
towards the more creative technological potentials of a
host country. If MNEs access these under-utilised elements
of a latent dynamic comparative advantage in a country
such as Romania they can greatly speed up the closing of
the gap between commerce and knowledge, to the mutual
advantage of the company and the country. Such an early
interjection of a creative basis for competitiveness in
Romanian industry should hopefully stimulate similar
momentum into indigenous firms, providing them also
with a dynamic view of their potential in international
competition.

Note

1. This concept of creative transition was best exemplified by the evolution of the Newly Industrialising Countries which started as cost-effective producers of unsophisticated standardised products, but used these assets in a way that enabled them to move forward to high-value-added production and exports.

9 The European R&D Operations of Japanese Multinationals

9.1 INTRODUCTION

Recent years have seen a massive rise in the number of R&D units set up overseas by Japanese MNEs.[1] This chapter will review the motivations and roles of these labs in order to argue that their emergence in Japanese MNEs is at the core of the latest distinctive phase in these companies' evolution as global competitors.

It has been persuasively argued by Ozawa (1991a, 1991b, 1992) that distinctive phases can be observed in the emergence of overseas activity of Japanese companies in the past 30 years, and that furthermore the characteristics of these phases have been closely related to the priorities of industrial restructuring in the home-country economy. Thus the re-emergence of Japan as a competitive force in the international economy was initially based around industries that benefited from low wage rates at home in order to successfully penetrate export markets for standardised labour-intensive goods. However, as the sheer success of this type of activity led to rising wage rates in Japan the firms that needed to retain low-cost access to their key input sought new sources of labour in countries such as Taiwan, S. Korea, Hong Kong, Thailand, etc., where it still remained abundant. Thus this 'elementary' stage of Japan's offshore production (Ozawa 1991a) involved the migration of standardised, low-technology labour-intensive industries.

In the face of the exodus of the labour-intensive industries Japanese industrial strategy moved towards the pursuit of another traditional source of competitiveness, with the encouragement of scale-economies-based sectors such as steel, aluminium, shipbuilding, petrochemicals and synthetic fibres. However the resource characteristics of these industries again soon ran up against severe constraints within Japan and 'led to the malignancies of pollution, congestion and ecological destruction as [they] tended to generate considerable environmental externalities' (Ozawa 1991a, p. 141). Once again the vulnerability of industries in Japan provoked a second phase of overseas investments, with the transfer abroad of some of these resource-intensive and pollution-prone operations and the pursuit of secure supplies of raw materials.

To replace the resource-consuming and polluting industries, the new emphasis in Japanese strategy turned to high-value-added knowledge-intensive industries such as electronics, automobiles and machine tools. This wave of Japanese industry also soon led to its own (the third) phase of overseas investment, though this time with rather different initial motivation and rather more profound implications for the nature of the enterprises involved. Thus the great exporting success of these industries from Japan soon led to protective barriers in other leading (North American and Western European) economies, which resulted in the decision to commence production within these markets. However, with the stimulus to this phase of overseas production emerging in the global rather than the local economy, it was possible for the Japanese companies to retain significant parts of their activity at home. Therefore 'this time the overseas operations complement strong continued activity in the industries in Japan (an intra-industry restructuring), rather than predominantly replacing them (an inter-industry restructuring)' (Pearce and Papanastassiou 1996, p. 9). One important implication of this was that, to a more profound extent than in either of the previous phases, the Japanese MNEs emerging in these industries had the scope and motivation to develop truly globalised perspectives on their strategic evolution. An increasingly important element in these strategies then related to the fact that the overseas operations in these companies can play a dynamic and creative role, rather than merely provide the efficient but passive application of established group capacities. In industries with ever-evolving tastes and technologies, Japanese subsidiaries operating in other advanced industrial environments have the scope to detect trends, and thus to participate proactively in both the improved commercial effectiveness of their group's current knowledge and its substantive regeneration through scientific research.

Whereas phases one and two of Japanese overseas investment responded respectively to 'efficiency-seeking' and 'resource-seeking' motivations (Dunning 1993a) within the current scope of their MNEs, phase three encompasses *inter alia* the attempt to extend that scope itself through 'strategic-asset-seeking' behaviour. The new strategies Dunning observes (1993b, p. 149)

> have been largely driven by the need of Japanese firms to transform themselves from exporters to 'insiders' in the major markets of the world, and to keep in touch with the latest technological and organisational developments.

In the same vein Ozawa (1991a, p. 137) observes that

> the rich cultural diversities and creative human resources in Europe are the new resources Japan needs – and can tap only through overseas operations – in its search for ideas and knowledge.

The view is that as contemporary Japanese MNEs seek sustained global competitiveness group-wide perspectives on the creation and use of technology become a key priority. A vital mechanism in implementing this approach is then the setting up of networks of overseas R&D labs. These labs may help improve the effectiveness with which the MNE's current knowledge achieves its commercial manifestation, by supporting associated subsidiaries in product adaptation or development, or contribute to longer-term competitiveness by carrying out precompetitive research in areas of special expertise of the host-country science base. Some useful evidence on Japanese MNEs' attitudes to decentralisation of R&D can be found in the eleventh annual survey of their European manufacturing operations carried out by Japanese External Trade Organisation (JETRO) during the second half of 1994 (JETRO 1995). The JETRO survey approached 720 Japanese manufacturing subsidiaries in Europe and 71 independent R&D facilities. In the next section evidence from the JETRO survey is used to derive indications of the emerging R&D strategies in Japanese MNEs. After that JETRO data provides clear documentation of the extensive growth of Japanese R&D units in Europe, whilst the subsequent two sections then interpret the roles and motivations of these labs.

9.2   R&D STRATEGIES OF JAPANESE MNES

Two questions reported in the JETRO survey asked respondents based in Europe to provide their views on the emerging approaches of their Japanese MNE groups to the decentralisation of R&D. The first of these questions requested the Europe-based respondents to say which of three group-level strategies they believed was most relevant to their company. The most strongly supported of these options was that the groups would 'entrust part of design to local offices to meet needs of clients'. As Table 9.1 shows, 57.1 per cent of the replies from manufacturing operations supported this as the most likely future R&D strategy of their group. In addition (JETRO 1995, p. 52) 40.4 per cent of the replies from independent R&D units also indicated the perception of this as the predominant future approach. This provides endorsement for the view that amongst Japanese MNEs there is a clear understanding of the need to implement decentralised creative operations in order to assist in the effective global extension of their current technology, through product development or adaptation that targets needs of local clients.

Table 9.1   Future R&D structure of Japanese MNEs[1]

Future structure (percent of respondents)			
	A	B	C	Total
Total by host country	22.5	57.1	20.4	100.0
UK	13.2	60.3	26.4	100.0
France	33.3	43.1	23.5	100.0
Germany	25.9	58.6	15.5	100.0
Benelux	26.7	62.2	11.1	100.0
Other	24.7	57.0	18.3	100.0
By industry				
Food	9.1	54.5	36.4	100.0
Textiles, apparel and textile products	23.1	53.8	23.1	100.0
Chemicals and pharmaceuticals	25.4	54.0	20.6	100.0
Metals[2]	38.2	50.0	11.8	100.0
General machinery	24.1	63.0	13.0	100.0
Electronic and electrical equipment	20.2	62.9	16.9	100.0
Electronic components	24.3	54.1	21.6	100.0
Transport equipment and parts	17.0	57.4	25.5	100.0
Precision instruments	21.1	57.9	21.1	100.0
Other	19.1	55.3	25.5	100.0

Notes:

[1] Responding Japanese manufacturers were asked which of the three future structures was most relevant to their company.
[2] Metal products, non-ferrous metals, iron and steel

Future R&D structure

A – will centralise both basic research and design in head office.
B – will entrust part of design to local offices to meet needs of clients.
C – will try to localise corporate activities by setting up bases of basic research, development of products or design centre.

Source: JETRO (1995).

The second most prevalent of the three R&D strategies offered for evaluation was that Japanese MNEs 'will centralise both basic research and design in head office'. This possibility was endorsed as most likely by 22.5 per cent of the manufacturing operations in Europe (Table 9.1). None of the independent R&D units that replied believed this type of centralisation would prevail in their group in the future. This perception is, of course, not surprising since these independent labs are likely themselves to be focusing on contributing to their group's basic research, or helping with the vital early phases of new product innovation (the transition from abstract scientific knowledge to radical new commercial potentials), so that expecting its complete centralisation in the future would imply, in effect, their own demise (or at least reduction to other less high- profile work).

Somewhat paralleling the second strategic R&D option the third was defined as 'will try to localise corporate activities by setting up bases of basic research, development of products or design centre'. In the main this strategy recognises the possibility that overseas R&D units can support longer-term corporate technology objectives of their group, by playing roles in those phases of the innovation process that work towards the generation of the core knowledge base that provides the scope for the eventual commercialisation of major new product concepts. Though only 20.4 per cent of respondents from manufacturing subsidiaries rated this as the most plausible future R&D strategy of their group the comparable figure for the independent laboratories was 59.0 per cent. This is likely to reflect the fact that the independent R&D units have a clearer perception of the benefits that their MNEs could secure, in terms of the enrichment of the core knowledge base, through decentralised work of the types they themselves carry out. Whether their response fully reflects the actual intentions of their group with regard to this phase of the technology creation and application process is perhaps less obvious.

Taking just the replies of the manufacturing subsidiaries (as reported in Table 9.1), these results may reflect on two levels of strategic decision making in the R&D programmes of the Japanese MNEs. Firstly it appears that 43.0 per cent of these respondents felt that the most important elements of the future R&D strategies of their group would be those that targeted corporate-level objectives, involving the pursuit of basic research and the development of the outlines of key new product concepts, i.e.

phase one of a global-innovation strategy. A small majority (52.5 per cent) of those respondents that rated this phase of the innovation process as likely to be most prevalent in future considered it probably would remain centralised in the Japanese head office. Secondly 77.5 per cent of the manufacturing subsidiary respondents believed that labs in Europe would make some contribution to the creation and commercial application of their group's technology in the future. The prevalent role of these European labs was then expected to relate to the second phase of a global-innovation strategy (i.e. development of a product for a regional market from a new group-level product concept), with 72.8 per cent of the replies that saw a role for such local units believing it was most likely to involve design to meet needs of clients.

The second question relating to these group-level dimensions of R&D strategy in Japanese MNEs was addressed to those that felt, in their replies to the previous question, that centralisation would remain the dominant approach.[2] It asked them to evaluate a number of reasons for the persistence of such centralisation, with respondents permitted to endorse any of the options that they felt contributed to this attitude. As Table 9.2 shows, the most pervasive factor contributing to centralisation of R&D involved resource constraints, with 55.6 per cent of respondents feeling that they 'cannot afford to decentralise power from the financial and personnel point of view'. Precisely one-third of respondents to this question considered that 'Japanese style ideas and designs are sufficient'. Though the earlier success of Japanese companies as exporters of products originally created in Japan may provide a basis for such confidence in their current generations of products, the wider evidence supports the view that as these companies have entered more profoundly into global competition through overseas production the benefits of responding positively to distinctive local-market needs have become decisively obvious to the majority of them. Finally 22.2 per cent of replies suggested that centralisation of R&D derived from the view that the 'growth of the

company is based on development of our own technology'.
This would appear to reflect a view that only home-country R&D can be relied on to underwrite the longer-term
evolution of a company's technological scope. Whereas it
is clear that some of the Japanese MNEs that have decentralised parts of their R&D programmes may still also

Table 9.2   Reasons for centralising R&D in head office of Japanese
MNEs

	Reasons (percentage)[1]			
	A	B	C	D
Total by host country	37.8	15.9	54.9	13.4
UK	31.3	12.5	68.8	18.8
France	35.3	23.5	52.9	11.8
Germany	46.7	13.3	60.0	20.0
Benelux	33.3	–	58.3	8.3
Other	40.9	22.7	40.9	9.1
By industry				
Food	–	–	–	100.0
Textiles, apparel and textile products	33.3	–	66.7	33.3
Chemicals and pharmaceuticals	25.0	6.3	62.5	12.5
Metals[2]	38.5	15.4	61.5	7.7
General machinery	69.2	7.7	53.8	–
Electronic and electrical equipment	38.9	22.2	61.4	5.6
Electronic components	44.4	–	44.4	33.3
Transport equipment and parts	42.9	28.6	42.9	28.6
Precision instruments	50.0	25.0	50.0	–
Other	22.2	33.3	55.6	–

Notes:
[1] Percentage of respondents that believed the reason was relevant to
the decision of their MNE to centralise R&D at head office in Japan.
[2] Metal products, non-ferrous metals, iron and steel.

Reasons for centralisation

A – Growth of company is based on development of our own techno-
logy.
B – Japanese style ideas and designs are sufficient.
C – Cannot afford to decentralise power from the financial and person-
nel point of view.
D – Other.
Source: JETRO (1995).

endorse this view of the need to centralise the key precompetitive phases, the relative unimportance of this reason for complete R&D centralisation seems more compatible with the perception that many Japanese firms do *not* feel confident in the ability to use home-country science to build their longer-term technology scope.

9.3 GROWTH OF JAPANESE R&D UNITS IN EUROPE

The growth in the total number of Japanese MNEs' R&D units in Europe has been considerable in recent years, almost precisely doubling from 147 at the end of 1989 to 292 at the end of 1994 (JETRO data, see Table 9.3). The UK has been the strongest participant in this, increasing its share of the total from 29.3 per cent in 1989 to 33.2 per cent in 1994. Germany retained a clear second place with 20.5 per cent in 1994 (slightly down from 21.1 per cent in 1989), with France then claiming third position with 12.7 per cent (up from 11.6 per cent) by displacing Spain which fell to fourth with 8.2 per cent (down from 12.9 per cent). Other notable host countries in 1994 were Netherlands (6.5 per cent), Belgium (5.8 per cent) and Italy (5.1 per cent).

The JETRO data distinguishes between two types of Japanese R&D units in Europe, which may be expected to have very different strategic objectives. Thus *independent* labs operate in a manner that involves no association with a local production facility and which may, therefore, be assumed to focus on roles in programmes that support corporate level (mainly precompetitive) R&D programmes. This type of unit accounted for 24.3 per cent of all Japanese MNE labs in Europe in 1994, which represented a slight increase from 20.4 per cent in 1989 (see Table 9.3). In the latter year, 32.4 per cent of these independent labs were in the UK, 23.9 per cent in Germany and 12.7 per cent in France. Amongst those countries that attracted large numbers of Japanese facilities the independent labs were relatively most prevalent in Germany where they accounted for 28.3 per cent of all units in 1994 (compared with 29.0 per cent in 1989). Next came France with 24.3 per cent (a notable rise from 17.6 per cent in 1989), closely followed by the UK with 23.7 per cent (a small rise from 20.9 per cent). These figures suggest that a clear separate strand of Japanese MNEs' technological commitments in Europe is focused on units that are based around types of work that have no immediate application to the operations of established production facilities in the region, but with a motivation that is instead much more derived from corporate knowledge-seeking programmes.

Table 9.3   Numbers of Japanese companies' R&D laboratories in Europe 1989 and 1994[1]

	Numbers of laboratories					
	Associated laboratories[2]		Independent laboratories[3]		Total laboratories	
	1989	1994	1989	1994	1989	1994
Total	117	221	30	71	147	292
UK	34	74	9	23	43	97
France	14	28	3	9	17	37
Germany	22	43	9	17	31	60
Netherlands	9	16	0	3	9	19
Belgium	6	13	3	4	9	17
Spain	18	22	1	2	19	24
Italy	6	9	2	6	8	15
Other	8	16	3	7	11	23

Notes:
[1] Figure for end of December in each year.
[2] Laboratories that work with a local production unit of the Japanese MNE.
[3] Laboratories that work independently of any local production operations of its Japanese MNE.
Source: JETRO (1995).

The second type of laboratory covered by the JETRO data does, however, derive its main motivation from the needs of production and marketing operations in Europe with which they have a direct working association. Though growing slightly slower than the former type these *associated* labs still accounted for 75.7 per cent of the total in

1994. The UK again accounted for the largest share of these labs in 1994 (33.5 per cent), followed by Germany (19.4 per cent), France (12.7 per cent) and Spain (10.0 per cent). If the number of associated labs is expressed as a proportion of total manufacturing subsidiaries[3] then the ratio rose from 24.0 per cent in 1989 to 30.7 per cent in 1994, suggesting that the commercial pressures of the European market caused an increasing proportion of Japanese producers there to detect the need for in-house R&D to support their competitiveness. In 1994 this ratio was highest for Germany at 40.2 per cent (up from 28.2 per cent in 1989), with the UK next at 36.1 per cent (from 26.2 per cent) followed at 33.3 per cent by the Netherlands (up from 29.0 per cent) and Spain (the only fall, from 36.7 per cent) and then by Belgium with 31.7 per cent (from 21.4 per cent) and France at 25.2 per cent (from 18.4 per cent).

9.4   TYPES OF R&D IN JAPANESE LABORATORIES

The eleventh JETRO survey provides some useful information on the prevalence of the different types of work carried out in the Japanese MNEs' labs in Europe (JETRO 1995, p. 57). The first of these, basic research, was included in the work of 36.2 per cent of the responding independent labs (where it was the second most pervasive type of work) but in only 10.3 per cent of the labs associated with production operations (which meant it was the least prevalent of the separately designated types of work in these units). This confirms the view that the presence of such precompetitive research is a key factor that defines the position of the independent laboratories.

'Development of products' emerged as perhaps the most generally pervasive type of work amongst the labs. Its inclusion in the activity of 69.0 per cent of the associated units (their second strongest role) is in line with the expectation that many Japanese production units in Europe now include a distinctive product development function. Development of products also emerged as the most prevalent type of work in the independent labs, being carried out by 51.1 per cent of them. Part of this may involve the carrying forward of their own basic research results towards the speculative definition of the technological characteristics of a new product (applied research), but before the precise commercial format of the new product is specified in collaboration with a particular production operation. Alternatively the presence of product development in independent labs may occur if the new goods are to be produced by several Japanese factories in Europe and it is decided, for reasons of efficiency or group politics, to keep the development process separate from all of them.

'Product design/change of specification' (i.e. the traditional overseas lab role of adaptation of established group products) was the most prevalent role in the associated labs (present in 76.1 per cent of them). It was also present in 29.8 per cent of the independent labs, where the provision of product adaptation support to a whole European network of factories producing established goods is the most likely explanation. The 'development of manufacturing process techniques' occurred in 37.4 per cent of the associated labs, but only 12.8 per cent of the independent ones, suggesting that close interaction with local conditions was of significance in achieving effective factory technology. Only 5.8 per cent of associated labs acknowledged the presence of undesignated 'other' types of work, compared with 10.6 per cent of the independent ones, whose wider knowledge scope may thus open them up to more idiosyncratic roles.

Further evidence on the extent and content of R&D in Japanese MNEs can be found in a survey carried out by Emmott (1992) in 1991–92.[4] Two questions in Emmott's questionnaire distinguished between the presence of research and development in the operations of these Japanese subsidiaries. In response to the question 'does your firm conduct research (as opposed to development) locally?' 53 (36.3 per cent) of 146 respondents[5] said that they did. The USA seemed rather more able than Europe to attract pure research, with 39.8 per cent of respondents there saying they did such work compared with 31.7 per cent of those in the UK and 29.4 per cent elsewhere in the EU. More commercially-oriented and market-focused development, however, proved to be generally more pervasive and widely dispersed. Thus when asked 'does your firm conduct any development or design locally?' 60.3 per cent of respondents said that they did. Though an average number of Japanese subsidiaries in the US (61.4 per cent) included this type of market-responsive work, this was at least matched by a similar tendency to carry out distinctive product development in Europe. Within Europe, however, the UK emerged as the prime location for this type of activity, with 63.4 per cent of subsidiaries there saying they included development or design compared with 47.1 per cent elsewhere in the EU. Thus it appears that at present it is the UK that is most able to attract the high-value-added creative activities of Japanese MNEs in Europe.

9.5 LOCALISATION OF JAPANESE R&D IN EUROPE

Two questions in the eleventh JETRO survey investigated aspects of the localisation of Japanese MNEs' R&D in Europe. The first of these asked respondents[6] to evaluate whether or not each of four separately designated factors contributed to the decision to set up local R&D operations in Europe. Of these influences the view that such facilities were needed 'because products manufactured locally should meet local needs' was considered as a relevant factor contributing to localisation of R&D by 86.4 per cent of the manufacturing subsidiary respondents (Table 9.4). Not only did these producing operations perceive the importance of R&D support for their desire to make their products responsive to local needs but this was also assessed to be a relevant influence on R&D localisation by 47.4 per cent of the independent labs. This may reflect the presence of such work in these independent labs or merely their understanding of the wider point that such work is likely to be a relevant element somewhere in the European R&D of their Japanese MNE group.

Table 9.4   Reasons for promoting localisation of R&D in Europe by Japanese MNEs

	Reason (percentage)[1]				
	A	B	C	D	E
Independent R&D units	47.4	65.8	65.8	34.2	9.4
Total manufacturing subsidiaries	86.4	20.4	57.9	40.4	6.4
By host country					
UK	86.3	18.6	58.8	42.2	7.8
France	84.8	27.3	69.7	57.6	15.2
Germany	95.3	23.3	58.1	25.6	4.7
Benelux	87.9	18.2	54.5	36.4	–
Other	81.2	18.8	52.2	40.6	4.3
By industry					
Food	80.0	–	10.0	30.0	10.0
Textiles, apparel and textile products	100.0	20.0	40.0	30.0	10.0
Chemicals and pharmaceuticals	80.9	12.8	53.2	42.6	2.1
Metals[2]	85.0	15.0	60.0	35.0	10.0
General machinery	87.2	20.5	48.7	35.9	2.6
Electronic and electrical equipment	85.9	23.9	69.0	38.0	5.6
Electronic components	89.3	14.3	46.4	57.1	3.6
Transport equipment and parts	86.5	32.4	64.9	43.2	18.9
Precision instruments	86.7	26.7	73.3	20.0	6.7
Other	92.1	23.7	63.2	47.4	–

Notes:

[1]   Percentage of respondents that believed a reason was relevant to the decision to localise R&D in Europe.

[2]   Metal products, non-ferrous metals, iron & steel.

Reasons for localisation

A – Because products manufactured locally should meet local needs.

B – To employ foreign researchers to broaden the range of research and development in ideas and ways of thinking.

C – To quickly grasp local trends and cope with sharpening technological competition.

(Contd. Overleaf)

D – To shorten lead time from research and development until starting
    production.
E – Other.
Source: JETRO (1995)

There has long been an understanding that decentralised
R&D in MNEs can support local production facilities
in adapting products to meet local market needs. However
more recent perceptions suggest that as global competition
becomes more intense such overseas labs can play a
more integral role in a dynamic global approach to
the technological evolution of these companies. This can
include monitoring and responding to global trends in
both markets and technology. Thus the JETRO
survey found a strong response to 'to quickly grasp local
trends and cope with sharpening technological competition' as a reason for promoting Japanese MNEs' R&D
in Europe. Though 57.9 per cent of the manufacturing
subsidiaries recognised the significance of this factor it
was perceived as relevant by even more (65.8 per cent)
of the independent labs. This may suggest that though
immediate direct response to these trends within Europe
by producing units is clearly vital, the independent
labs (with their often more interdependent position in
their Japanese group's overall technological evolution)
can also see such emerging localised knowledge as key
inputs into wider perceptions of longer-term technological
and commercial developments. Alongside this the
importance of quick application of new possibilities was
reflected in the fact that 40.4 per cent of manufacturing
subsidiaries and 34.2 per cent of independent R&D units
rated 'to shorten lead time from research and development
until starting production' as reasons for carrying out R&D
in Europe.

The last of the separate influences on R&D localisation
covered in Table 9.4 was described as 'to employ foreign
researchers to broaden the range of research and development in ideas and ways of thinking'. This would reflect
a view of Japanese MNEs that their R&D programmes

can be enriched by tapping into distinctive technological traditions in Europe through the employment of local scientific personnel that have been educated within this unique knowledge heritage. Such idiosyncratic original inputs are likely to be more relevant to the longer-term precompetitive group-level research programmes of MNEs than the more day-to-day commercial application of knowledge through local development work. Thus it is not surprising that 65.8 per cent of the independent labs (at least part of whose activity is likely to support group-level programmes) endorsed the availability of such high-quality researchers as being relevant to R&D localisation, compared with only 20.4 per cent of manufacturing subsidiaries.

In its previous (i.e. tenth) survey, JETRO (1994, table V-3, p. 53) included three additional potential factors in its investigation of reasons for promotion of localised R&D in Europe by Japanese MNEs. Though none of those proved of great significance (perhaps justifying their exclusion from the next survey) it is worth drawing attention to them here as they do help extend our knowledge of those factors which do, or do not, help explain decentralisation of R&D in these companies. The first related to the possibility of the implementation of such R&D units 'because joint study with foreign enterprises and institutions will be a future task to perform'. This further means of extending the research scope of Japanese companies through technological collaborations set up by their overseas R&D units (including with local laboratories, etc; see Pearce and Papanastassiou 1996, Papanastassiou and Pearce 1994a, 1996) was only perceived as relevant by 15.8 per cent of manufacturing subsidiaries but did appear rather more important to independent R&D units, where 40.6 per cent endorsed it as a valid influence. This tends to suggest (in line with interpretation of the desire to recruit talented local scientists, as noted above) that such access to distinctive local knowledge traditions and research scope is more likely to be used by Japanese MNEs to assist in the evolution of their underlying technological capacity (through independent labs) than to support immediate commercial operations (through labs associated with production units).

Next it was suggested that Japanese MNEs carry out R&D in Europe 'because they are short of personnel engaged in research and development in Japan'. Though we have seen that distinctive qualitative characteristics of European researchers had some influence on attracting R&D, a purely quantitative scarcity of such personnel in Japan was revealed as much less relevant as a motivation. Thus this explanation was only endorsed by 9.7 per cent of producing units in Europe and by 3.1 per cent of independent labs. The third of these extra factors was defined as 'part of a measure to increase in-house sourcing'. This would suggest that localised R&D would serve to support the ability of European operations of these companies to extend their value- added scope into input supply (perhaps replacing inputs from elsewhere in the group and lessening criticism of 'screwdriver' operations). Overall 10.9 per cent of production operations and 15.6 per cent of independent labs felt this was of relevance.

The second of this pair of questions in the eleventh JETRO (1995) survey looked at factors influencing the location of Japanese R&D centres in Europe. As Table 9.5 suggests, communication seems a key element here, with proximity to an existing plant or office of pervasive importance. Thus 70.7 per cent of the manufacturing subsidiaries felt that laboratories supporting such operations were 'attached to existing plant', whilst 10.0 per cent more considered these labs were 'close to existing plant or office'. In line with definition none of the independent R&D units were attached to an existing plant, but 17.1 per cent were close to a plant or office. The latter case may stem from the possibility of sharing certain overheads, or because the independent lab does supply certain types of support to a production unit but also feels that too close a proximity to it might compromise its autonomy in terms of other, more group-related, work (Casson, Pearce and Singh 1991, pp.256–7).

Table 9.5   Factors influencing location of Japanese R&D centres in Europe

	Factor (percentage)[1]				
	A	B	C	D	E
Independent R&D units	–	17.1	39.0	73.2	22.0
Total manufacturing subsidiaries	70.7	10.0	8.6	22.1	11.4
By host country					
UK	53.3	8.9	6.7	20.0	24.4
France	68.4	15.8	15.8	31.6	5.3
Germany	83.3	8.3	4.2	12.5	4.2
Benelux	73.7	10.5	15.8	21.1	5.3
Other	84.8	9.1	6.1	27.3	6.1
By industry					
Food	66.7	–	33.3	–	–
Textiles, apparel and textile products	80.0	–	–	20.0	–
Chemicals and pharmaceuticals	66.7	14.3	9.5	23.8	9.5
Metals[2]	50.0	–	–	–	75.0
General machinery	85.7	7.1	–	21.4	–
Electronic and electrical equipment	69.2	15.4	12.8	23.1	17.9
Electronic components	86.7	–	13.3	20.0	13.3
Transport equipment and parts	78.3	8.7	4.3	21.7	8.7
Precision instruments	50.0	20.0	20.0	40.0	–
Other	71.4	4.8	4.8	19.0	14.3

Notes:

[1] Percentage of respondents that believed a factor was relevant to the decision on location of European R&D unit.

[2] Metal products, non-ferrous metals, iron and steel.

Factors affecting location decision

A – attached to existing plant.
B – close to existing plant or office.
C – infrastructure including traffic network and communications network are ready for use.
D – can employ excellent researchers, designers, etc.
E – Others.
Source: JETRO (1995).

Another facet of the importance of communication in this question related to the influence of 'infrastructure including traffic network and communication network are ready for use'. Only 8.6 per cent of manufacturing subsidiaries felt that this was a relevant factor in location of associated R&D units. This suggests that the local inter-functional communications achieved by proximity to a plant are the main priority for this type of lab, with communications with the 'outside world' of much less relevance. By contrast, 39.0 per cent of the independent labs did consider that scope to facilitate wider communication was a significant location influence. This reflects the more cosmopolitan (group-level) objectives of much of the research done in such labs. Thus the work of these labs is often part of globally-coordinated precompetitive programmes of the overall MNE group, and needs mobility of personnel and good telecommunications to facilitate the networking essential to full integration into these projects.

As a location factor the ability to 'employ excellent researchers, designers, etc.' within the specific area was rated as of relevance by 22.1 per cent of the laboratories associated with manufacturing subsidiaries. However, this supply-side influence was much more decisive for the independent labs, 73.2 per cent of which confirmed its relevance to their location choice. This is again in line with the expectation that the ability to carry out the more extensive and ambitious aims of these labs depends on the availability of personnel with at least a generalised high level of expertise, and most probably also embodying distinctive types of knowledge that reflect specific areas of strength in the local technological heritage. Also such independent labs are able to respond more freely to such factors in their location choice because they are not tied into operating in association with other functions (notably manufacturing) whose location decision may take priority and be motivated by other factors.

As in the case of the previous question, JETRO's tenth survey (1994, table V-7, p. 57) had incorporated some extra location influences that were not replicated in the next investigation (as reported in Table 9.5). The first of these, 'there are related industries nearby', was considered to be

of relevance by only 7.0 per cent of the manufacturing
subsidiaries. It was, however, of somewhat more importance to independent labs (endorsed by 21.2 per cent of
them), perhaps reflecting possible synergies to be gained
from a creative agglomeration of technologically interdependent industries in the region. Another perhaps synergistic influence, 'you can enjoy good conditions for
procuring materials and parts', was only seen as relevant
by 9.6 per cent of manufacturing subsidiaries and by 6.1
per cent of independent labs. Clearly it is knowledge inputs
that prevail as location-determining influences on R&D
units.

The last pair of the supplementary location factors
investigated in JETRO's tenth survey relate to government
inducements. They are 'you were actively approached by
the Government of the nation and organisation for inviting
investment' and 'you can enjoy preferential treatment on
tax and subsidies'. Though never of really 'front line'
relevance these factors are rather more important to the
independent labs than to those associated with production
facilities, this perhaps merely reflecting the scope of the
former labs to respond directly to any such approaches
rather than under constraint as an integral part of a
wider-motivated operation. Thus 21.2 per cent of
independent labs felt the first factor to be of relevance and
15.2 per cent assessed the second that way, whilst the
comparable figures for manufacturing subsidiaries were
only 4.3 per cent and 7.0 per cent.

9.6 CONCLUSIONS

The survey evidence reviewed in this chapter is compatible
with a view of a strategic approach to technology in Japanese MNEs in which a response to *localised* characteristics
of particular host countries is built into wider *globalised*
dimensions of the pursuit of group-level competitiveness.
Though with some degree of overlap within particular
laboratories two distinctive motivations emerge for decen-

tralised R&D facilities within Japanese companies that are trying to sharpen their current global competitiveness and to ensure the basis of their longer-term technological viability. Thus one strand of the R&D activity of Japanese MNEs in Europe is found to focus on precompetitive work (basic and/or applied research) that mainly seeks to enrich the core technological scope of the groups. The primary reason for locating such units in Europe appears to be the desirability of accessing specific areas of local knowledge strength, and current research capacity, into which Japanese companies either wish to extend their competence or where there is a perceived weakness in existing technology in Japan. The second strand invokes R&D operations to support the effective commercial use of the MNEs' existing technology. This reflects the need to respond to European taste characteristics within global product development programmes. As the survey evidence again indicates, Japanese MNEs increasingly understand that international competitiveness involves a need to both discern, and respond swiftly to, trends that may be emerging in different segments of the global marketplace. Overall, then, it is realistic to conclude that the growth of their R&D operations in Europe is a key manifestation of the emergence of Japanese MNEs as true global competitors, imposing decentralised and interdependent dimensions on their approach to technology and its positioning at the core of the pursuit of self-sustaining international competitiveness.

Notes

1. See Pearce and Singh (1992a), Papanastassiou and Pearce (1994a; 1995). For evidence of the contrasting situation in the early 1980s, see Dunning (1986, pp. 154–5).
2. Eighty-two firms replied to this question in the JETRO survey, compared with 83 that endorsed centralisation as their future R&D strategy.
3. Data on numbers of production units obtained from JETRO (1995, table 1.1).

4. The survey was sent to 500 subsidiaries of Japanese manufacturing firms in US, UK and the rest of the European Union.
5. Overall 150 subsidiaries replied to Emmott's questionnaire, but four (all in USA) did not answer the question on R&D. Of respondents to the R&D question 88 were in USA, 41 in UK and 17 in the rest of the EU.
6. Replies were received from 280 of the 285 manufacturing subsidiaries that endorsed one or other of the two R&D localisation strategies covered in Table 9.1, plus from 38 of the independent R&D units.

10 The Globalisation of R&D in Pharmaceuticals, Chemicals and Biotechnology: Some New Evidence

with Gurkanwal Singh Pooni

10.1. INTRODUCTION

The recent wave of studies of overseas R&D operations in MNEs[1] has clearly delineated the broad strategic positioning of such decentralised laboratories in the evolution of these globally-competing companies. Thus it emerges that whilst they sometimes still support the ability of overseas production operations to apply existing technology most effectively to their local markets through product *adaptation*, the increased pressure of global competition means that there is now a pervasive momentum towards allowing subsidiaries to *develop* products (i.e. to play a role in the innovation process itself) for particular (regional or even global) markets, through high-value-added creative operations that usually need to incorporate an extensive in-house R&D competence. Beyond this the studies also observe a growing tendency for some decentralised R&D labs in MNEs to stand aside from a direct association with production facilities and instead to carry out precompetitive (basic and/or applied) research using access to local scientific personnel and (through collaborative associations) host-country institutions (university laboratories; industry or independent research facilities).

A major implication of the broadening of the strategic roles of overseas R&D units in MNEs, again extensively

239

observed and documented in the recent studies, is that it brings into play in a more decisive manner the influence of supply-side factors on decision making relating to such units. Clearly the precompetitive labs will be located where the quality, and specialised knowledge tradition and research competence, of the host-country science base is of a standard and nature that fits the needs of the MNE group's research programme. Even where a lab supports directly the work of a product-development subsidiary supply-side elements may prove significant. Thus such a product-creating operation tends to be aimed at the supply of a wide market (well beyond the national market of the subsidiary), so that it could be located anywhere in the region. Given the creative high-value-added nature of its mandate the location decision relating to such a subsidiary is likely to depend more on its host-country's ability to support the technological and skill needs of its activities than pure cost elements in its production process. Central to this is likely to be the capacity to implement an R&D unit that can acquire the scope and competences to play its role in the subsidiary's product generating activity.

However, against this broadly perceived background momentum in R&D decentralisation, the received studies also reveal different emphases of priority according to industry, the home country of the MNE and the host country of the lab. Thus the extent and nature of overseas R&D in an industry may depend on the intensity and forms of its current global competition and the degree of maturity of its prevailing mainstream technology. The extent of outward R&D in firms from a particular country may again reflect their industry composition and also the ability of the home-country science capacity to continue to support the evolving needs of technological competition in its traditionally established sectors. In ways already suggested above the degree of R&D in a country that is controlled by foreign MNEs will reflect the fit between strategic needs of such companies and the characteristics of the country's knowledge and research competences.

This chapter reviews new information on decentralised R&D in the chemicals and allied group of industries, seeking to provide new evidence on the broad factors driving overseas knowledge creation and access, but also to discern patterns of differences in motivation and performance between three complementary but distinctive components of the sector. These are traditional industrial chemicals, pharmaceuticals, and the technologically-volatile and commercially-immature biotechnology. The evidence also allows the observation of differences in behaviour according to home country of MNE.

The information discussed here is derived from a questionnaire survey carried out by G.S. Pooni in 1995. The questionnaire was sent to the parent R&D units of 150 of the world's largest enterprises in the chemicals and allied sector, and investigated *inter alia* a number of issues relating to the strategic positioning and organisation of their overseas R&D. Here we review evidence, from the 63 replies received, relating to the broad strategic influences that underpin the emergence of global perspectives on the creation and use of knowledge, through decentralised R&D units, in these industries.[2]

10.2 STRATEGIC PRIORITIES OF CHEMICAL AND ALLIED SECTOR COMPANIES

Before looking in detail at the position of decentralised R&D we investigate, in this section, elements of the current strategic priorities of companies in the chemical and allied sector industries. In Table 10.1 we present a summary of replies to a question which asked respondents to specify in which of five countries/areas they had producing operations. This data immediately supports the view of the prevalence of interactive competitive strategies in these industries. Thus it is clear that the majority of leading companies were using a network of operations in most of the leading countries as a means of developing their approach to global competitiveness.

Further information on the strategic evolution of leading companies in the chemicals and allied sector was
obtained in a question which asked respondents from their
parent R&D laboratories to evaluate the relevance of six
possible factors in their current development. Though
these replies did come from R&D units it seems reasonable
to expect that leading scientific decision makers in such
technology-driven industries would be likely to possess the
information and breadth of perception to derive a clear
understanding of the major factors in the strategic momentum in their enterprise.

It appears from the replies as summarised in Table 10.2
that the most prominent strategies are those that are associated with consolidation and progress along established
lines with existing technologies. Thus the strongest priority
emerged as to continue producing 'high-value-added products in existing business fields', complemented by a similarly high commitment to 'strengthening total business
capabilities'. However, relatively positive and dynamic attitudes may be reflected in the greater emphasis on 'business
diversification' compared to 'streamlining, including withdrawal from non-profitable markets'. 'Globalisation,
including offshore business' emerges quite prominently as
a means of implementing medium-term global strategic
development, but there seems to be less perception of the
need for 'strengthening basic R&D' as a longer-term priority.

Amongst the individual industries Table 10.2 reveals
quite positive perspectives for the pharmaceutical companies. There seem to be no signs of problems in existing
business fields (moderate average response [AR] for role
D), but a relatively strong commitment to basic research
and to diversification and globalisation. Chemicals, by
contrast, suggests a rather more defensive business posture,
with a limited role for diversification and basic research
and a relatively strong commitment to streamlining.
Against this background the globalisation that is occurring
in chemicals may be defensive rationalisation of operations, rather than part of a more aggressive growth

Table 10.1 Proportion of respondents with production subsidiaries in particular host countries, by home country of company

	Host country (per cent[1])				
	USA	Germany	UK	Other Europe	Japan
By home country					
USA	100	50	72	70	93
Germany	72	100	72	83	78
UK	80	50	100	72	85
Other Europe	80	50	72	100	57
Japan	68	50	54	83	100

Notes:

[1] Percentage of respondents from a particular home country with a production subsidiary in the particular host country.

Source: Gurkanwal Singh Pooni database.

strategy. In biotechnology there is a strong commitment to those strategies (D and E in Table 10.2) that tend to reflect a current momentum towards growth within the relatively precisely defined areas of new technology. Thus participants in the biotechnology industry do not feel the need to seek for fundamental extra areas to 'escape' into (relatively low need for basic research), though the natural momentum of its technological development does appear to open up strategic scope for diversification whilst limiting any need for streamlining of operations.

In terms of the companies' home countries those from USA seem mostly content to grow positively along established lines (strong response to strategy D), with relatively little interest in either expansion of scope through diversification, globalisation or basic research, or in retrenchment through streamlining. German respondents, by contrast, seem to present a posture of strategic vulnerability. Thus they appear threatened and negative in established areas (low values for positions D and E), leading to very high commitment to streamlining of operations. This current defensiveness is not reflected in any strategic pursuit of medium or longer-term enhancement of scope through either globalisation or basic research. UK firms appear to envisage a strategy that continues a quite dynamic momentum in established areas. Thus a notable commitment to extension of high-value-added products in existing business fields is backed by strong use of basic research, with little perceived need for either streamlining or diversification.

Respondents from Other European countries seem to be most decisively motivated by the need to seek new opportunities. Thus a high commitment to both diversification and basic research supports a perceived need to strengthen

Table 10.2 Evaluation by central laboratories of aspects of their group's current operations

| | Group business strategies (*average response*[1]) | | | | | |
	A	B	C	D	E	F
By industry						
Pharmaceuticals	2.27	2.16	2.36	2.69	2.52	1.76
Chemicals	1.94	1.97	2.27	2.60	2.29	1.88
Biotechnology	2.33	2.00	2.25	2.75	2.75	1.75
Total	2.18	2.05	2.28	2.66	2.38	1.81
By home country						
USA	1.84	1.72	2.08	2.76	2.30	1.61
Germany	2.16	1.50	1.67	2.20	2.00	2.50
UK	1.70	2.30	2.11	2.80	2.22	1.60
Other Europe	3.00	3.00	2.00	2.50	2.50	2.50
Japan	2.85	2.38	2.76	2.64	2.64	1.71
Total	2.18	2.05	2.28	2.66	2.38	1.81

Note:

1 Respondents were asked to evaluate each strategy as either, 'a main objective', 'one of our objectives', 'not our objective'. The average response was calculated by allocating responses of main objective the value 3, one of our objectives the value 2 and not an objective the value 1.

Group business strategies

A – business diversification.
B – strengthening basic R&D.
C – globalisation, including off-shore business.
D – high-value-added products in existing business fields.
E – strengthening total business capabilities.
F – streamlining, including withdrawal from non-profitable markets.
Source: G.S. Pooni database.

total business capabilities, alongside a very high need for streamlining and relatively low momentum in existing business fields. However, the need to pursue these new technological and product dimensions seems to preclude a strong role for globalisation in the immediate future strategies of these European companies.

Japanese companies indicate a significant role for the continued growth of the current direction of their activity (an average position for strategy D, along with a notable need to strengthen overall business capabilities), but also reveal the desire to seek wider sources of dynamism (with high values of diversification, basic research and globalisation). Thus, alongside the enhancement of what they appear to perceive as a sound base in their established business fields, the Japanese enterprises in these industries are developing emphatic global perspectives (decisively the highest valuation of a globalisation strategy), which may well be strategically related to new basic research and to development of new product scope.

10.3 CHEMICAL AND ALLIED SECTOR R&D STRATEGIES

The central labs surveyed were also asked to provide an evaluation of five elements in the overall R&D strategies of their companies. As Table 10.3 illustrates, the responses clearly exemplify the view that in the chemicals and allied sector R&D takes a key position in the enterprises' strategy, supporting both the fundamental evolution of their technology and its effective use in the dynamic global competition of the industries. Thus the two most strongly supported strategic motivations for R&D are 'to respond to intensified competition for technological supremacy in the industry' and 'to shorten lead times for product innovation'. This clearly places R&D and technology at the centre of dynamic competition in the sector, suggesting that firms need to both continually strengthen their core knowledge base and to speed up the commercial application of its new capacities. Another dimension of the competitive use of technology in a fully formulated global strategy is also supported as a key role of R&D, in the form of its application 'to help manufacture products that meet local needs in key markets worldwide'. Thus, as new knowledge brings forth innovative new product concepts, their effective commercial application worldwide may need another level of decentralised R&D facilities in order to

Table 10.3   Central laboratories' evaluation of the R&D strategy of their parent company

	R&D strategies (average response[1])				
	A	B	C	D	E
By industry					
Pharmaceuticals	2.42	2.64	2.23	2.24	2.48
Chemicals	2.58	2.45	2.00	2.12	2.56
Biotechnology	2.67	2.83	2.58	2.25	1.83
Total	2.49	2.57	2.11	2.20	2.53
By home country					
USA	2.72	2.32	1.76	1.80	2.56
Germany	2.00	3.00	3.00	3.00	1.83
UK	2.22	2.60	2.00	2.10	2.63
Other Europe	2.50	3.00	2.50	3.00	3.00
Japan	2.69	2.61	2.71	2.57	2.64
Total	2.49	2.57	2.11	2.20	2.53

Note:

[1] Respondents were asked to evaluate each strategy as either 'a major objective', 'one of our objectives', 'not our objective'. The average response rate was calculated by allocating responses of main objective the value of 3, one of our objectives the value 2, not our objective the value of 1.

R&D strategies

A – to help manufacture products that meet local needs in key markets worldwide.

B – to respond to intensified competition for technological supremacy in the industry.

C – to broaden the horizon of our R&D activity (geographically and/or technologically).

D – to actively seek joint ventures with foreign companies and research institutions.

E – to shorten lead times for product innovation.

Source: G.S. Pooni database.

facilitate the creation of separate variants that can respond to the differential tastes and production conditions of particular geographical segments of global markets. Though clearly less centrally significant than the three facets so far noted, Table 10.3 also suggests that the R&D strategies implemented by the chemicals and allied sector firms include important supporting awareness of the need 'to broaden the horizon of our R&D activity (geographically and/or technologically)' and 'to actively seek joint ventures with foreign companies and research institutions'.

Amongst the separate industries pharmaceuticals provides a fairly conventional set of responses, with a somewhat below average support for current products (role A), and (by comparison with chemicals, amongst the 'traditional' parts of the sector) quite strong pursuit of new research inputs (roles C and D). Despite a strong interest in shortening of product innovation lead times, chemical industry replies otherwise suggest a quite undynamic strategic position for its R&D, with an emphasis on support of current production (role A) and little pursuit of new research scope (C and D). Biotechnology respondents indicated that their R&D plays a very significant role in the support of effective global manufacture of current products, but with little perception of a need to seek a shortening of innovation lead times. Otherwise R&D strategies in the biotechnology firms are decisively motivated by the intensity of technology-based competition in the industry (role B), with this reflected in a very strong desire to widen their research scope (role C) including through international joint ventures (role D).

The R&D perspectives of US respondents (along with their wider strategic positioning as noted in the previous section) appear somewhat undynamic. Whilst there is a strong commitment of R&D to the support of current products, and also an average interest in backing those commercial orientations with shortening innovation lead times, the US enterprises show themselves to be relatively little concerned with the revitalisation of their underlying technological competitiveness and research scope (roles B, C, D in Table 10.3). By contrast, German respondents provide limited R&D support for their current products, or for shortening lead times, which seems to reflect the negative attitude to the vulnerability of their current products and operations which was noted in the previous section. However their very strong replies to the other three roles does suggest a decisive attempt to place R&D in a key regenerative position in their operations (though not through basic research according to replies to the previous question reported in Table 10.2).

The UK companies seem to see their R&D in a relatively dynamic and forward-looking commercial context (strong response to roles B and E less so to role A), but (like US firms) manifest relatively little interest in expanding the range of their research inputs (roles C and D). The Other European firms clearly see R&D as being vital to gaining a new commercial momentum in these industries, emphasising (like UK companies) the need to respond to technology competition and to shorten lead times and (unlike UK and US) they are clearly strongly motivated to pursue these objectives through new sources of inputs. The relatively strong evaluation of all the R&D strategies by Japanese respondents may reflect a perceived need to overcome a technological vulnerability *vis-à-vis* longer-established global competitors in these industries. The especially strong response to the widening of R&D scope would clearly be in line with this perspective.

10.4   ROLES OF OVERSEAS R&D

The previous two sections have shown decisively that firms in the chemical and allied sector clearly perceive the need to articulate their competitive strategies on a global basis, and also see their ability to sustain competitiveness at this level as being driven by a dynamic approach to the creation and use of a technological advantage. The juxtaposition of these core elements in their strategic motivation

suggests an obvious position for an increasingly internationalised position for R&D in such enterprises, with overseas laboratories potentially supporting both the
generation of new technological scope and its effective
commercial application in the process of product development. To investigate this the central labs surveyed were
asked whether or not their company conducted R&D
abroad. Overall 83.9 per cent of respondents said that their
technology operations did include overseas R&D. This was
very pervasive in each of the three industries, with 88.8 per
cent of pharmaceuticals respondents having overseas
R&D, 83.3 per cent of those in biotechnology and 74.4 per
cent in chemicals. By home country of firm, all those from
Other European enterprises had overseas R&D, 92.8 per
cent of those from Japan, 88.0 per cent from USA, 72.7 per
cent from UK, but only 50.0 per cent of those from Germany.

Reflecting the twin strategic forces that drive these companies, their need to incorporate overseas R&D units may
be a response to two different types of factors. Pursuit of
the efficient continual upgrading of the core knowledge
capacities, from which market-leading innovations can
then emerge, may need a number of specialised quality
inputs that can be accessed most effectively from a range
of locations. Thus supply-side research factors may motiv-
ate the use of a dispersed network of labs. However, efficient global application of new products, often driven by a
need for shortened innovation lead times and responsiveness to diverse location-specific product characteristics in
drug and other medical needs, also provides a role for
demand-side influences on overseas R&D, where decentralised labs support the ability to comply with such factors.

To investigate those perspectives the survey asked the
central labs to evaluate four possible reasons for choosing
to conduct some of their groups' R&D abroad. As Table
10.4 shows, the demand-side motivation 'to assist production units to adapt or develop products that meet the needs
of their local markets' emerged as an extremely pervasive
factor that influenced the choice to implement overseas

R&D units. Of the supply-side factors the most prevalent was 'to secure high-quality specialised research personnel'. The strength of this confirms that the technological momentum in these industries enhances the need of leading firms for increasingly specialised knowledge inputs and research abilities, which are then most often effectively accessed through an internationalised network of mutually-supportive R&D units. The relevance of this type of globalised perspective to the technological regeneration of the competitive advantage of these firms is further confirmed by the quite strong influence of the need 'to perform basic research in areas with relevant established specialised research resources and skills'. To further complement the view of local (host-country) competences as an influence on the choice of overseas R&D, there was quite strong support for the relevance of the desire 'to widen the base of our research collaboration with major universities and research institutions' as mediated through such decentralised laboratories.

At the industry level, the clearest pattern of influences on the choice to conduct R&D abroad emerges in biotechnology, where all three supply-side factors are more important than in the other two industries and the demand-side factor is less so. This suggests that in an industry that is at an early stage in its technological trajectory the main preoccupation of its firms is with support of the fast-evolving technology itself, with commitment of resources to the detailed commercial refinement of products being both difficult and unnecessary. With its technological momentum provoking this set of general priorities in biotechnology, overseas R&D there is clearly motivated by its ability to provide specialised inputs into the research process rather than to achieve the detailed commercial refinement of products that are themselves likely to be subject to substantial technological reformulation or obsolescence, due to that high rate of progress of underlying core knowledge in the industry. By contrast in chemicals, with a much more mature technological trajectory, the knowledge base of a large part of the product

range is accepted as relatively stable, so that detailed
support for its effective application becomes a higher
priority in technological operations. Thus the demand-
side influence on overseas R&D is at its strongest in
chemicals, with all supply-side factors of below
average relevance. In terms of the motivations of overseas
R&D, pharmaceuticals takes an intermediateposition,
with much less preoccupation with the demand-side
influence than in chemicals but a greater pursuit of

Table 10.4   Central laboratories' evaluation of reasons for choice to
conduct R&D abroad

| | Reason for choice (*average response*[1]) | | | |
	A	B	C	D
By industry				
Pharmaceuticals	2.32	2.18	2.55	2.31
Chemicals	2.72	2.20	2.40	1.92
Biotechnology	2.25	2.40	2.80	2.60
Total	2.48	2.22	2.53	2.14
By home country				
USA	2.65	1.95	2.39	2.05
Germany	2.67	2.67	3.00	2.33
UK	1.88	2.50	2.37	2.00
Other Europe	2.33	2.66	2.83	1.67
Japan	2.69	2.15	2.61	2.54
Total	2.48	2.22	2.53	2.14

Note:

[1] Respondents were asked to evaluate each reason as either 'very
important', 'of some importance', 'not important'. The average
response rate was calculated by allocating responses of 'very important' the value of 3, 'of some importance' the value of 2 and 'not
important' the value of 1.

Reason why firms choose to conduct R&D abroad

A – to assist production units to adapt or develop products that meet
the needs of their local markets.
B – to perform basic research in areas with relevant established special-
ised research resources and skills.
C – to secure high-quality specialised research personnel.
D – to widen the base of our research collaboration with major uni-
versities and research institutions.
Source: G.S. Pooni database.

specialised research personnel and, especially, willingness to establish collaborations with host-country research institutions.

US firms emerge as the most decisively focused on the use of overseas R&D to support the effective commercial application of their products which, it would appear, mainly emerge from a relatively self-sufficient home-country science capability, with all three supply-side factors of below average influence. Having previously observed the relatively small proportion of German respondents that have overseas R&D, it is interesting to note that those that do seem to find a highly committed and dynamic role for it, with all four influences of above average relevance. By contrast only the accessing of specialised basic research resources (factor B in Table 10.4) is of above average importance for UK respondents, with the demand-side factor of notably limited relevance. The UK companies, therefore, seem relatively confident of home-country competences in terms of both overall technological evolution and product development, but do seek to access some complementary specialised elements of basic research inputs. Other European companies have a strong drive to acquire specialised basic research inputs and high-quality personnel (factors B and C) through overseas R&D, but are relatively reluctant to develop collaborations with host-country institutions through such labs. Apart from a below average desire to access specialised basic research resources, the Japanese respondents rated all the influences as of significant relevance to the decision to have overseas R&D, with a notable enthusiasm for the ability to establish research collaborations with host-country university and other laboratories.

Further elaboration of the motivation for overseas R&D in chemical and allied industries was sought in the survey of parent laboratories through two questions that were directed to those respondents that did not yet have labs abroad. As there were in fact relatively few companies in this position the breakdown of results by industry or home country did not prove meaningful. Nevertheless the overall responses to the factors investigated in the two questions do enhance our broad understanding of the process of R&D decentralisation in globally-competing industries.

The first of this pair of questions asked respondents without overseas labs to evaluate five possible reasons for not conducting R&D abroad. They were invited to rate each reason as either very important, of some importance or of no importance, with average responses [AR] calculated by allocating very important a value of 3, some importance a value of 2 and no importance a value of 1. Of the five offered reasons the two that took most prominence were 'we are satisfied with our home-country technology' with an AR of 2.50, and 'we expect our centrally-designed products to satisfy worldwide market needs' with an AR of 2.46. Both of these clearly reject the supply-side motivation for overseas R&D by embodying a strong belief in the ability of centralised technological competence and creative scope to derive both the knowledge base and commercial product development to underpin the longer-term evolution of global competitiveness. The second of these factors also partially rejects the demand-side motivation for overseas R&D by suggesting that centrally-designed products will be acceptable in a range of potentially differentiated markets worldwide.

A traditionally-argued reason for expecting centralisation of R&D in some industries has been that there might be major economies of scale in research activities, with the implication that there would then be serious costs involved in breaking up and decentralising such programmes. In the survey those firms without overseas R&D were asked to evaluate 'economies of scale prevent fragmentation of R&D efforts' as a contributing factor. The AR of 2.28 did indicate some relevance for this influence. Another traditional argument against overseas R&D has been that decentralised programmes are difficult to coordinate, so that they could engender unnecessarily high costs alongside diminished efficiency of work. However 'concern for management of decentralised R&D' only received an AR of

1.61, suggesting that even central laboratories without overseas R&D perceive few likely management problems being generated by such decentralised approaches. The last possibility is that overseas R&D programmes need extra financing to an extent that compromises their implementation. This seems to be only a moderate constraining factor, with 'we cannot generate adequate funds to support overseas operations' receiving an AR of 1.97.

The second of these questions invited parent laboratories without overseas units to evaluate, as possible reasons for starting such decentralised R&D, the same four influences that were assessed by those that do have facilities abroad (see Table 10.4). Here the demand-side factor 'to assist production units to adapt or develop products that meet the needs of their local market' emerges as decisively the most influential, with an AR of 2.36. By contrast, none of the supply-side factors were perceived as being of substantial relevance to the consideration of possible overseas R&D, with 'to secure high-quality specialised research personnel' receiving an AR of 1.75, 'to perform basic research in areas with relevant established specialised research resources and skills' one of 1.64, and 'to widen the base of our research collaboration with major universities and research institutions' only 1.44. This supports the perspective derived from the first of these two questions in suggesting that some central labs may still tend to have a somewhat myopic view of competence, persisting in perceiving their own research scope as fully adequate to underpin their group's technological evolution and only worrying about a certain vulnerability in their ability to respond to different market needs in overseas operations. This may also be compatible with the substantially greater evaluation of the supply-side factors by those central respondents with overseas labs (Table 10.4), in supporting a view of overseas R&D as an evolutionary process. Thus labs that are set up to mainly support the application of existing technology (adapting existing products) may then be able to expand their creative scope in response to both an improved knowledge of local market needs and, in particular, the availability of the distinctive specialised host-country scientific and research capacities. In this light as overseas labs become more firmly embedded in their host-country technological environment they can then respond to and assimilate particular elements from its distinctive competences to build up their own capacities and, therefore, their position in their group's research network.

10.5   FACTORS INFLUENCING R&D LOCATION IN CHEMICAL AND ALLIED INDUSTRIES

To further extend our perceptions of the globalisation of strategic perspectives on R&D in chemical and allied industry firms the parent lab respondents were asked to evaluate the relevance of six reasons for their decision to locate labs in each of the five countries/regions in which they possessed such facilities. Tables 10.5(a) to 10.5(f) summarise the evidence derived from this question.

The first factor evaluated in this question was 'the existence of particular national research and technological expertise'. This suggests that firms may choose to locate labs in particular countries because the distinctive areas of specialised expertise available there can make a valuable contribution to the scope of their current R&D programmes. The overall AR of 2.31 (Table 10.5(a)) suggests that this type of supply-side attribute is very often a significant factor in choosing the locations of R&D units in this sector. Biotechnology firms emerge as the most responsive to this characteristic of national science capacities, reflecting the pursuit of radical and idiosyncratic inputs at the volatile and speculative early phase of the industry's technological trajectory. From the same viewpoint the fact that the lowest response to this factor came from chemical companies can then be interpreted as reflecting a position as the most technologically mature of the three industries.

When we turn to home countries, firms from Japan and Other European countries emerge as the most strongly responsive to the relevance of this first influence. Interestingly respondents from both of these origins provide a very low rating for their home countries with regard to this characteristic (as, indeed, is also the broad evaluation of these countries by USA, UK and German respondents). In response to this assessment of notable home- country vulnerability in what they clearly perceive as a crucial element in articulating the technological dimension in their competitive evolution, these firms then generally provide a very strong evaluation of the importance of this factor in choosing to locate labs in USA, UK and Germany. German firms also rate the importance of this location characteristic relatively highly but, compared with Other European and Japanese companies, assess its availability at home at a much more considerable level. Though this confidence leads to a very limited influence for this factor on German companies' R&D elsewhere in Europe, it is decisively significant for their operations in the USA and is also rated relatively highly (compared with firms from other countries) in Japan. Generally US firms have a rather low evaluation of such distinctive elements in research and technological scope as reasons for carrying out R&D in particular locations. This is compatible with the already apparent view that US enterprises in the chemicals and allied sector seem to be currently more motivated to use R&D in the enhanced application of existing technology through the development of new products from it, or the improvement of established ones, than in generating substantial new scientific knowledge that might be relevant to their longer-term competitive revitalisation. The low overall evaluation of this influence in UK companies' R&D-location decisions is a reflection of its limited relevance to labs elsewhere in Europe (including Germany) and in Japan. By contrast, the factor is strongly influential for home-country R&D operations and in UK firms' labs in USA.

Table 10.5(a)   Evaluation by central laboratories of reasons for locating R&D laboratories in particular locations: the existence of particular national research and technological expertise

	Host country (location) of R&D labs (average response[1])					
	USA	*Germany*	*UK*	*Other Europe*	*Japan*	*Total*
By industry						
Pharmaceuticals	2.57	2.47	2.64	2.22	2.12	2.41
Chemicals	2.36	2.44	2.20	1.91	1.95	2.25
Biotechnology	3.00	3.00	2.80	2.33	1.83	2.50
Total	2.50	2.45	2.48	2.10	1.94	2.31
By home country						
USA	2.11	2.08	2.36	2.07	2.00	2.13
Germany	3.00	2.67	1.67	1.66	2.33	2.27
UK	2.60	1.80	2.60	2.00	1.00	2.06
Other Europe	2.33	3.00	2.50	1.80	2.00	2.41
Japan	2.93	2.91	2.75	2.38	1.91	2.42
Total	2.50	2.45	2.48	2.10	1.94	2.31

Note:

1. Respondents were asked to evaluate, for each relevant host country, a reason as either 'very important', 'of some importance', 'of no importance'. The average response was then calculated by allocating responses of very important the value of 3, of some importance the value of 2, of no importance the value of 1.

Source: G.S. Pooni database.

Overall, this type of distinctive research and technological expertise is marginally most significant as a motivation for locating labs in the USA, with German, Japanese and UK companies all finding particularly strong reasons for building such competences into their global R&D portfolios. Notably, it is the US companies themselves that rate the factor lowest, though this is mainly a reflection of its generally small role amongst their current technological imperatives rather than an explicit rejection of US capacity. The UK closely matches the US in the overall assessment of this type of competence. Indeed US firms provide an evaluation of UK capacity in this characteristic that somewhat belies their normal disregard of its relevance.

By contrast German companies are notably unenthusiastic about the UK's capacity to provide them with aspects of distinctive expertise that are relevant to their needs. Germany itself also rates highly as a location attracting R&D through this characteristic of its science capacity though, in a remarkable mirror-image of the earlier result, it is here that UK firms are least impressed in this respect. It may be that if the UK and Germany have distinctively different traditions in terms of their areas of particular expertise in chemical and allied industry related knowledge, and their firms have then formulated the needs of their ongoing technology trajectories in especially strong reflection of their home-country characteristics, then the strongly different needs and competences implied could generate the type of 'mutual-alienation' that is suggested. Part of such differences may be indicated by the generally higher evaluation of pharmaceutical expertise, and the lower rating of chemicals, in the UK compared with Germany. As already noted Japan and the Other European countries are generally less highly rated in terms of the availability of these types of distinctive expertise, with both vulnerable in chemicals and Japan also notably weak in biotechnology.

The second of this group of location factors relating to R&D facilities was 'the concentration of scientists, engineers and technologists in the area'. This indicates strong generalised technological competences in a country, which can give firms confidence to embark on knowledge-related operations there, rather than reflecting particular elements of specialised expertise as would be embodied in the first factor. Though this characteristic is still likely to provide significant support to the implementation of the types of precompetitive (basic and applied) research that is especially attracted by the first factor, it can also provide an essential basis for the ambitious, but less scientifically distinctive, technological operations involved in product development and the commercial application of knowledge. Perhaps reflecting its relevance to a wider range of technological activities this second factor received an overall AR of 2.44 (Table 10.5b), somewhat above that of the first.

Once again this supply-side attribute is of greatest relevance to location decisions in biotechnology laboratories and least so in chemicals. Japanese firms emerge as most likely to give consideration to this factor in their R&D location decisions and, despite a relatively high evaluation of its availability in their home country, it clearly provides a major influence on their labs in overseas countries. US firms are revealed as notably more responsive to this supply-side factor than they are to the first. Bearing in mind that we believe this generalised competence has more relevance to operations involving the effective commercial application of technology than the more distinctive elements of the first, its stronger endorsement by US enterprises is then compatible with the suggestion that their main current preoccupation is in this area rather than with the generation of distinctive new knowledge. By contrast, Other Europe firms are somewhat less concerned with this supply-side characteristic than with the former one. This may reflect a rather diminished sense of their vulnerability with regard to this facet of technological competence, with this perhaps also indicated by its relatively high evaluation in these Other European countries by US and Japanese enterprises. German firms generally have only a moderate interest in this factor, whilst UK companies are least reactive to it, with a high regard for home-country capability reflected in limited response to it elsewhere (except in the USA).

The third reason for siting labs in particular locations was described as 'the strategic importance of corporate presence in particular local markets'. This reflects the relevance of an R&D facility within the functional scope of those subsidiaries that represent an MNE's strategic presence in key markets. Though this is most likely to have a strong demand-side motivation, in the form of helping these subsidiaries to use group technology most effectively to meet the needs of markets that are vital components of an overall programme of global competitiveness, it may also encompass the supply-side motivation with such strategic subsidiaries detecting and accessing the types of local research capacity that can be used to enhance the group's overall knowledge scope. The overall AR of 2.40 for this factor (Table 10.5c) places it amongst the most relevant reasons for choice of particular R&D locations.

Table 10.5(b)   Evaluation by central laboratories of reasons for locating R&D laboratories in particular locations: the concentration of scientists, engineers and technologists in the area

| | Host country (location) of R&D lab (average response) | | | | | |
	USA	Germany	UK	Other Europe	Japan	Total
Total						
Pharmaceuticals	2.52	2.40	2.61	2.39	2.06	2.41
Chemicals	2.52	2.44	2.25	2.47	2.21	2.32
Biotechnology	2.90	2.88	2.71	2.71	2.00	2.69
Total	2.53	2.52	2.45	2.50	2.16	2.44
By home country						
USA	2.40	2.46	2.18	2.33	2.07	2.31
Germany	3.00	2.67	2.33	2.00	2.67	2.27
UK	2.60	1.80	2.67	1.67	1.50	2.19
Other Europe	2.50	3.00	2.33	2.00	2.00	2.29
Japan	2.77	2.50	2.67	2.92	2.25	2.59
Total	2.53	2.52	2.45	2.50	2.16	2.44

Differences between industries in their overall responses to this factor are very small. For biotechnology this represents a modest retreat from its prevalent position for the two previous (more decisively supply-side) influences. This would be in line with the view that the dominant technological imperative in biotechnology firms is at present much more concerned with securing a strong position in the creation of core technology relevant to the sector than with the application of their current knowledge to particular geographic market segments. By contrast, this factor achieves somewhat greater relative prominence for chemicals, supporting the alternative perspective of a prevalent preoccupation with the effective commercial use of a fairly mature and stable core technology. The strong evaluation of this factor in pharmaceuticals firms may reflect the presence of both the supply-side and demand-side aspects of technological activity in strategic subsidiaries in the industry, with their operations not only helping to access valuable local research and knowledge competences, but also playing a significant commercial role in applying technology as effectively as possible to the subsidiaries' markets.

This factor is of strongest relevance in the R&D location decisions of US firms, which provides a very decisive contrast with their relatively low evaluation of the two previously discussed influences. This reinforces the view that US chemicals and allied enterprises tend at present to be more concerned to use their R&D operations to support the optimal commercial use in global competition of their existing technology than to seek strong precompetitive research capacity in order to enrich this core knowledge scope. The position of R&D in supporting the operations of strategic subsidiaries also emerges strongly in both UK and Other European firms. In these cases it may be that the role encompasses a wider technological dynamism than for the US companies, perhaps not only supporting the shortening of innovation lead times as a commercial objective but also playing some role in the widening of their knowledge perspectives that is often sought by these companies (especially those from Other Europe). For German firms a strong endorsement for this motivation in their home-country operations, and in USA and Japan, contrast with a much less strong position for it in the UK or Other Europe, which may perhaps reflect the retention of key strategic activity for Europe in Germany. Japanese enterprises are least likely to see this type of motive affecting their overseas R&D, especially in USA, UK and Germany (where strong responses to the previous supply-side factor may suggest a tendency to embody those capacities in labs that are independent of other strategic presence of the group in these markets).

We observed earlier that most of the companies in the survey had production operations in most of the key

Table 10.5(c)   Evaluation by central laboratories of reasons for
locating R&D laboratories in particular locations:
(the strategic importance of coprorate presence in particular
local markets

	Host country (location) of R&D labs (average response)					
	USA	Germany	UK	Other Europe	Japan	Total
By industry						
Pharmaceuticals	2.35	2.56	2.47	2.53	2.47	2.49
Chemicals	2.38	2.50	2.14	2.43	1.95	2.40
Biotechnology	2.43	2.33	2.71	2.17	2.67	2.47
Total	2.38	2.44	2.40	2.46	2.45	2.40
By home country						
USA	2.72	2.70	2.41	2.78	2.46	2.63
Germany	2.67	2.67	1.33	2.00	2.67	2.27
UK	2.57	2.40	2.71	2.75	2.33	2.50
Other Europe	1.67	3.00	2.50	2.00	3.00	2.47
Japan	2.07	2.08	2.08	2.30	2.42	2.19
Total	2.38	2.44	2.40	2.46	2.45	2.40

market areas, suggesting the strong presence of the forms
of strategic interdependency that are typical of a globally-
oligopolistic industry. We have also observed an extensive
commitment to internationally-decentralised R&D as a
part of the way in which these enterprises approach various aspects of their technological evolution. It therefore
becomes logical to speculate as to whether the oligopol-
istic-interactive 'mindset' of leading players in the chemicals and allied sector extends into R&D location decision
making. Thus it could be the case that some labs are set-up
in particular locations, not because of a strong independent
positive evaluation by their enterprise of other objective
motives for doing so, but instead because a number of their
leading competitors have implemented research facilities
there. Fear that some (perhaps not clearly perceived) attributes of the location may then contribute to a source of
technological leadership for the first movers may lead other
firms to match them with new labs of their own. Therefore
respondents were asked to evaluate 'the high level of competitors R&D activity in that location' as a reason for

extending the geographical scope of their technology programmes. The overall AR of 2.37 (Table 10.5d) suggests a
clear presence for this type of behaviour in the technological positioning of leading chemical and allied firms.

Table 10.5(d)   Evaluation by central laboratories of reasons for
locating R&D laboratories in particular locations:
the high level of competitors' R&D activity in that location

	Host country (location) of R&D labs (average response)					
	USA	Germany	UK	Other Europe	Japan	Total
By industry						
Pharmaceuticals	2.33	2.20	2.53	2.22	2.23	2.31
Chemicals	2.34	2.22	2.24	2.22	2.00	2.28
Biotechnology	3.00	2.55	2.71	2.71	2.17	2.67
Total	2.35	2.28	2.41	2.29	2.09	2.37
By home country						
USA	2.19	2.00	2.16	2.13	1.92	2.09
Germany	2.00	1.67	1.00	2.00	2.00	1.86
UK	2.20	1.60	2.20	1.00	1.67	1.81
Other Europe	2.00	3.00	2.50	1.47	2.50	2.14
Japan	2.92	2.42	2.75	2.76	2.33	2.65
Total	2.35	2.28	2.41	2.29	2.09	2.37

The response to location of competitors R&D is most
notable amongst biotechnology firms, especially in their
operations in USA, UK, Other Europe and Germany. This
is clearly in line with the view that in biotechnology the
generation of new knowledge through quite basic or
applied research (strong response to the two supply-side
factors) is seen as perhaps the most crucial level of current
competitive activity, so that close observation of, and often
response to, the siting of rivals' R&D can influence the
direction of extension of a firm's own programmes. This
behaviour pattern is also of quite extensive relevance in
pharmaceuticals (especially in the UK) and chemicals.
Japanese firms reveal a consistently above average
responsiveness to this pattern of behaviour in R&D

location. Amongst these firms, that are often relative new-
comers to global competition in these industries and who
have been revealed earlier as having a very strong motivation to seek new sources of knowledge and research inputs,
the response to high levels of leading firm R&D in a
particular location may be more as an indicator of its
quality and scope rather than as a competitive move
against the existing incumbents. By contrast where firms
have a low reaction to this form of location behaviour (e.g.
those from UK, Germany and to some extent USA) it may
be that a relatively well-established commitment to dispersed R&D has led to a balanced global programme
which is now articulated in response to an understanding
of the real virtues of various locations, and is relatively
immune to any desire to react to less clearly comprehended
moves by rivals.

The next factor evaluated in terms of its influence on
R&D location was described as 'to provide technical support to other parts of the group'. This would be most likely
to cover the rather *ad hoc* provision of information and
problem solving advice to other MNE-group operations on
a relatively informal basis, rather than being encompassed
within a systematic ongoing relationship. Table 10.5e
reveals that this function does take a quite significant
position within the scope of many chemicals and allied
industry R&D units. The table also shows that this type
of technological support activity is generally most prominent in the parent company R&D facilities of these enterprises, with the home-country evaluation being above
average for all countries/areas. This perhaps reflects the
fact that the mainly *ad hoc* nature of the support required
may mean that the central laboratory, with probably the
broadest overview and understanding of group technology,
is most likely to provide adequate answers (or at least
provide the most logical starting point for a process of
investigation). Nevertheless some overseas labs do also
carry out this role to a significant degree, perhaps indicating cases where a very distinctive knowledge competence
within the group is accessed to provide support to opera-

tions beyond those with which it has a more dedicated and systematic relationship.

Table 10.5(e)   Evaluation by central laboratories of reasons for locating R&D laboratories in particular locations: to provide technical support to other parts of the group

	Host country (location) of R&D labs (average response)					
	USA	Germany	UK	Other Europe	Japan	Total
By industry						
Pharmaceuticals	2.45	2.27	2.28	2.27	1.82	2.28
Chemicals	2.22	2.00	1.40	2.33	2.38	2.22
Biotechnology	2.57	2.50	2.28	2.67	2.50	2.52
Total	2.36	2.24	2.09	2.36	2.18	2.27
By home country						
USA	2.47	2.18	2.23	2.33	2.14	2.29
Germany	2.33	2.67	1.67	2.67	2.33	2.53
UK	2.67	1.60	2.33	2.00	1.00	2.11
Other Europe	2.00	3.00	2.83	3.00	2.00	2.57
Japan	2.23	1.83	1.83	2.15	2.38	2.13
Total	2.36	2.24	2.09	2.36	2.18	2.27

The presence of this support role is strongest and most widely pervasive in the operations of biotechnology industry laboratories. This is likely to be another reflection of the volatility of the core knowledge base of companies in an industry that is at an early exploratory phase of its technological trajectory. Thus, with the essential technology of biotechnology enterprises still relatively speculative, strong mutually-supportive associations between group labs are necessary to define and refine the MNE's overall R&D programme, to delineate the evolving position of individual research units within it, and to facilitate an unusually high level of knowledge transfer. In addition, the nature of the unresolved commercial potentials of the industry at this phase requires a particularly intense and direct communication between the often quite pure-research-oriented labs and other functions in the groups. German and Other European enterprises appear relatively likely to use labs to support other parts of their group's activity within Europe (with the exception of German labs in the UK), but the practice has emerged somewhat less strongly in their operations in US and Japan. By contrast, UK chemicals and allied companies seem to rely on their home-country labs for technical support to their operations in Europe, with the role most extensively developed elsewhere within their US facilities. Such wider support activities are so far relatively rare in the mainly recently created overseas labs of Japanese companies in the sector.

The last of these R&D location influences was 'to forestall entry of another firm', indicating the possibility that a strong pre-emptive move into a particular technological environment could deter rivals from seeking comparable benefits within the host country and thus coopt for a MNE a distinctive source of potential competitive strength. The overall AR (Table 10.5f) of 1.33 clearly shows that this form of technological strategic positioning does not play a major role in the R&D location patterns of chemical and allied enterprises. It is, however, perceived as distinctively relevant to the way in which Japanese (especially biotechnology) firms feel they can defend their position in their home country. Elsewhere Other European firms find relatively strong relevance for this motivation in their US, German and UK labs. At the industry level biotechnology firms seem most likely to find some scope for this behavioural factor, indicating that where industry technology is still very speculative and volatile even a temporary monopoly of a distinctive source of knowledge inputs may be worth pursuing within the strategic motivation of R&D expansion.

10.6 SOURCES OF OVERSEAS LABORATORIES' R&D FUNDING

An organisational issue that also reflects on the strategic motivations for the globalisation of R&D programmes in chemical and allied industry firms is the sources through which their overseas labs receive their funding. In the survey a question asked of respondents was to evaluate the importance of five potential sources of funding for their overseas R&D units. The results are summarised in Table 10.6.

The first of these funding sources was 'corporate (group) funds'. This form of central financial support for decentralised R&D activity emerged as the strongest of the five sources. This is clearly compatible with the view of the chemical and allied sector as one where leading firms retain a strong awareness of the need to reinforce their underlying group-level technology capacity and find great value in decentralised R&D operations in pursuing this objective. Where overseas labs provide such precompetitive research inputs in support of programmes aimed to enrich the group's overall technology trajectory it is usually necessary for this element in their work to be centrally funded from corporate-level resources. This type of funding is most decisively the predominant one in biotechnology.

Table 10.5(f) Evaluation by central laboratories of reasons for locating R&D laboratories in particular locations: to forestall entry of another firm

	Host country (location) of R&D labs (average response)					
	USA	Germany	UK	Other Europe	Japan	Total
By industry						
Pharmaceuticals	1.43	1.20	1.41	1.11	1.65	1.36
Chemicals	1.28	1.11	1.10	1.17	1.90	1.27
Biotechnology	1.43	1.00	1.71	1.00	2.33	1.62
Total	1.31	1.14	1.29	1.10	1.96	1.33
By home country						
USA	1.11	1.20	1.18	1.21	1.21	1.18
Germany	1.00	1.00	1.00	1.00	1.00	1.00
UK	1.20	1.40	1.40	1.00	1.00	1.24
Other Europe	2.16	2.00	1.67	1.00	1.00	1.93
Japan	1.30	1.00	1.25	1.07	2.53	1.44
Total	1.31	1.14	1.29	1.10	1.96	1.33

Thus in firms where both the underlying knowledge and the nature of its commercial application remain in a state of considerable flux, their overseas R&D labs are likely to be predominantly responsible to central decision making (it is too early for them to establish stable supporting relationships with other group operations) and thus are extensively centrally funded. Though still of substantial relevance this funding source is of least significance in chemicals, in line with the perception that it is there that technology is most mature and least priority is placed on precompetitive work. As reflected in funding patterns UK, Other European and Japanese MNEs appear to be more notably oriented to use of decentralised R&D in support of centrally-motivated strategic technology programmes.

Another, perhaps somewhat more *ad hoc*, way in which overseas labs can support a quite wide level of technological ambition in their group is by 'undertaking contract research for operating divisions'. Table 10.6 shows that funding earned in this manner is overall the second most important source in these labs. The current lack of clear definition of strategic and commercial purpose in many biotechnology firms probably accounts for the difficulty in articulating this type of technical support as a role played by decentralised labs, whilst the more coherent organisation structures in place in chemicals and pharmaceuticals do allow it to emerge quite strongly there. It is in German and Other European enterprises that labs have the strongest propensity to receive funding at the operating division level.

In the context of decentralised R&D as part of a MNE's approach to global competitiveness it is very plausible that such labs could work directly with particular production subsidiaries in order to help them apply group technology effectively. In this way 'an associated production subsidiary's own funds' represents a potential source of finance for these R&D units. In fact this emerged as a relatively limited funding source, again indicating that the prevalent motivation of these labs in chemical and allied MNEs is to support a wider strategic imperative. Funding from an associated production subsidiary does emerge as decisively strongest in US companies, strongly confirming the view

derived earlier that in these MNEs the current technological priorities do seem to be much more with the effective
use of a relatively stable knowledge base than with the
pursuit of new sources of technology.

The remaining sources of funding take account of the
possibility that the knowledge and competences available
within the labs of MNEs could allow them to earn supplementary income by providing services to clients outside
their own group. However, as Table 10.6 reveals, neither
'undertaking contract research for external clients' nor
'conducting analysis and tests for external clients' actually
took very strong positions in the finance secured by the
labs. Generally biotechnology and pharmaceutical labs are

Table 10.6   Sources of funding of R&D in overseas laboratories

| | Source of funding (average response[1]) | | | | |
	A	B	C	D	E
By industry					
Pharmaceuticals	2.57	2.33	2.08	1.44	1.39
Chemicals	2.35	2.29	2.05	1.09	1.09
Biotechnology	2.70	1.71	1.88	1.67	1.33
Total	2.46	2.27	1.94	1.32	1.24
By home country					
USA	2.11	2.18	2.42	1.06	1.12
Germany	2.00	2.67	1.00	1.67	1.33
UK	2.63	2.17	1.17	1.83	1.50
Other Europe	3.00	2.83	1.67	1.50	1.17
Japan	2.77	2.27	1.44	1.33	1.33
Total	2.46	2.27	1.94	1.32	1.24

Note:

[1] Respondents were asked to evaluate each source of funding as either a
major source, a minor source, not a source. The average response rate
was calculated by allocating responses of major source a value of 3,
minor source a value of 2 and not a source a value of 1.

Funding source

A – from corporate (group) funds.
B – undertaking contract research for operating divisions.
C – an associated production subsidiary's own funds.
D – undertaking contract research for external clients.
E – conducting analysis and tests for external clients.

more likely to operate in this way than are those in chemicals, suggesting that clients for such services are more likely to exist in areas where the technology is less mature.

10.7 CONCLUSIONS

The evidence reviewed has confirmed the industries of the chemicals and allied sector as being ones where clearly globalised perspectives on competition continue to need to be backed up by a strong commitment to R&D, as both a means of ensuring the effective commercial application of existing technology and also of regenerating this knowledge base itself as a source of sustained future competitiveness. The notable commitment to overseas R&D as a key element in the strategic evolution of these companies was then revealed as serving to support both elements of their technological objectives, by assisting in product development for distinctive segments of the global market and by accessing original research inputs in particular host countries. However, as anticipated, the positioning of overseas R&D units (in terms of the roles played and the influences to which they responded) varied according to industry and home country of the parent MNE.

Biotechnology emerged as the most distinctive case, with the technological imperatives of firms decisively focused on articulating responses to the dynamic and volatile nature of the industry's core knowledge. Competitiveness appeared to be pursued through attempts to detect, access and harness developments in this core technology itself, whilst the uncertainty generated by its volatility and speed of evolution seemed to diminish the potential returns to committing major technological resources to support of product development and marketing. The strong commitment to R&D that emerges from these imperatives in biotechnology was found to include a significant overseas component, which encompassed a notably strong motivation to access particular types and qualities of knowledge inputs alongside a relatively low orientation to support current market- focused activities. Thus the overseas R&D of these firms appears to fully reflect the central elements of their technological momentum, by helping them to keep up with the volatile core knowledge itself rather than by emphasising support for the detailed commercial refinement of current products.

By contrast with the biotechnology companies' necessarily aggressive and positive reaction to the technological incoherence of their emergent industry, those from chemicals seemed to be more driven by a defensive response to a mature and stabilised knowledge base. Generally their R&D priorities seemed to be to support current products rather than to pursue major elements of new knowledge in order to underwrite long-term evolution. In line with this chemical companies' overseas R&D focused mainly on support of current production and marketing operations, with relatively limited interest in seeking access to the specific types of technology inputs that could invigorate precompetitive research. The attitude of pharmaceutical companies was distinctly more positive, with an apparent confidence in the state of the competitiveness in their current fields of activity not precluding support for the pursuit of expansions in technological scope and new commercial horizons. Thus, by comparison with chemicals, R&D in pharmaceutical enterprises was somewhat more oriented towards the acquisition of distinctive new knowledge inputs and rather less towards support for current products. In line with this overseas R&D in pharmaceutical companies reflected a mixture of demand-side and supply-side influences that placed it between the dynamic precompetitive-research-oriented biotechnology companies and the mature market-focused chemicals enterprises.

US firms in these chemicals and allied sectors seem mainly content to continue their growth within their existing profiles, with little apparent pursuit of major new dimensions to their activities either in terms of industrial or geographical diversification. Within this constrained context their overseas R&D, reflecting the predominant motivations of their current technological ambitions, is most clearly oriented towards the support of the commercial application of established products, with a limited response to the supply-side factors indicating little interest in using such labs to help enhance their wider knowledge base. Though UK companies share with their US counterparts an apparent preference to remain within their established lines of operation, they do seem considerably more actively concerned to ensure a dynamic momentum in these areas and embody a relatively strong commitment to basic research to underwrite this objective. With these UK chemicals and allied enterprises manifesting quite a strong degree of confidence in their home-country creative capacity the most prevalent role for their overseas R&D units seems to be to pursue specialised basic research inputs that can complement the scope of their parent companies' competences.

By comparison with US and UK companies those from Germany appear to suggest a sense of surprising vulnerability in their current lines of development, and in several respects indicate rather negative and defensive postures. However, whilst their R&D priorities reflect this vulnerability in terms of limited support for current products, other elements are rather more indicative of attempts to use such programmes as part of a regenerative process. Also, whereas overseas R&D is less prevalent in these German enterprises compared to those from other home countries, where it occurs it does seem to both seek to harness distinctive host-country capacities to the regenerative process and also to provide some support for current products. The respondents from Other European countries seem strongly motivated by the need to find new sources of commercial opportunity. In this R&D is seen as central to gaining a new commercial momentum, and the enterprises from these countries seem more motivated than, for example, those from the UK to seek new sources of inputs to achieve this. In line with this their overseas R&D is notably driven by supply-side influences and by the pursuit of specialised inputs.

Finally, Japanese companies show a clear support for the continued growth of their current lines of operations, but also demonstrate an active pursuit of additional sources of dynamism. Thus their R&D programmes seem to both provide support for the application of existing knowledge and also to seek to generate new sources of forward-looking technology. Apart from a, perhaps surprising, below average interest in basic research Japanese MNEs' overseas R&D units respond to all other factors, with a relatively strong interest in research collaborations with host- country institutions.

Notes

1. Florida and Kenney (1994); Hakanson and Nobel (1993a,b); Howells and Wood (1993); Pearce (1989); Pearce and Singh (1992a,b); Papanastassiou (1995); Pearce and Papanastassiou (1996).
2. Valuable earlier contributions to understanding decentralised R&D in these sectors include Burstall and Dunning (1985) and Taggart (1989, 1991).

Part IV
Policy Conclusions

11 Industrial Policy, MNEs and National Technology

The papers in this book are about a

> world in which comparative advantage, international competitiveness, and the international division of labour results in large measure from corporate strategies and national policies rather than from natural endowments. (Gilpin 1988, p. 164).

> In this world the scope for competition is no longer limited by national boundaries so that, at the firm level, it becomes a matter of 'internalising on a worldwide scale key assets such as knowledge, finance, production experience and market access, that can lead to the development and to the effective commercialisation of a wide variety of products and services. (Ernst and O'Connor 1989, p. 25)

Countries now create rather than inherit comparative advantage. This creation and competitive application of comparative advantage is achieved through collaborations with firms. However, for a particular country, the firms that contribute to the formulation of its comparative advantage need not be uninational companies. Both the home-country operations of indigenous MNEs and the activity of local subsidiaries of foreign MNEs are likely to be involved in the creative processes that help generate national comparative advantage.

This then parallels the new global creative horizons of the contemporary MNE. For these companies the sources of competitiveness no longer emerge from a uninational background, but from creative interdependencies with the knowledge traditions and current research scope of many countries. The position of technology in these views of created comparative advantage also has resonances in its increasingly active position in recent theories of international trade and factor movements.

The Heckscher–Ohlin model, which has served as 'the dominant model of comparative advantage in modern economics' (Södersten and Reed 1994, p. 41) assumes that countries have identical technologies for the products traded (so that trade patterns reflect national endowments of other factors, e.g. capital and labour). One way of interpreting the assumption would be that if new technology did emerge in an isolated location (country or firm) it would diffuse instantly to all potential users of it. A further implication of that is that no one would have any motive to invest in creation of new technology. Yet the twentieth century has seen increasing firm-level commitment to R&D (aimed at product innovation), and countries increasingly have committed themselves to technological education and support of scientific research.

Once technological change was accepted as a continuous and differentiated process there was obvious scope for it to emerge as an explanation of trade. This was formalised in the imitation- gap theory of Posner (1961). Thus, provided the demand for the product diffused internationally quicker than the technology underpinning the ability to produce it, the country innovating it would have a period as a unique source of exports. Building on this perception the product-cycle theorists (Vernon 1966 Hirsch 1967) demonstrated the ways in which, once a technology did begin to diffuse internationally (i.e. Posner's imitation gap began to close), the firms responsible for the original innovation would initiate overseas production in order to defend their market lead. This overseas production might occur first in other high-income markets where demand for the product was already strong (stage two of product cycle) and then, in pursuit of cost-effective production, in low cost economies (stage three).

As we have already noted in Chapter 1, once the overseas production units that emerge in the fashion explained by the product cycle have fully assimilated their position in both their firm (which will now have become an MNE) and their host country, they have great potential to *inter alia* alter the positioning of technology as a competitive resource (of firms and countries) in the contemporary global economy. At the very least, such overseas subsidiaries offer the scope to speed up the diffusion of established commercial technology and then perhaps, more ambitiously, to involve decentralised facilities in the innovation process itself. Beyond that, MNEs may deepen their interdependencies with host-country science bases (often through stand-alone R&D units, rather than production subsidiaries) in pursuit of more radical progress in core technologies.

These various theoretical perspectives on the emergence of technology as a distinctive factor in understanding the main determining forces of the contemporary international economy have clear resonances in those strategic developments in MNEs that have provided the main themes of this book. One dimension of this can be seen if we readopt two assumptions implied in the discussion of Chapter 1, namely that MNEs possess a very large proportion of the current stock of commercially-relevant technology and that another of their key ownership advantages is an ability to organise the effective international and intragroup transfer of such knowledge. If this is so then MNEs are likely to seek to apply this technology in locations where the relevant complementary productive factors are available in the most cost-effective forms. By speeding up the international diffusion of standardised technology in this way MNEs could be interpreted as taking us at least part of the way towards the relevant assumption of the Heckscher–Ohlin theory, with the concomitant implication that the dominant sources of comparative advantage of host countries again become the traditional static ones (e.g. homogeneous labour and raw materials). This efficiency-seeking mode of behaviour can be related both to the third stage of the original product cycle and to the presence of rationalised product subsidiaries in the strategic portfolio of contemporary MNEs (see Chapter 2).

However, whilst this type of behaviour may be a necessary facet of the current competitiveness of MNEs and of the industrialisation processes of certain countries, it is unlikely to be sufficient to allow the achievement of the wider aims of either party. MNEs will seek not to just apply their current stock of technology effectively but also to extend its scope and regenerate the science that underpins it. Countries need to move beyond a technologically-dependent use of cost-effective sources of comparative advantage towards the generation of elements of distinctive indigenous knowledge scope and their embodiment in higher-value-added activity. As our discussion of the process of creative transition (Chapter 3) has argued the achievement of part of these more dynamic and scope-enhancing aims can benefit from a deeper interdependence between MNEs and host countries. This can be embodied in regional product mandate subsidiaries which apply local research, marketing and managerial competences to the development of distinctive new products (responsive to the needs of their own market areas) using new group-level technology. By creating a set of distinctive variants of a new product, each of which responds to a key segment of the world market, this globalised approach to innovation eliminates the imitation lag and assists in the operationalisation of host-country technology and research capacity as a source of comparative advantage.

A further deepening of the technological interdependence between host countries and MNEs can occur when the latter set up international interdependent laboratories (Chapter 2). These carry out basic or applied (precompetitive) research embodying distinctive local competences, which reflect the stronger elements of the national technological tradition, but as part of wider international programmes that reflect the needs of the MNE group. Though the activity of these labs is unlikely to reinforce the more immediately commercially-applicable comparative advantage of the host country it may build on the scope of the local science base in ways that do eventually support the competitiveness of indigenous industry.

The re-emergence of technology as an element in theoretical perceptions of the international economy, and its embodiment in new conceptions of created comparative advantage, do not reduce the validity of concern with more traditional elements of comparative advantage. This is, of course, especially true of labour. Thus the ways in which national policies pursue competitiveness in the global economy still need to be compatible with the quantitative aim of full employment. What the new viewpoints emphasise is that the dynamic aspects of global competition make it possible, indeed necessary, for national policies to be actively concerned with the qualitative aspects of the factors (again notably labour) that are embodied in comparative advantage. The importance of national support for the technological and skill base is crucial in this context. How this base is operationalised by enterprises for competitiveness in the global economy is then also vital. We have been concerned here with the ways in which foreign firms can be involved in both the longer-term evolution of a national technology base and also with its shorter-term commercial application.

We have argued that whereas MNEs fully understand the need to produce current generations of products as cost effectively as possible (and create international supply networks to achieve this), they also know that the evolution of better products (more appropriate to particular nation's/ region's tastes) and of innovative new generations of products, is central to their long term growth and survival. International programmes operating through creative product-development subsidiaries and decentralised R&D units are crucial to this forward-looking phase of MNEs' activity. National industrial strategies therefore have to recognise the need for a longer-term view of their own industrial evolution, and should understand the ways in which MNEs can support this wider creative perspective. It can be argued that an obsession with attracting MNEs through low labour costs misunderstands, in a potentially very harmful manner, both the true meaning of a national competitive strategy and the needs of contemporary MNEs and therefore the nature of the contribution these companies can make to the *growth* of national competitiveness (rather than just the use of its current comparative advantage).

These policy dimensions may be illustrated through the background to the rise of Japan and the newly industrialised countries (NICs) as sources of globally-competitive enterprises. It can be suggested that the true nature of the success of these countries, and of their challenge to older industrial economies, is often misinterpreted. The decisive factor in their strategic evolution is, ultimately, not their initial success as cost-effective producers but the way that they used the resources and assets created in this phase to move forward into higher-value-added operations through investment in education, training and research. There seems to be a danger that some established industrial countries are articulating too much of their response to the competitive challenge of the NICs in terms of the past (low-cost) profile of these countries, rather than in terms of an understanding of the ways in which they have made the transition to quality- and innovation-based sources of competitiveness. In fact the NICs are only one element in a very heterogeneous international competitive environment. Countries need to comprehend their current status in this environment and seek the policy basis for moving forward qualitatively in it. The early understanding of this may be the crucial source of the successes to date of Japan and the NICs.

Overall, it is clear that the obvious policy perspective underpinning much of the discussion in this book has been that countries need to take a dynamic view of their sources of comparative advantage and to have a perpetual commitment to their renewal and expansion. It is also likely that any such dynamic view of comparative advantage will include emphasis on at least some elements of technological scope, if the latter is seen broadly to encompass a spectrum running from pure scientific research to training of shop-floor engineering personnel. It is not argued here that this process of upgrading of national comparative advantage can only be achieved through the types of technological interdependencies between MNEs and host countries that have been analysed throughout this book. What *is* suggested is that once a country has decided that it wishes to involve inward foreign direct investment quantitatively in its industrial base, *then* it does need to understand qualitatively the ways in which MNEs pursue their own global competitiveness, and to have very clear views on how it expects to benefit from a position in the global strategies of these companies.

Bibliography

ACS, Z. J. and AUDRETSCH, D. B. (1991) *Innovation and Technical Change, An International Comparison* (Hertfordshire: Harvester Wheatsheaf).

BARTLETT, C. A. (1986) 'Building and Managing the Transnational: The New Organisational Challenge', in M. E. Porter (ed.), *Competition in Global Industries* (Harvard: Harvard Business School Press) pp. 367–401.

BARTLETT, C. A. and GHOSHAL, S. (1990) 'Managing Innovations in the Transnational Corporation', in C. A. Bartlett, Y. Doz and G. Hedlund (eds), *Managing the Global Firm* (London: Routledge) pp. 215–55.

BARTLETT, C. A. and GHOSHAL, S. (1989) *Managing Across Borders – The Transnational Solution* (London: Hutchinson Business Books).

BARTLETT, C. A. and GHOSHAL, S. (1986) 'Tap Your Subsidiary for Global Reach', *Harvard Business Review*, 64, 6, pp. 89–94.

BEHRMAN, J. N. and FISCHER, W. A. (1980a) *Overseas R&D Activities of Transnational Companies* (Cambridge, Mass: Oelgeschlager, Gunn and Hain).

BEHRMAN, J. N. and FISCHER, W. A. (1980b) 'Transnational Corporations: Market Orientations and R&D Abroad', *Columbia Journal of World Business*, xv, 3, pp. 55–60.

BIRKINSHAW, J. M. (1994) 'Approaching Heterarchy – A Review of the Literature on Multinational Strategy and Structure', *Advances in Comparative Management*, 9, pp. 111–44.

BONIN, B. and PERRON, B. (1986) 'World Product Mandates and Firms Operating in Quebec', in H. Etemad and L. Séguin Dulude (eds), *Managing the Multinational Subsidiary* (London: Croom Helm) pp. 161–76.

BUCKLEY, P. J. and CASSON, M. C. (1976) *The Future of the Multinational Enterprise* (London: Macmillan).

BURSTALL, M. and DUNNING, J.H. (1985) 'International Investment in Innovation', in N. Wells (ed.), *Pharmaceuticals Among the Sunrise Industries* (London: Croom Helm).

CANTWELL, J. A. (1991) 'The International Agglomeration of R&D', in M. C. Casson (ed.), *Global Research Strategy and International Competitiveness* (Oxford: Blackwell) pp. 104–32.

CASSON, M. C. (1994) 'Enterprise Culture and Institutional Change in East and Central Europe', in P. J. Buckley and P. N. Ghauri (eds), *The Economics of Change in East and Central Europe* (London: Academic Press).

285

CASSON, M. C., PEARCE, R. D. and SINGH, S. (1991) 'A Review of Recent Trends', in M. C. Casson (ed.), *Global Research Strategy and International Competitiveness* (Oxford: Blackwell) pp. 250–71.

COHEN, W. M. and LEVINTHAL, D. A. (1989) 'Innovation and Learning: The Two Faces of R&D', *Economic Journal*, 99, pp. 569–96.

CORDELL, A. J. (1973) 'Innovation, the Multinational Corporation: Some Policy Implications for National Science Policy', *Long Range Planning*, 6, 3, pp. 22–9.

CORDELL, A. J. (1971) *The Multinational Firm, Foreign Direct Investment and Canadian Science Policy*, Science Council of Canada, Special Study No. 22 (Ottawa: Information Canada).

CROOKELL, H. (1986) 'Specialisation and International Competitiveness', in H. Etemad and L. Séguin Dulude (eds), *Managing the Multinational Subsidiary* (London: Croom Helm) pp. 102–11.

CROOKELL, H. and CALIENDO, J. (1980) 'International Competitiveness and the Structure of Secondary Industry in Canada', *Business Quarterly*, 45, 3, pp. 58–64.

D'CRUZ, J. (1986) 'Strategic Management of Subsidiaries', in H. Etemad and L. Séguin Dulude (eds), *Managing the Multinational Subsidiary* (London: Croom Helm) pp. 75–89.

DUNNING, J. H. (1994) 'The Prospects for Foreign Direct Investment in East and Central Europe', in P. J. Buckley and P. N. Ghauri (eds), *The Economics of Change in East and Central Europe* (London: Academic Press).

DUNNING, J. H. (1993a) *Multinational Enterprises and the Global Economy* (Wokingham: Addison-Wesley).

DUNNING, J. H. (1993b) *The Globalisation of Business* (London: Routledge).

DUNNING, J. H. (1988) *Explaining International Production* (London: Unwin Hyman).

DUNNING, J. H. (1986) *Japanese Participation in British Industry* (London: Croom Helm).

DUNNING, J. H. (1980) 'Toward an Eclectic Theory of International Production: Some Empirical Tests', *Journal of International Business Studies*, 11, 1, pp. 9–31.

DUNNING, J. H. (1977) 'Trade, Location of Economic Activity and the Multinational Enterprise: A Search for an Eclectic Approach', in B. Ohlin, P. O. Hesselborn and P. M. Wijkman (eds), *The International Allocation of Economic Activity* (London: Macmillan) pp. 395–418.

DUNNING, J. H. and PEARCE, R. D., (1994) 'The Nature and Growth of MNEs', in C. Nobes and R. Parker (eds), *Issues in International Accounting* (Oxford: Philip Allan Publishers) pp. 1–26.

DUNNING, J. H. and PEARCE, R. D. (1985) *The World's Largest Industrial Enterprises 1962–1983* (Aldershot: Gower).

EMMOT, B. (1992) *Japan's Global Reach* (London: Century).

ERNST, D. and O'CONNOR, D. (1989) *Technology and Global Competition* (Paris: OECD).

FLORIDA, R. and KENNEY, M. (1994) 'The Globalisation of Japanese R&D. The Economic Geography of Japanese R&D Investment in the United States', *Economic Geography*, 70, 4, pp. 344–69.

GILPIN, R. G. (1988) 'Implications of the Changing Trade Regime for US–Japanese Relations', in Inoguchi (ed.), *The Political Economy of Japan. The Changing International Context, Vol. 2* (Stanford: Stanford University Press).

GRANSTRAND, O. and SJOLANDER, S. (1992) 'Internationalisation and Diversification of Multitechnology Corporations', in O. Granstrand, L. Häkanson and S. Sjolander (eds), *Technology Management and International Business* (Chichester: Wiley) pp. 181–207.

HÄKANSON, L. (1981) 'Organisation and Evolution of Foreign R&D in Swedish Multinationals', *Geografiska Annaler*, 63B, pp. 47–56.

HÄKANSON, L. and NOBEL, R. (1993a) 'Foreign Research and Development in Swedish Multinationals', *Research Policy*, 22, pp. 373–96.

HÄKANSON, L. and NOBEL, R. (1993b) 'Determinants of Foreign R&D in Swedish Multinationals', *Research Policy*, 22, pp. 397–411.

HAUG, P., HOOD, N. and YOUNG, S. (1983) 'R&D Intensity in the Affiliates of US-owned Electronics Companies Manufacturing in Scotland', *Regional Studies*, 17, pp. 383–92.

HEDLUND, G. (1993) 'Assumption of Hierarchy and Heterarchy, with Applications to the Management of the Multinational Corporation', in S. Ghoshal and D. E. Westney (eds) *Organisational Theory and the Multinational Corporation* (London: Macmillan) pp. 211–36.

HEDLUND, G. (1986) 'The Hypermodern MNC – A Heterarchy?' *Human Resource Management*, 25, 1, pp. 9–35.

HEDLUND, G. and ROLANDER, D. (1990) 'Actions in Heterarchies: New Approaches to Managing the MNC', in C. A. Bartlett, Y. Doz and G. Hedlund (eds), *Managing the Global Firm* (London: Routledge), pp. 15–46.

HIRSCH, S. (1967) *The Location of Industry and International Competitiveness* (Oxford: Oxford University Press).

HOOD, N. and YOUNG, S. (1982) 'US Multinational R&D: Corporate Strategies and Policy Implications for the UK', *Multinational Business*, 2, pp. 10–23.

HOWELLS, J. and WOOD, M. (1993) *The Globalisation of Production and Technology* (London: Belhaven Press).

JAPANESE EXTERNAL TRADE ORGANISATION, (1995) *The 11th Survey of European Operations of Japanese Companies in the Manufacturing Sector* (Tokyo: JETRO).

JAPANESE EXTERNAL TRADE ORGANISATION (1994) *The 10th Survey of European Operations of Japanese Companies in the Manufacturing Sector* (Tokyo: JETRO).

KLINE, S. J. and ROSENBERG, N. (1986) 'An Overview of Innovation', in R. Landau, and N. Rosenberg (eds), *The Positive Sum Strategy, Harnessing Technology for Economic Growth* (Washington, DC: National Academy Press).

KOJIMA, K. (1978) *Direct Foreign Investment – A Japanese Model of Multinational Business Operations* (London: Croom Helm).

LUNDVALL, B. A. (1992) *National Systems of Innovation, Towards a Theory of Innovation and Interactive Learning* (London: Pinter Publishers).

LUNDVALL, B. A. (1988) 'Innovation as an Interactive Process – From User–Producer Interaction to the National System of Innovation', in G. Dosi *et al.* (eds), *Technical Change and Economic Theory* (London: Pinter Publishers).

MCGUINNESS, N. W. and CONWAY, H. A. (1986) 'World Product Mandates: The Need for Directed Search Strategies', in H. Etemad and L. Séguin Dulude (eds), *Managing the Multinational Subsidiary* (London: Croom Helm) pp. 136–58.

OZAWA, T. (1992) 'Cross-investments Between Japan and the EC: Income Similarity, Technological Congruity and Economies of Scope', in J. A. Cantwell (ed.), *Multinational Investment in Modern Europe* (Aldershot: Elgar) pp. 13–45.

OZAWA, T. (1991a) 'Japanese Multinationals and 1992', in B. Burgenmeier and J. L. Mucchielli (eds), *Multinationals and Europe 1992* (London: Routledge) pp. 135–54.

OZAWA, T. (1991b) 'Japan in a New Phase of Multinationalism and Industrial Upgrading: Functional Integration of Trade, Growth and FDI', *Journal of World Trade Law*, 25, 1, pp. 43–60.

PAPANASTASSIOU, M. (1995) 'Creation and Development of Technology by MNEs' Subsidiaries in Europe : The Cases of UK, Greece, Belgium and Portugal', Thesis submitted for the Degree of Doctor of Philosophy, University of Reading.

PAPANASTASSIOU, M. and PEARCE, R. D. (1996) 'The Creation and Application of Technology by MNEs' Subsidiaries in Europe', in F. Burton, M. Yamin and S. Young (eds), *International Business and Europe in Transition* (London: Macmillan) pp. 207–30.

PAPANASTASSIOU, M. and PEARCE, R. D. (1995) 'The Research and Development of Japanese Multinational Enterprises in Europe', in F. Sachwald (ed.), *Japanese Firms in Europe* (Luxembourg: Harwood Academic Publishers) pp. 265–310.

PAPANASTASSIOU, M. and PEARCE, R. D. (1994a) 'The Internationalisation of Research and Development by Japanese Enterprises', *R&D Management*, 24, 2, pp. 155–65.

PAPANASTASSIOU, M. and PEARCE, R. D. (1994b) 'Technology Sourcing and the Strategic Roles of Manufacturing Subsidiaries in the UK: Local Competences and Global Competitiveness', University of Reading, Department of Economics, Discussion Papers in International Investment and Business Studies, No 191.

PEARCE, R. D. (1994) 'The Internationalisation of Research and Development by Multinational Enterprises and the Transfer Sciences', *Empirica*, 21, pp. 297–311.

PEARCE, R. D. (1993) *The Growth and Evolution of Multinational Enterprise* (Aldershot: Elgar).

PEARCE, R. D. (1992) 'World Product Mandates and MNE Specialisation', *Scandinavian International Business Review*, 1, 2, pp. 38–58.

PEARCE, R. D. (1989) *The Internationalisation of Research and Development by Multinational Enterprises* (London: Macmillan).

PEARCE, R. D. and PAPANASTASSIOU, M. (1996) *The Technological Competitiveness of Japanese Multinationals* (Ann Arbour: The University of Michigan Press).

PEARCE, R. D. and SINGH, S. (1992a) *Globalizing Research and Development* (London: Macmillan).

PEARCE, R. D. and SINGH, S. (1992b) 'Global Strategy and Innovation: The Role of Internationalised Research and Development', in *World Trade and MNE in the 21st Century*, proceedings of the Fifth International Conference on Multinational Enterprise (Taipei: Chinese Culture University).

PEARCE, R. D. and SINGH, S. (1992c) 'Internationalisation of R&D Among the World's Leading Enterprises: Survey Analysis of Organisation and Motivation', in O. Granstrand, L. Häkanson and S. Sjolander (eds), *Technology Management and International Business* (Chichester: Wiley) pp. 137–62.

PITELIS, C. N. (1994) 'Industrial Strategy for Britain in Europe', *Journal of Economic Studies*, 21, 6.

PORTER, M. E. (1986) 'Competition in Global Industries: A Conceptual Framework', in M. E. Porter (ed.), *Competition in Global Industries* (Boston: Harvard Business School Press) pp. 15–60.

POSNER, M. V. (1961) 'International Trade and Technical Change', *Oxford Economic Papers*, 13, pp. 323–41.

POYNTER, T. A. and RUGMAN, A. M. (1982) 'World Product Mandates: How Will Multinationals Respond?', *Business Quarterly*, 47, 3, pp. 54–61.

RONSTADT, R. C. (1978) 'International R&D: The Establishment and Evolution of R&D Abroad by Seven US Multinationals', *Journal of International Business Studies*, 3, 3, pp. 3–15.

RONSTADT, R. C. (1977) *Research and Development Abroad by US Multinationals* (New York: Praeger).

RUGMAN, A. M. (1983) 'Multinational Enterprises and World Product Mandates', in A. M. Rugman (ed.), *Multinationals and Technology Transfer* (New York: Praeger) pp. 73–90.

RUGMAN, A. M. and BENNETT, J. (1982) 'Technology Transfer and World Product Mandating in Canada', *Columbia Journal of World Business,* 17, 4, pp. 58–62.

SCHUMPETER, J. A. (1969) *The Theory of Economic Development* (Cambridge, Mass: Harvard University Press).

SÖDERSTEN, B. and REED, G. (1994) *International Economics*, 3rd edn (London: Macmillan).

STENT, A. Y. (1980) 'East–West Technology Transfer: European Perspectives', The Centre for Strategic and International Studies, Georgetown University, Washington DC.

TAGGART, J.H. (1991) 'Determinants of the Foreign R&D Location Decision in the Pharmaceutical Industry', *R&D Management*, 21, 3, pp. 229–40.

TAGGART, J.H. (1989) 'The Pharmaceutical Industry: Sending R&D Abroad', *Multinational Business* (Spring), pp. 10–15.

TEECE, D. J. (1977) 'Technology Transfer by Multinational Firms: The Resource Cost of Transferring Technological Knowhow', *Economic Journal*, 87, pp. 242–61.

TEECE, D. J. (1976) *The Multinational Corporation and the Resource Cost of International Technology Transfer* (Cambridge, Mass: Ballinger).

UNITED NATIONS CONFERENCE ON TRADE and DEVELOPMENT (1993) *World Investment Report – Transnational Corporations and Integrated International Production* (New York: United Nations).

VERNON, R. (1979) 'The Product Cycle Hypothesis in a New International Environment', *Oxford Bulletin of Economics and Statistics*, 41, 4, pp. 255–67.

VERNON, R. (1966) 'International Investment and International Trade in the Product Cycle', *Quarterly Journal of Economics*, 88, pp. 190–207.

WEX, S. (1984) *Instead of FIRA: Autonomy for Canadian Subsidiaries?* (Montreal: Institute of Research on Public Policy).

WHITE, R. E. and POYNTER, T. A. (1984) 'Strategies for Foreign-Owned Subsidiaries in Canada', *Business Quarterly*, 9, 2, pp. 59–69.

WITTEN, M. (1981) 'Branch Plants Bear New Fruit', in K. C. Dhawan, H. Etemad and R. W. Wright (eds), *International Business, A Canadian Perspective* (Don Mills, Ontario: Addison-Wesley) pp. 600–10.

WOLF, B. M. (1983) 'World Product Mandates and Freer Canada–United States Trade', in A. M. Rugman (ed.), *Multinationals and Technology Transfer* (New York: Praeger) pp. 91–107.

YOUNG J. P. (1977) *Quantification of Western Exports of High Technology Products to Communist Nations*, US Department of Commerce (Washington, DC: Government Printing Office).

YOUNG, S., HOOD, N. and HAMILL, J. (1987) *Foreign Multinationals and the British Economy* (London: Croom Helm).

Index